Harbingers of the Turning of the Ages Presents:

THE SHAMANIC ASTROLOGY HANDBOOK

The Archetypes And Symbols Of The Signs And Planets And Their Role In Shamanic Astrology

Daniel Giamario & Carolyn Brent

JCAU Publications
Tucson, Arizona

Fourth Edition
Cover design: Gene King and Jeff Brent
Original astrological mandala design: Howard Hansen
Book design: Carolyn Brent
Computer Graphic Medicine Wheel design: Jeff Brent
Printing: http://www.instantpublisher.com/

ॐ This is the symbol for Galactic Center
honoring the place in the sky marking
The Current Turning Of The Ages
(See A Shamanic Look At The Turning Of The Ages
starting on page 9 for details)

ISBN: 0-614-09459-3

Dedication, Lineage and Vision Statement

We as Shamanic Astrologer's honor our ancestors, predecessors, and the prior lineages of Shamanic Astrology including, but not limited to:

The Ancient Ones
The Greater Shamanic Council of Light
The Great Shining Ones
Thoth/Hermes Trismegistus and The Ark of Grace
The Prophetic Traditions of Ezekiel and Daniel
The Merlin Traditions
Avalon
The Magi
The Calendric Shamans of The Anasazi and Other Native Americans
The Sky Shamans of the Maya
The Star Priests and Priestesses of Egypt and all other Ancient Traditions
The Mystery Teachings of Neolithic Peoples
And more recently
The Astrosophy of Rudolph Steiner
The Cosmology of Dane Rudhyar
And The Archetypal Vision of C.G. Jung

We as Shamanic Astrologers are committed to the fullest expression of life grounded on the foundation of As Above, So Below, As Without, So Within; a life recognizing and celebrating the union between Soul and Spirit, between Land and Sky, between Feminine and Masculine, between Body and Mind, and between Shadow and Light. We are committed to a Life of Service, in facilitating the assistance of any sentient being desiring connection or reconnection to the magical link between Earth and the Heavens. Our highest priority and deepest motivation is love; and it is our love of the Magical connection between Land and Sky, and the Celestial Cycles, which animates our great privilege and joy in participating and co-creating with 'Great Mystery.'

We believe this experience and commitment facilitates greater understanding, acceptance, inspiration and support for the joyous fulfillment of our individual and collective destinies, assisting in eliminating fear, separation, power over others, false classes and hierarchies, and other relationships not in accordance with Spirit. Lastly, we are committed to participating in Dreaming the Dream Onwards.

We recognize these as the skills of a Shamanic Astrologer including but not limited to:
*Shamanic Astrology Counseling
*Night Sky Teaching
*Personal Attunement to Astronomical Cycles
*Intuitive Connection to Land & Sky through Geomantic Alignments & Hierophanies
*Knowledge of the Turning of the Ages

CONTENTS

ACKNOWLEDGMENTS

No book is ever brought into form without the inspiration and dedication of many individuals whose talents, gifts, and insights help to give it birth. This work is no exception. Our deepest gratitude and appreciation go to everyone who influenced this work either directly or indirectly. Special thanks go to Jeffrey Brent for his loving and unwavering support, keeping the computer on line, tending to other technical matters, and figuring out the computer graphics for the Medicine Wheel in the front of the book, Merilyn Massey for her proofing and editing work, Susan Alley for her assistance in helping us find a printing company and graphic design advice, Gary Wolf for his legal advice, Gene King for her great cover artwork, and to the many individuals who have directly supported and promoted this work.

I, Daniel Giamario, desire to thank and acknowledge the teachers who were my greatest inspirations. While in college studying philosophy I met a remarkable woman of Celtic magic, Jane Hoskinson, who soon became my teacher and I her apprentice. Her unique approach to understanding the Moon and Rising sign gave me a truly supportive foundation. An early instruction of hers was to refrain from reading any other astrology books until I had finished all of those by Dane Rudhyar. This instruction I gladly carried out. There can be no greater philosophical and theoretical foundation for astrology available than to be grounded in Rudhyar. I am deeply thankful for his contribution to my life.

Another great formative influence on my life during my university days was my philosophy professor, the amazing Dr. Alfonso Verdu, who expanded my mind with a cross-cultural understanding of the world's greatest formulators of the philosophy of interpenetration. Beyond the academic comparisons uniting Hellenistic idealism, German phenomenology, and Oriental Mahayama Buddhism, his child-like exuberance and passion for teaching influenced me most.

In the 1970's I was greatly privileged to have studied with the late Tony Joseph, a greatly under-acknowledged and too little known astrologer, who did more to remythologize astrology than *anyone*. He was also especially instrumental in bringing the Goddess back into astrology. Jungian and archetypal psychology heavily influenced my astrology work during the time I worked with Tony, and these experiences have played a big part in the development of this work.

In the 1980's, my greatest teachers were not human beings. Shamanism and direct teaching from the night sky dominated. In particular, there was a special large rock formation located in the Joshua Tree National Monument "Wonderland of Rocks" that gave me specific and detailed instructions in formulating the Astrological Vision Quest. During these years my friend, Howard Hansen, shared many of these Vision Quest adventures, and his presence was an inspiration to me.

I also wish to acknowledge my parents who were supportive of my non-traditional life choices. They are people of great integrity who have always made choices of honesty and idealism, instilling those values in me rather than the prevalent lowest common denominators of expediency, materialism, and valueless ambition.

In the 1990's I am extremely thankful for two amazing women. First, to Carolyn Brent, who has so tirelessly and with so much dedication, almost single-handedly produced this book. In addition to her hard work on this project and others, she has also been busy raising four children! I look forward to further work together.

Most importantly, I express my deepest gratitude to my most sweet and loving wife, Debby Joy, for her unconditional support and belief in my work. When we first met, she told me she saw "three books in my aura." Well, here is the first. More than anyone, she knows that without her, *the work*, as represented by this book, would be rather meaningless.

I am also greatly indebted to the ancient ones, and the keepers of the sacred ancient traditions of the land and sky by the indigenous people of this most beautiful living planet. I aspire to be of that lineage. I feel a special connection to the Celtic teachings of the Western tradition, particularly as represented by the great standing stones of Scotland. Lastly, I must express my appreciation to the many dedicated students, the hundreds who have participated in the vision quests, workshops and classes, the special friends who have been promoters and supporters of this work, and to all whom I have known on this path. I am thankful for each and every one of you who have supported this work and have participated in dreaming the dream onwards.

PREFACE

"In that time before there was *time*, there was Grandfather Fire. Around Grandfather Fire sat the circle of Animal Brothers, beyond them was the darkness. Each, in their own turn, would tell their tellings in that sacred language of spirit. Through their tellings, Grandfather Fire would express creation. There came *time* when the two-leggeds got up and wandered away from the fire and into the darkness..."

And so the sacred aberration of our spirit's sojourn through the realm of the time oriented physical domain began. Our heart's desire is the return home to the circle, and Grandfather Fire. This journey of self-realization, assisted by the tellings (myths) of the twelve members of the circle of animal brothers, is the mystery and history of our quest. The structure and syntax of this magnificent mystery is encoded within each of us.

Herein, Daniel Giamario has brought forth the tools with which we can begin to understand and apply the messages expressed through the sacred language of spirit, by the twelve of the circle.

As a shaman of lineage, mine is the awesome responsibility of the caretakership of a compendium of knowledge, myths, ceremonies, and spiritual powers that has been passed from generation to generation from archaic times, and to the generations yet to come. A caretakership held in sacred trust for all peoples.

In the person of Daniel Giamario, I have met, and recognized, a man of like dedication. With courage, humor, insight, and unswerving service to the unfoldment of the human spirit in its movement towards individuated consciousness, Daniel has re-revealed a map of the mythos, through Shamanic Astrology, which is well informed and true-to-course.

It is rare when two such diverse paradigms as astrology and shamanism can converse. And yet, in the many conversations between Daniel and myself, we have found a singularity of essence and principle in the dynamics of creation and co-creation expressed through the translations of each our own archetypal systems.

This was most profoundly impressed within me upon the first occasion of our meeting in Sedona, Arizona, in 1987. For the first time I had met an astrologer who, when discussing the art, lifted eyes to the starry heavens and said pointing upwards, "See there, that is the constellation which gives your myth expression in your life's purpose."

"What?!" My mind screamed. "How could he possibly know that?" I had just met a person, not of a shamanic culture, who understood the central basis of all primary shamanic ceremonials: shamanic ceremony is the re-enactment of the mythos of cosmological phenomena. This was but the first of many such cross-paradigm revelations we were to enjoy together.

My personal definition of adventure is: *A life threatening experience you live to tell about.* To journey through the archetypal landscape Daniel presents, is to partake of an adventure that is life-threatening to the invested beliefs one may have in the outmoded astrology of the pop culture we were raised with.

As with any successful adventure, we gain a confident sense of self in relationship to who we are, where we've been, where we are going, and most importantly, how to get there.

Welcome home to Grandfather Fire.

Jade Wah'oo
American Shaman
February 1994
Sedona, Arizona

INTRODUCTION

Shamanic Astrology is an evolving system developed by Daniel Giamario that has emerged from the direct experience of Daniel and others in their relationship to the unfolding mysteries. The following is an in depth description by Daniel of the current understanding of these mysteries.

Since a Mt. Shasta vision quest experience in August of 1981, I have been involved with an approach to astrology called Shamanic Astrology. First I'll explain what I mean by the use of this phrase. One definition of shamanism describes it as the process of "death by intent".[*1] This is not accidental death and coming back into body, but a conscious *choice* to die and be reborn back into the same body, many times. This "death", can be emotional, physical, spiritual, or a literal physical death and rebirth.

I do not consider myself a shaman. I am neither of blood lineage nor on a formal path of shamanic initiation. However, certain basic tenants of the Shamanic Astrology approach are relevant to understanding this approach. These principals include:

1. *The foundational philosophical truth of Shamanic Astrology (and arguably of everything) is from the opening lines of the* Emerald Tablets of Hermes, *"As Above, So Below, As Without, So Within."*[*2] This is considered to be a literal, kinesthetic, organic reality, not an intellectual or spiritual abstraction. The patterns of the constellations and the cycles of the Sun, Moon and planets are the *same* as the patterns and cycles of the human psyche and the seasons of our lives. The relationship is *not* cause and effect.

2. *Shamanic Astrology is experiential and earth-centered.* The sky that can be directly experienced without telescopic or cybernetic enhancement has the greatest importance and power. Therefore, Shamanic Astrology would be as effective in a non-technological age. This view can be termed Neo-Ptolemaic, an astrology for terrestrial humans experiencing the sky, perceivable with unaided vision without light pollution.[*3] The modern scientific reality of the heliocentric, Copernican worldview is essentially irrelevant to this approach.

3. *Shamanic Astrology is ceremonial and participatory, and operates from a mythic perspective.* Jade Wah'oo, an American Shaman, states, "All true shamanic ceremonies are the dramatic mythic re-enactment of cosmological phenomena." Over time, the cultural ceremonies and mythic stories created by the various civilizations are draped onto the actual physically observed cycles of the planets and patterns of the constellations.

4. The *death and rebirth* motif of shamanism inspires Shamanic Astrology in two basic ways: First, the understanding and experience of the natural rhythm and cycles of the planetary bodies are linked to the initiatory process in human beings. The universe is supportive of, and power is accessed by, human beings who consciously participate with their initiation cycles. And second, Planets (especially Venus, Mercury, and Mars) disappearing below the horizon, are seen as entering the underworld, dying and later

being reborn when they rise above the horizon.

5. *Shamanic Astrology links to modern psychology through the use of archetypes.* An ancient shamanism using gods, goddesses, spirits and animal essences, can now be expressed through a comprehensive, cross cultural, full spectrum approach to archetypes. (Note the elucidation of the 24 prime archetypes of the masculine and feminine on page 14).

Shamanic Astrology is archetypal and symbolic. It is the study of intent, not a static description of how people are. Archetypes are the fastest way to have astrology work in people's lives. The archetypal material gives us a sense of all the possibilities that are available and which ones apply to us. Let's take the issue of enlightenment for an example. Using the astrological model we find there are twelve valid ways of reaching an enlightenment experience. One person's approach might be through conscious partnership. Another person's approach might be through having a family, or having adventures, or karma yoga, or transcendent union with the absolute. There are different paths for different people. All are equally valid. Shamanic Astrology makes no judgment about one path being better than another.

Astrology today is totally different than at other time periods in history. During a more "normal" time, astrologers could look at a chart and absolutely, deterministically know what type of job the person would have, when and what type of person they would marry, how many children they would have and so on. However, as we are now in the final few years an entire 26,000 year cycle, what we are experiencing today, is not a "normal" time.

The largest cycle the human senses can perceive is the cycle of the procession of the equinoxes and the solstices. It is a subtle movement. They move one degree every seventy-two years against the backdrop of the stars. The movement of the Solstice and Equinox points completes one entire circuit of the zodiac in 25,820 years. For short we call this a 26,000 year cycle. This is similar to the cycle spoken of in the Mayan Calendar. Throughout most of history, the majority of the calendric traditions on the planet began with the winter solstice. The winter solstice point has been, and still is in some cultures, the beginning and the ending of a calendar. In May, 1998 the winter solstice point in the sky, for the only time in 25,820 years, formed an exact alignment with the place in the sky where the Milky Way intersects the solar system in the direction of galactic center.[4] The plane of our solar system is seen in the sky as the zodiac. To tell where a circle begins, something outside of the circle must intersect it. The plane of the Milky Way Galaxy intersects the plane of our solar system in the vicinity of Sagittarius and Scorpius. In May of 1998, the winter solstice exactly aligned with this intersection point, dramatically heralding the end and the beginning of an entire 26,000 year cycle.

What is the effect of this event on humanity? There are two important phenomena occurring now called *acceleration* and *recapitulation*. Acceleration is the speeded up effect almost everyone is feeling in their life today. Today, a year of living can feel like several lifetimes, or six weeks (or even six days) in a relationship is what six years in a relationship was like in a more normal time. We can extend this even further. If there are five or ten people left on your time track for relationship, it is very likely you will meet all of them in the next few years.

These are not "normal" times. This is not the time where you will necessarily find one person and the relationship will last a whole lifetime, as is the case in a Golden Age, or more traditional time. Some people will still do that, but it is not the predominant cultural mode at the Turning Of The Ages, because of the speeded up affect. Recapitulation, or summary is a phenomenon where the main themes of your entire time track reoccur in a concentrated form. The individual horoscope is now a summary of the entire 26,000 year time track. What a person has done with relationships over the course of their 26,000 year time track is now summarized and recapitulated in an extremely powerful form. This includes any unfinished business. It is a chance to work everything out in a short period of time.

The whole speeded up effect also means anyone with any karma to work out on this plane, who has been alive at any point over the past 26,000 years; will be born now. They want to be here at the celebration, or great Saturnalia festival at the end of the cycle. A Saturnalia festival is a Winter Solstice festival that happens at the end of an entire cycle. Depending on the culture it lasted three to twelve days. The Romans celebrated Saturnalia at the Winter Solstice just prior to the New Year by turning the law upside down. It was a time of great chaos and confusion. It was sanctioned by the culture to have the festival just prior to the New Year. From the perspective of the entire 26,000 year cycle, including the phenomenon of the Winter Solstice point having reached the aforementioned intersection point in May 1998, we are celebrating Saturnalia for collective humanity right now!

There is another amazing event taking place in the sky that has to do with the connection between male and female. (Incidentally, in describing masculine and feminine I am never talking about gender. There are many men working on feminine issues and vice versa.) The image of the sphinx, (variously depicted as a female lion with a pharaoh's head, or a lion with a woman's head), is the blending together of the constellation of the Lion and the constellation of Virgo. This image is representative of the phenomenon now taking place in the sky. Throughout the ages, the constellation of the Lion, or Leo, represented Yang energy, the masculine principle to its greatest extent, the "I am, that I am." Leo has an independent, sovereign self-identity.

Right next to the Lion constellation, is the constellation of Virgo. Virgo through out the ages is the symbol of the autonomous, sovereign, independent, female principle. Not the woman as mother, or girlfriend, who defines who she is by who she is with, or the proverbial nurse who takes care of other people, but the aspect of the feminine complete unto itself. The original meaning of virgin did not mean "no sex," it described a woman who did not need to be with anyone to know who she was, she was one unto herself. These two constellations are right next to each other. Twice in the entire 26,000 year cycle can an equinox point hit the border between the Lion and the Virgin. Either when the autumnal equinox point hits there, or when the spring equinox point hits there. Right now the autumnal equinox point is right in between Leo, the Lion and Virgo, the Virgin Goddess. The autumnal equinox is always the zero degree Libra point. Zero degrees of Libra astrologically symbolizes the balance between the male and the female force. It also represents the mystery of partnership and relationship itself. Libra asks the question, "What is the nature of partnership and relationship?" We now have the zero degree Libra point aligned between the two main symbols in the sky, of the independent autonomous male, the Sun King, Leo, and the autonomous, sovereign, female principle, the Virgin Priestess, Virgo. They are right next to each other at the equilibrium point.

What does this mean? We are *not* in a position where the excesses of patriarchy (and are there ever many), will be overwhelmed by an emerging matriarchy that takes over again. It will not be a continued battle of one winning over the other. In fact, there comes a point where, finally, true androgyny is possible, when the male principle is at its fullest individuated point, and the female principle is at its fullest individuated point, and they meet again, not needing each other, but out of choice. At that point we have a completely new set of mysteries concerning how male and female come together.

Shamanic Astrology is a powerful tool for sorting out the symbols and archetypes of the past. It also gives clues about what the new archetypes will look like on the other side of the Turning Of The Ages. This method of interpreting the horoscope provides a way of quickly getting to the most important issues for an individual in the current life. This knowledge empowers people and gives them techniques for progressing on their intended path. It helps us to understand and participate with our individual cycles, as well as the cycles of the collective. In these speeded up times where confusion and chaos are predominant, and even necessary, to bring in the new operating manual, this information is indeed timely. It gives us permission to relax, not know anything, be open, expand our vision of possibilities, and even enjoy the process of the Turning Of The Ages.

Notes
1) Described as such by Jade Wah'oo American Shaman of lineage, a personal friend and colleague of the authors. See Preface.
2) From the rendition favored by Val Valerian and *The Leading Edge* publication.
3) A phrase frequently used by astrological astrosophy, a form of stellar science inspired by Rudolph Steiner, and elucidated through the works of Willi Suker, Norman Davidson who wrote, *Astronomy And The Imagination and Sky Phenomena,* and Joachim Schultz who wrote, *Movement And Rhythms Of The Stars.*
4) According to the calculations of astronomer Jean Meuss

A SHAMANIC LOOK AT THE TURNING OF THE AGES

Writers note: This writers note was added to preface the appearance of this writing in the February/March 1998 issue of The Mountain Astrologer. These thoughts are important so they are included here. The essence of this information, developed in the late 1980's, has been a regular part of my classes and workshops for years. For me, the original spark igniting this investigation came from a wonderful essay written by Robert Hand in Essays On Astrology[1] (also similar information is mentioned in some of his tape sets) concerning the movement of the solstice and equinox points into new constellations. Hand's essay was inspired by C. G. Jung's treatment of the same subject in his book, The Aeon.*

Over the years, my experiential and ceremonial work with the night sky, as well as the process of teaching the night sky to others, crystallized the workability of these ideas. In those days, nearly a decade ago, very few in the astrological community were interested in this material. The only other person I knew of, who was aware of the solstice galactic alignment, was constellational astrologer Raymond Mardyks, whose fine work can be accessed as an example of other directions this same data can lead.

In the late 1980's, I began corresponding with European master astronomer Jean Meuss, via a recommendation from astronomer-publisher Guy Ottewell, concerning the precisely calculated dates of entry, into different constellations, of the solstices and equinox coordinates. I sent a communication to Meuss in 1991 asking him to calculate the exact date of the winter (December) solstice alignment with the intersection of the galactic plane and the plane of the solar system. His response was May 1998. I have been sharing this date in my talks and workshops ever since. Jean Meuss references the May 1998 date in his recently published book Mathematical Astronomy Morsels.[2]

Within the last few years, spontaneously and intuitively, many people, from many different backgrounds, have become aware of this larger context calendric frame of reference. I suspect this awareness and understanding has occurred at other times in history, then was forgotten for a time and remembered again. In any case, these insights are not necessarily original or new. I've recently seen flyers from different organizers, of mainly ceremonial and shamanic events, referencing the upcoming alignments. These events are occurring in various places ranging from the British Isles, Mt Shasta, the Yucatan, and others. Lately, more and more astrologers are showing interest in these events, and this article is responding to that interest. What is offered here is not dogma, or copyrighted material, but rather is intended to inspire speculation and imagination. The clues are all in the sky. All we need do is look and be open.

Nearing the end of this millennium there is much speculation about the so-called "end times." Catastrophes, apocalypses, various end points of cultural calendars, as well as world renewal and oncoming Golden Ages are common themes. In an astrological context this is often referred to as the beginning of the Aquarian Age.

Within this century, literally scores of scenarios have developed claiming conclusive dating for the beginning of the Aquarian Age.[3] The question of when the Aquarian Age actually begins is a highly interesting field of inquiry, and worthy of several entire books. However, I prefer to investigate a *larger context*, which can answer questions and raise issues that render the timing of the "Aquarian Age" moot. I believe *shamanic methodology* demonstrates that humanity is exactly at the end and beginning of an entire 26,000 year cycle (with 1997-1998 as the center point).

The longest cycle in the natural world that can be apprehended by the human senses, in a single lifetime, is the 26,000 year cycle marked by the precession of the equinoxes and solstices.*4 This phenomenon is caused by the interaction of the twenty-three-and-a-half degree tilt of the Earth's axis (creating the seasons) and the wobble of the Earth's axis (causing entirely different stars to mark "North" over the 26,000 year cycle, among other things). The interaction of the tilt and wobble of the Earth's axis causes the solstice and equinox points to move backwards or precess one degree every seventy-two years through the zodiac.

There is a huge amount of available literature concerning the so-called astrological ages, their connection synchronistically to history, and their remarkable relationship to esoteric and occult mystery schools. Personally, I consider that the western scientific view (also held by some astrologers) contending that the precession of the equinoxes and solstices was *unknown* before Hipparchus is pretentious and oblivious to the obvious. It is on par with the belief that no culture, prior to the age of western science, had any awareness of the eighteen to nineteen year Lunar Standstill Cycles. Within the last ten years, scores of astro-archetypelogical sites have been shown to have as their basis the extremes of the Moon's orbit.*5 Yet, even if no one knew about the precession of the equinoxes and solstices prior to 300 BC, it still serves as a valid basis for the investigation at hand, which is a *shamanic investigation* of The Turning Of The Ages.

The Neo-Platonists compared an entire 26,000 year cycle to one year, and referred to it as a "Platonic Year." This analogy is extremely useful. Just as one year has twelve months and four seasons, a Platonic Year also has twelve *months* and four *seasons*. However, one *month* in a Platonic Year is 2160 years long and each *season* is 6480 years long. These figures are arrived at using simple math, but where do we *start* the Platonic Year or the 26,000 year cycle? What establishes the boundaries for beginning and ending the Platonic Year? This is identical to the problem of where to begin a circle. In this case the circle represents the plane of the solar system, or the ecliptic, marked by the signs and constellations of the zodiac. The best way to begin a circle is to cut through the circle from the outside. For example, Aries is the first sign of the zodiac (or circle), because conventionally it is the first thirty degrees following the spring equinox. Therefore it is the spring equinox that cuts the circle of the zodiac to begin a standard solar year. However, where do we begin marking the beginning and ending of the entire 26,000 year cycle? Is there something else we can use to determine the beginning and ending of the circle relative, not to one standard solar year, but to an entire Platonic year? If so, this issue of where to begin and end the *greater cycle* could be resolved. This also means that the smaller issue of where to begin and end one of the Platonic months (i.e. Aquarius) becomes far less significant.

A *mytho-shamanistic* approach to astrology involves the direct observation of the night sky, connecting with natural phenomena using the human senses. It is not based on an abstract, complicated computer-generated solution to a problem. In the night sky, there is one very clear and even dramatic phenomenon that cuts the circle of the zodiac. It is the Milky Way! The plane of our galaxy cuts the zodiac/ecliptic belt at about a sixty-six degree angle in the region of the zodiacal constellations of Sagittarius and Scorpius. The Milky Way intersects the zodiac near the *center* of the galaxy in an extremely rich and thick field of stars. Looking in the opposite direction out towards deep space, another intersection takes place in the vicinity of the constellations of Gemini and Taurus where the Milky Way is barely noticeable. The phenomenon of precession does not change these intersection points. The Milky Way's fixed star relationship to the zodiacal constellations creates a visible framework far grander, and much longer lasting, than even the 26,000 year precessional cycle.

While we have now established what cuts the circle and defines a wider context than one year, a *timer* is still required to determine the end and the beginning of the 26,000 year cycle. The majority of the world's cultures have chosen solstice or equinox points within a solar year to determine the beginning of the New Year. The only exceptions to this are locations on the planet, close to the equator, where the seasons are similar and not much difference is noticed between solstice time and equinox time. These cultures, such as the Hawaiian, have chosen the rising of a star or constellation (i.e. the Pleiades), and then calibrate that event with a new Moon to mark the New Year. Most cultures, however, have chosen the spring equinox, winter solstice, autumnal equinox, or occasionally the summer solstice as the New Year's point. For example, our modern western secular calendar, which begins on January 1, *originally* began on the winter solstice. Both astrologers and astronomers today begin their coordinate and calendric systems with the spring equinox.

The solstice and equinox points can also be used as the timer for the wider 26,000 year framework. These points can be used to determine the astrological age, or Platonic Month, the Platonic Season, as well as the Platonic Year, because they precess at approximately one degree every seventy-two years. It's the arrival of the solstice and equinox points at the intersection of the Milky Way and zodiac that clearly determine the Platonic Seasons, which occur about every 6480 years. But what Platonic Season determines the end and beginning point of the Platonic Year? Which of the two intersection points is more important? And which of the four solstice and equinox points has precedence?

The intersection in the Sagittarius/Scorpius part of the zodiac is visually impressive, and is also the area of Galactic Center.[6] If the Sun is central to the solar system, galactic center is like the central Sun that all the stars of the galaxy circuit. When the equinox or solstice points are aligned with the Sagittarius/Scorpius intersection, *the Sun rises at galactic center* on those dates! This occurs about every 6480 years and marks a change of Platonic Seasons. It's happening now. According to the calculations of Astronomer Jean Meuss[7] (famous for calculating stellar occultations), the winter solstice coordinate exactly reached the intersection of the plane of the Milky Way with the zodiacal plane in May of 1998. This is the only time in the 26,000 year precessional cycle that the December solstice (or winter solstice in North America) is aligned with galactic center.

The Sumerian/Babylonian civilizations chose a spring equinox calendar and modern astrologers and astronomers still use it. There are two possible reasons for this choice. For one thing, around 4000 BC, the equinoxes were in alignment with the Milky Way/Zodiac intersection. This was one whole Platonic season before now. The cosmic frame of reference had an equinox priority then. Secondly, during the third millennium BC, the spring equinox formed precise alignments with the royal star Aldebaran and then with the Pleiades. The rising Sun at spring equinox was conjunct the Pleiades during the very same years that the Sun rose at summer solstice with the royal star Regulus. All that must have been quite impressive and worthy of creating a calendar! So, at that time, the Sun rising in the Sagittarius/Scorpio zone (or Galactic Center) at the autumnal equinox was overshadowed by the dramatic celestial events occurring in the constellations of Taurus and Gemini.

When sharing this material over the past ten years, I have found it is the native and traditional peoples of shamanic orientation who most easily resonate with this information. This is largely because they ceremonially "work" the cycles of the Earth and Sky. They know what the winter solstice is. It is the time of the greatest density, the deepest descent of spirit into matter, the longest night, and then the return, or rebirth, of the Sun. It is the turning of the year. It was also not a coincidence that the winter solstice was chosen by the current world culture (through its secular calendar) to be the most important of the four calendar turning points, to mark the turning of a solar year.

Due to the primacy the shamanic and traditional cultures give to the December solstice, I feel the higher calendric priority (in this case, more than the equinoxes) for marking the end and beginning of an entire Platonic year is the December solstice. However, there can be a great stimulating debate on this issue. At the very least, we know humanity is at a seasonal shift. If now isn't the end and beginning of the Platonic year, then my feeling is the next most likely possibility is the "mirror image" of now, 12,500 -13,000 years ago, when the December solstice was at galactic anti-center, in the Gemini/Taurus region. This marked the time when the vernal (spring) equinox was entering the constellation of the Lion (represented by the Lion Sphinx of Giza, facing due east as silent witness to those historical events). Today, the Sphinx witnesses the spring equinox's entry into the constellation of the Waterbearer, or Aquarius.

Recent trips to Peru, Bolivia, and Scotland, have provided me with impressive direct experiences of ancient monuments built to capture the precise rising and/or setting of the December solstice Sun. It is as if these monuments were built with this time in mind. For only now, (and the mirror image time 12,500 -13,000 years ago) can the rising and setting Sun be experienced at the solstice, Milky Way, and zodiacal intersection.

I propose that all shamanically and experientially oriented individuals continue creating conscious ceremony and festivals, especially during the winter solstices[8] at this current time now symbolizing the end and beginning of a galactic year. The rising Sun at winter solstice is a marvelous opportunity to receive a transmission of galactic intelligence directly from galactic center, for dreaming and co-creating the next great age.

Notes

1) Robert Hand, *Essays on Astrology,* Whitford Press, 1982

2) Jean Meuss, *Mathematical Astronomy Morsels*, Willman-Bell, 1997.

3) Some of the more interesting proposals are:

   1962 AD   The great conjunction of planets in Aquarius

   2018 AD   The movement of the star Regulus into the sign of Virgo

   (from Dane Rudhyar)

   2376 AD   Vernal Equinox enters the constellation of Aquarius as defined

   by the sidereal zodiac of Fagan and Bradley

   If we use the tropical zodiac to create twelve equal ages, then each age is about 2160 years long. If we date the beginning of the Piscean age at approximately 100 BC, then the current time is very near the entry into the next constellation of Aquarius. If we use the constellational boundaries of Ptolemy, the vernal equinox will not reach Aquarius until after 2600 AD.

4) Various numbers of years have been given for this cycle. The number of years is probably not entirely stable and may oscillate a bit over time. Dane Rudhyar uses 25,868 years because that is used in Blavatsky's <u>Secret Doctrine</u>. Charles Jayne uses 25,694 years. Most popular literature currently uses 25,920 years. My personal favorite exact figure is 25,800 years used by many astronomers such as Guy Ottewell. To simplify, I use the rounded figure of 26,000 years for the cycle.

5) Chimney Rock, Colorado, Chaco Canyon, New Mexico, Callanish, Scotland and many others

6) The precise location of Galactic Center, currently at about 27 degrees Sagittarius, lies below the ecliptic and thus below and to the right of the intersection of the Milky Way and zodiacal constellations. But it's pretty close.

7) From a personal correspondence

8) These are important ceremonial timings, but remember the greater planetary festival has already begun and lasts until at least 2012.

The Shamanic Astrology
Medicine Wheel Mandala

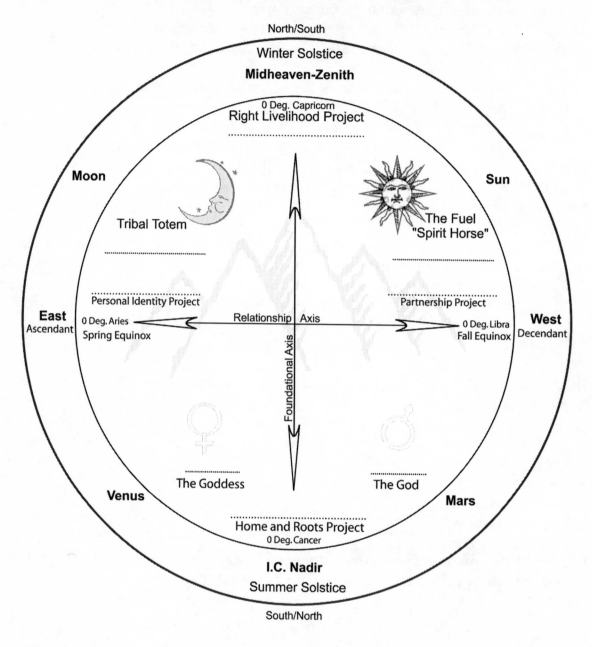

North/South

Winter Solstice
Midheaven-Zenith

0 Deg. Capricorn
Right Livelihood Project

Moon

Tribal Totem

Sun

The Fuel
"Spirit Horse"

Personal Identity Project

0 Deg. Aries   Relationship Axis   0 Deg. Libra
East   **West**
Ascendant   Decendant
Spring Equinox   Fall Equinox

Partnership Project

Foundational Axis

The Goddess   The God

Venus

Mars

Home and Roots Project
0 Deg. Cancer

I.C. Nadir
Summer Solstice

South/North

Note: Use the dotted lines to personalize the Medicine Wheel

Design by www.jcau.com

THE GODDESSES AND GODS
The Archetypes And Images Of The Signs
For the Feminine and Masculine Principle

SIGN	ARCHETYPES, IMAGES, AND GODDESSES FOR THE FEMININE
ARIES ♈	Wild Woman Archetype, "Women Who Run With The Wolves," Warrior Amazon, Fighting For A Cause, The Tom Boy, Joan of Arc, The Goddess: Queen Bodicca
TAURUS ♉	Aphrodite, The Lover, The Courtesan, The Artist, Musician, Dancer, Model
GEMINI ♊	The Eternal Youth, The Female Peter Pan, The Divine Comedienne, ShapeShifter, Heyokah-Coyote Woman, The Entertainer Connected To Her Creative Muse
CANCER ♋	The 'Great Mother' In Her Nurturing Aspects, The Woman Primarily Connected To Her Clan, Tribe, Or Family, Serious And Responsible Giving Of Love To Progeny Or 'Seeds' Until Maturity Is Reached
LEO ♌	The Leading Woman, The Amazon Queen, The Star, Women Who Lead With Spontaneous Will and Who Have A Tremendous Amount of Self-Love
VIRGO ♍	The High Priestess Dedicated To The Sacred Work, Spider Woman The Goddesses: Hestia (Vesta), Demeter (Ceres)
LIBRA ♎	The Wife, The Partner, Women Who See Relationship As The Path To God, The Goddesses: Hera (Juno)
SCORPIO ♏	The Sorceress Witch, The Tantrika, The Mistress of Magic, The Goddesses: Kali, Pele, Hecate, Cretan Snake Goddess
SAGITTARIUS ♐	The Vision Quest Amazon In Search Of Spiritual Truth And The Meaning Of Life, The Spiritual Adventurer, The Trailmate
CAPRICORN ♑	The Central Woman, Queen Bee, The Matriarch Herself, The Business Woman Responsibly Commanding Her Domain, The Counselor, The Elder, The Wise One
AQUARIUS ♒	The Avant-Garde Revolutionary, The Female Avatar, The Grand Experimenter, The Cosmic Visionary, The Lover Of The Devic Kingdoms, Goddess of Democracy
PISCES ♓	The Empathic Woman, Nurse/Caregiver, The Boddhisattva, The Mystical Dreamer

SIGN	ARCHETYPES, IMAGES, AND GODS FOR THE MASCULINE
ARIES ♈	The Rugged Individualist, Aggressive Play, Spontaneous, Willful, Self-Centered Boy With The Toys, The Warrior/Competitor
TAURUS ♉	The Lover, Intimacy Expert, Pleasure Lover, Dancer, Artist, Model, Musician
GEMINI ♊	The Trickster Magician, The Troubadour Minstrel, The Court Jester, The Coyote, The Fool, The Shape Shifter, The Information Networker, Hermes (Mercury), Loki
CANCER ♋	The Good Father And Family Man, The Nurturer, The Protector, Identity Base On Giving Love From Responsibility And Commitment
LEO ♌	The King Archetype, The Born Leader, The Leading Man, Apollo
VIRGO ♍	The Priest Dedicated To The Sacred Work Or Craft, The Servant Of The Goddess, The Gods: Hephaestus (Vulcan)
LIBRA ♎	The Husband, The Partner, The Peacemaker, The Diplomat
SCORPIO ♏	The Sorcerer Magician, The King-Stag, The Horned-God, Pan, The Green Man, The Gods: Pluto, Hades, Cernonoss
SAGITTARIUS ♐	The Hero's Quest, Vision Quest For Meaning And Truth, The Philosopher-Pioneer
CAPRICORN ♑	The Elder, The Prime Minister, The Lawgiver, The Responsible Elder And Good Provider, The Practical Business Man, The Exiled Scapegoat
AQUARIUS ♒	The Cosmic Visionary, The Idealistic Scientist, The Universal Free-Spirit, The Avant-Garde Revolutionary, The Meditator Seeking To Ascend
PISCES ♓	The Empath, The Boddhisattva, Deep Mystical Vision, The Rapture Of Transcendental Union, The God Dionysus

THE SCRIPT

The script consists of three distinct aspects, or movements, as in a symphony. These aspects are the *thesis*, or first movement, the *antithesis*, or second movement, and the *synthesis*, or third movement. The *thesis* deals with the past life themes, or original identity. The *antithesis*, or counterpoint, deals with the tools, equipment and strategy for the current life. The *synthesis* is the current life purpose or the personal medicine wheel. The following is an outline of how this works.

THE SYMBOLS FOR THE THESIS

- **MOON ☽**
- **HOUSE POSITION OF THE SOUTH LUNAR NODE ☋**
- **PLANETS NEAR THE SOUTH NODE ☋**

WHAT THEY SYMBOLIZE

➢ Lineage - Past life themes, family history, genetic encoding, the tribe you come from
➢ The training you have already taken
➢ The Gods and Goddesses of our lineage are located in these symbols
➢ The House Position of the South Node indicates the job you had in your tribe or the specialty you had in your previous training
➢ Any planet near the South Node represents a specific skill from previous training

THE SYMBOLS FOR THE ANTITHESIS

SUN ☉

➢ The fuel, not "life purpose," but the fuel we burn to reach "life purpose"
➢ Not archetype specific unless conjunct Venus or Mars
➢ Only two-fifths of people are anything like their "Sun Sign" descriptions

VENUS ♀

➢ Principle archetype of the feminine
➢ On a woman's chart the specific feminine imagery for the current life
➢ The emerging Goddess
➢ On a man's chart this represents the anima or the magical feminine
➢ On a man's chart frequently associated with physical attraction and romantic love; and the "sacred marriage" i.e. union with one's inner partner

MARS ♂

➢ Principle archetype of the masculine
➢ On a man's chart the specific masculine imagery for the current life
➢ The emerging God
➢ On a woman's chart this represents the Animus or inner masculine
➢ On a woman's chart frequently associated with physical attraction and romantic love; and the "sacred marriage" i.e. union with one's inner partner

MERCURY ☿

➢ Current life mental and thinking and cognitive capacities
➢ A style of perception and communication

THE STRATEGY

The hard aspects (conjunctions, squares, and oppositions) of the five outer planets represent the strategies set up by the individual for eventually accomplishing the life purpose projects.

JUPITER ♃
  ➢ Symbolizes the kinds of activities that promote reaching current life goals as fast as possible
  ➢ Suggests the appropriate "path of enlightenment"
  ➢ Planet of the "vision quest"

SATURN ♄
  ➢ Boundaries and limit conditions
  ➢ Our relationship with the operating manuals of life
  ➢ Third dimensional reality
  ➢ Where things are not intended to work

URANUS ♅
  ➢ Unplanned, unexpected, uncontrollable events that bring on dramatic change

NEPTUNE ♆
  ➢ Dreams, visions, new awareness through identity crisis

PLUTO ♇
  ➢ The descent into the underworld, the incorporation of the "shadow," facing the deepest fears, and events producing chaos

THE SYNTHESIS
The Life Purpose Projects
Your Personal Medicine Wheel
The Astrological Mystery Schools

The four main angles of the chart are the indicators for the current life purpose projects:

ASCENDANT (ASC or AS
  ➢ The Personal Identity Project
  ➢ "The 12 Paths of Enlightenment"
DESCENDANT (DSC or DS)
  ➢ The Partnership Project
MIDHEAVEN (MC)
  ➢ The Right Livelihood Project
BOTTOM OF CHART (IC)
  ➢ The Home And Roots Project

NORTH NODE ☊
The House Position of the North Node further clarifies the life purpose projects. Used in combination with any of the four angles it helps determine your new job in your new tribe or your new specialty in your new training.

The progressive reading of a chart has all the tools and equipment, the lineage, and the strategy serving the Life Purpose projects.

The regressive reading of a chart has all the tools and equipment, the strategy and an unclear idea of the Life Purpose projects attempting to hold on to the lineage, and perpetuate the already established identity.

Note On Use Of The Whole House System In Shamanic Astrology
Addendum To The Script Material

Since this book was first published in 1994, a new yet ancient House System has been adopted by Shamanic Astrologers. This was catalyzed and inspired in part through two articles written by Robert Hand for the Mountain Astrologer Magazine in 1999. Hand explained that the translation of ancient Sumerian and Babylonian astrological texts led to the discovery of the oldest known house system used called the Whole Sign System. This system simplifies the houses and eliminates confusion around planetary placements near house cusps. From the perspective of the archetypal approach utilized by Shamanic Astrology the Whole House system beautifully aligns with this, equating the archetypal meaning of a house with that of a sign. For example, the first house of 30 whole degrees always has the connotation of the sign Aries, the second house, Taurus and so on.

In the Whole House System each house cusp begins with zero degrees of the sign, placing the ascendant or sign that is rising somewhere in the first house. So for example, if a person is born with 29 degrees Capricorn Rising the first house cusp is zero degrees Capricorn, the second house cusp is zero degrees Aquarius, etcetera. The difference is the Ascendant/Descendant are not defining the first or seventh house cusp but fall within the context of those houses. Other benefits of this system are how it effectively eliminates the confusion concerning what house a planet or node is really occupying. It also eliminates 'intercepted' signs in houses and is a tremendous resolution to the long-standing problem regarding the distortion of house size at more extreme northern latitudes. During the last few years, the use of this house system has eliminated one of the last remaining ambiguities in the Shamanic Astrology system resolving important inconsistencies in interpretation.

All in all, this system is philosophically in perfect accord with an archetypal system of exact 30 degree units with an original intent of equality and correspondence between sign and house. The fundamental priority of the degree of the Ascendant and Midheaven hasn't been altered; rather they now appear as prominent placements within houses, successfully uncoupling the angles with the 1st and 10th houses.

You can order natal and other charts from the back of the book based on the Whole House System, or Solar Fire, Win Star and other astrology programs do have a Whole House or Whole Sign Option. Our suggestion is to look at your chart and other charts using Whole Sign Houses. It may take some time to develop familiarity with this system especially if you are practiced in looking at charts on the Placidus or Koch or some other house system. Give it some time, approach it with an open mind and decide for yourself what system works best for you. There is no one right or wrong way to look at the astrological mysteries and that includes the house system. Finding what works for you is the key. It is interesting to note that as this edition goes to press, this house system has been added as an option by Astro Communications Services (800-888-9983), under the name of the Shamanic House System. We are pleased!

QUICK GUIDE
To The Astrological Signs, Archetypes And Planets

SIGN	KEY WORDS	ELEMENTS
Aries ♈	Aggressive Play	Cardinal/Fire/Masculine
Taurus ♉	Intimacy and Aesthetics	Fixed/Earth/Feminine
Gemini ♊	Freedom of Mind/Communication	Mutable/Air/Masculine
Cancer ♋	Responsible Nurturing	Cardinal/Water/Feminine
Leo ♌	Radiant Self-Love	Fixed/Fire/Masculine
Virgo ♍	Sacred Work	Mutable/Earth/Feminine
Libra ♎	Relatedness, Partnership	Cardinal/Air/Masculine
Scorpio ♏	Command of Feelings & Desires	Fixed/Water/Feminine
Sagittarius ♐	Quest For Meaning Of Life	Mutable/Fire/Masculine
Capricorn ♑	Management and Control	Cardinal/Earth/Feminine
Aquarius ♒	Life as a Grand Experiment	Fixed/Air/Masculine
Pisces ♓	Selfless Service To Others	Mutable/Water/Feminine

SIGN	THIS MYSTERY SCHOOL INVESTIGATES:
Aries ♈	Pure Centered-On-Self Awareness, Spontaneity, Aggressive Play, Protect The Cosmic Order
Taurus ♉	Aesthetics, Intimacy As An Art Form, Receptivity, Brings Spirit Into Matter To Enjoy
Gemini ♊	The Nature Of Analytical Mind And Its Forms Of Communication, The Entire Spectrum Of Logical And Mental Interconnectedness, To Go Beyond Linear Processes
Cancer ♋	Responsible Nurturing, Home And Roots, New Themes For Home And Family
Leo ♌	The Nature Of The Sovereign Autonomous Central Self Develop Radiant Self-Love, Essence Of Leadership
Virgo ♍	The Patterning Of The Organic World And Of Soul, To Discover And Then Dedicate Self To The "Sacred Work," Brings Spirit Into Matter To Honor It
Libra ♎	To Discover Conscious Equal Partnership, Balance Individual Truth & Consensus Reality
Scorpio ♏	Life Force Energy And The Deepest Emotions Through The Full Experience Of The Interaction Of Will And Desire, Intimacy As Tantra And Eros
Sagittarius ♐	Truth And The Meaning Of Life By Expanding The Self To The Widest Possible Horizons, Through The Hero's Journey And Vision Quests
Capricorn ♑	The Rules And Principles That Govern The Structure Of The Universe, Brings Spirit Into Matter To Manage And Administer It
Aquarius ♒	Freedom Through Awareness Of Cosmic Overview & Spiritual Or Intellectual Detachment, Enrichment Of Life's Possibilities Through Unique Eccentricity & Revolution
Pisces ♓	The Ecstasy Of Mystical & Empathic Union With Humanity And God, Selfless Service, The Bodhisattva Ideal

PLANET	WHAT IT REPRESENTS
Sun ☉	The Fuel You Burn, The Type Of Energy Required To Reach Your Goals
Moon ☽	Tribal Ancestral History, Lineage
Mercury ☿	Communication, How A Person Thinks
Venus ♀	Feminine Energy, Universal Anima
Mars ♂	Masculine Energy, Universal Animus
Jupiter ♃	Fastest Path To Liberation, Expansion
Saturn ♄	Manmade Law, Creative Encounter With Limit Conditions
Uranus ♅	Whatever It Takes To Bring About Change
Neptune ♆	Brings In New Visions/Dreams Through Identity Crisis
Pluto ♇	Law Of Life, Deepest Fears, Incorporating The Shadow

QUICK GUIDE
ASTROLOGICAL HOUSES, ANGLES AND ASPECTS

HOUSE	RULERS	REPRESENTS
First	♈ Aries/Mars ♂	The Autonomous Sovereign Self
Second	♉ Taurus/Venus ♀	Pleasure, Aesthetics, Receiving
Third	♊ Gemini/Mercury ☿	Communication, Mind
Fourth	♋ Cancer/Moon ☽	Roots, Home And Family
Fifth	♌ Leo/Sun ☉	Fun, Radiant Self-Love, Children
Sixth	♍ Virgo/Vesta ⚶	Sacred Work, Service, Health
Seventh	♎ Libra/Juno ⚵	Partnership And Relationship
Eighth	♏ Scorpio/Pluto ♇	Death/Rebirth, Intensity Of Sexuality
Ninth	♐ Sagittarius/Jupiter ♃	Expansion Of Self To Widest Horizons
Tenth	♑ Capricorn/Saturn ♄	Career, Contribution, Duty
Eleventh	♒ Aquarius/Uranus ♅	Cosmic Overview, Community, Friends
Twelfth	♓ Pisces/Neptune ♆	Selfless Service, Mystical/Transpersonal

ANGLE	AREA OF CHART	REPRESENTS
Rising Sign (ASC or AS)	The East Point	The Personal Identity Project
Descendant (DSC or DC)	The West Point	The Relationship Project
Midheaven (MC)	Top of the Chart	The Right Livelihood Project
Nadir (IC)	Bottom of the Chart	The Home and Roots Project

ASPECTS	ANGLE/DEGREE	REPRESENTS
Conjunction ☌	0 Degrees/Orb of 10	Burst Of Energy, Powerful Synthesis
Sextile ⚹	60 Degrees/Orb of 6	Easy Integration
Square □	90 Degrees/Orb of 10	Crisis In Action, At The Effect Of
Trine △	120 Degrees/Orb of 10	Easy Flow, Inherent Talents
Opposition ☍	180 Degrees/Orb of 10	Forced Awareness, High Intensity
Quincunx ⚻ or ⊼	150 Degrees/Orb of 3	Disconnect

SQUARES ENERGY			OPPOSITIONS		SIGN
Aries □ Cancer and Capricorn	♈□♋	♈□♑	Aries ☍ Libra	♈☍♎	Cardinal Signs
Taurus □ Leo and Aquarius	♉□♌	♉□♒	Taurus ☍ Scorpio	♉☍♏	Fixed Signs
Gemini □ Virgo and Pisces	♊□♍	♊□♓	Gemini ☍ Sagittarius	♊☍♐	Mutable Signs
Cancer □ Aries and Libra	♋□♈	♋□♎	Cancer ☍ Capricorn	♋☍♑	Cardinal Signs
Leo □ Taurus and Scorpio	♌□♉	♌□♏	Leo ☍ Aquarius	♌☍♒	Fixed Signs
Virgo □ Gemini and Sagittarius	♍□♊	♍□♐	Virgo ☍ Pisces	♍☍♓	Mutable Signs
Libra □ Capricorn and Cancer	♎□♑	♎□♋	Libra ☍ Aries	♎☍♈	Cardinal Signs
Scorpio □ Leo and Aquarius	♏□♌	♏□♒	Scorpio ☍ Taurus	♏☍♉	Fixed Signs
Sagittarius □ Virgo and Pisces	♐□♍	♐□♓	Sagittarius ☍ Gemini	♐☍♊	Mutable Signs
Capricorn □ Aries and Libra	♑□♈	♑□♎	Capricorn ☍ Cancer	♑☍♋	Cardinal Signs
Aquarius □ Taurus and Scorpio	♒□♉	♒□♏	Aquarius ☍ Leo	♒☍♌	Fixed Signs
Pisces □ Sagittarius and Gemini	♓□♐	♓□♊	Pisces ☍ Virgo	♓☍♍	Mutable Signs

TRINES		ELEMENTS
Aries △ Leo △ Sagittarius	♈△♌△♐	Fire/Masculine
Taurus △ Virgo △ Capricorn	♈△♌△♐	Earth/Feminine
Gemini △ Libra △ Aquarius	♈△♌△♐	Air/Masculine
Cancer △ Scorpio △ Pisces	♈△♌△♐	Water/Feminine

THE SHAMANIC ARCHETYPES OF THE SIGNS

These Are Not Sun Sign Descriptions. These sign descriptions are designed to give a feeling or flavor of the nature of the twelve archetypes. Once each of the archetypes is understood, they can then be plugged into the script in many different ways. For example, the Moon position describes the area of mastery, or talents and skills, a person has already attained. It also describes the areas where there may be addictions or attachments. The Rising sign and Venus or Mars, describes what type of training a person intends to undergo in the current life. The understanding of each archetype provides a quick and simple way to start unraveling the symbols found in the script.

♈ ARIES ♈

Aries is the rugged individualist, who is very competitive. These qualities are partly responsible for patriarchy's mistranslation of Aries as war-related. Really, Aries has less to do with war and more to do with aggressive play, or competitiveness. The image of two Rams butting heads with each other does not mean they are trying to kill each other; rather they are egging each other on. Aries is also associated with the innocence of a child. That's why the enlightenment motif for Aries is what Christ meant when he said, "To enter the kingdom of heaven you must enter as a small child." So Aries training includes learning a combination of trust, innocence and courage.

One of my favorite images for giving a flavor of the Aries archetype is the story of what happened after the 1976 World Series with Pete Rose. Pete Rose's team had just lost the sixth and deciding game and it was one of the most astounding games ever played in any World Series. The winner of the series had to be determined in an extra inning, and at the end of that inning Cincinnati had lost. The reporters expected to find the losing team with their heads down, going through the agony of defeat when they entered their dugout. However, after this particular game, Pete Rose was in a state of elation. An interviewer asked; "Pete, how does it feel to have just lost?" Pete responded by saying; "Wasn't that the greatest game you've ever seen? It was just incredible." The interviewer was stunned. Pete's reaction was not what he expected. For Pete it was the pure sense of joy of having been engaged in such a great competitive event. That's the Aries sense of play and competitiveness. Aries love getting paid big bucks for doing something that is like a kid's game.

The essence of Aries is absolutely straightforward and dualistic, black and white, good and bad. Whenever there is a war, or a battle against the dark lords, you want to have Aries on your side. Hence, the Gods and Goddesses most associated with Aries are the defenders of the Cosmic Order. This is in contrast to Scorpio where the Goddess images are the creators of disorder and chaos, preparing the ground so new things can grow in the spring. The down side of Aries shows up as ruthless fundamentalism, which is every bit as black and white.

With this in mind, it is important to note that Aries, per se, is not a householder sign. However, Aries can choose to be a householder. Among the twelve archetypes it is difficult to find a husband who is a greater defender of the family than the Aries man. He is also more possessive and more black and white about his beliefs. He may be defending the outer framework of a householder arrangement, but he may not fully understand what the content of a relationship and a family really is. Cancer, Capricorn, and Libra are cardinal signs (the cardinal signs are initiators of action, intending to act directly and decisively) and are considered householder paths. The householder path is the path of family, community and relationship. Aries is also a cardinal sign, but is less immediately seen as being a part of the householder path. However, when Aries chooses to stand up for the way the society is set up, to protect a relationship, to protect the family, or to protect a country, then Aries aligns with householder values. The Aries archetype may not fully identify with householders, but it can be a defender of householders. An example of how this might polarize is when the Aries man, married with children, ready to protect his family to the death if necessary is also having an outside love affair at the same time. The Aries archetype doesn't' have the subtleties and complexities of intimacy, but as long as Aries is on your side, and as long as they are motivated to defend something, they will be one-pointed, consistent, and thorough about it.

The Aries archetype can also show up as footloose and fancy free on the trail, charging at life as if experiencing it for the very first time. Archetypal Aries as the adventurer is not about having to take responsibility or play by society's rules. An example of how an Aries might operate today is they are the ones who know that if they show up late to a concert or a play, they can butt to the front of the line and go right to their seat. What allows them to do that? It is their total lack of any feeling towards what others are experiencing. They can only experience themselves. Aries is not a giving or receiving sign; it is neutral, and it operates out of pure selfishness and narcissism. This is not a negative value judgment, because when Aries is healthy and in balance it operates out of innocence, and there is something charming and childlike about it.

For a woman, Aries is most often expressed as the Virgin Amazon. Virgin, in this case does not mean they do not have sex. The original meaning of the word simply meant unmarried. What it does mean is a woman who is whole and complete unto herself, determining her own course of action for her life. Amazon refers to a woman whose identity is based upon her own accomplishments and achievements, and not on whom she is with. A great Aries image for women is the wild and rugged Celtic Warrior Goddess astride her war stallion; her flaming red hair blowing in the wind, as she fearlessly leads her army into battle. She is so fierce and determined that when the invading army sees her they flee the battlefield.

Today a woman with strong Aries (Venus in Aries, Moon in Aries, or Aries Rising) is more likely to demonstrate the nontraditional, or non-householder version of Aries, unless she has other strong householder aspects, such as Cancer, or Libra. Then her Aries side might be expressed as the defender of her family in a dualistic way, like a fundamentalist Christian woman, who follows the dictates of the Bible exactly. For her there is nothing other than the literalism of it, the black and whiteness of it. If the Aries woman is not a householder, then she will be a wild and free Amazon all the way.

ARIES TRAINING is about developing a strong, individuated self. An important Aries theme is "I do what I want, don't tell me what to do!" The challenge for those undertaking Aries training is to live their life as if they are doing it for the first time. To be successful in this training a person must learn to play--be spontaneous, independent and free. They must also develop qualities of trust, innocence, and courage. One way to approach Aries training is to learn to be two years old, to look at everything in life as if seeing it for the first time. Two-year-olds insist on exploring everything. "I want to taste this, I want to touch that, I want to do that, I want to check that out, and don't tell me what to do." Like two-year-olds, Aries are learning about the first pure expression of individual will.

♉ TAURUS ♉

Taurus training was originally associated with Aphrodite, who represented the qualities of deep personal intimacy. The gift of intimacy was her greatest contribution to humanity. The following statement is an example of how Aphrodite expressed herself: "I am beautiful by definition, and I don't even have to work on it. I am beautiful just the way I am. Know this, you may be with me if you honor, love, and savor me, in a manner befitting my status, and one more thing, you don't own me. I shall be this way with whomever honors me according to these standards." Therefore, originally Aphrodite was not a pair bonder, or a monogamous married type, but she was also not promiscuous. She had the highest standards and requirements for deep personal intimacy, and no one could be with her unless they met her standards.

The marvelous work of Jean Bolen, _The Goddesses in Every Woman_ is like an astrological textbook, even though astrology is never mentioned in it. She describes three categories of Goddesses. First, there are the autonomous, or virgin Goddesses. Again, virgin doesn't refer to women who don't have sex, but rather to women who are complete unto themselves. These women don't have to be with anyone to know who they are. Next, there are the vulnerable Goddesses. They choose to marry and define themselves by their relationship, and/or define themselves by their children, and family connections. The third category has only one Goddess, Aphrodite. She is paradoxical, because she doesn't pair bond, or marry, and she isn't known for being a mother, so she is not vulnerable in that sense. But, she must be intimate with someone to know who she is, so she is not a virginal autonomous type, either. Instead, she merges or blends autonomy and intimacy together. In the old days, it was the Aphrodite woman who initiated the young boys into the art of intimacy and sexuality, and it was the Aphrodite woman who was invited into the bridal chamber to make sure the newlyweds knew what they were doing.

Taurus is a tantric mystery school, as is Scorpio. It has to do with life force energy, the essence of intimacy. Taurus training has two pillars. One pillar is aesthetics, not the knowledge of, but the full sensual experience of what is beautiful. The other pillar is intimacy per se. Taurus training involves becoming a master of intimacy, where intimacy is an art form. The Taurus archetype, for both men and women, has been violated and invalidated by patriarchy. No Goddess has been more violated than Aphrodite. This is plain to see when we realize how the exploitative advertising of women, in the current culture, is a major violation of the Venus/Aphrodite image. Why? Because, when Aphrodite becomes beautiful, she is not doing it for the men or anyone else. She is doing it for herself. This violation has taken place at the hands of the men and women who have willingly gone along with the exploitation of this image in the advertising industry. It is important to know that this has nothing to do with what the original essence of Aphrodite represented.

Taurus, like Aries, is centered on self and narcissistic. That's why Aphrodite is often seen looking at herself in the mirror. Ideally, the intent of Taurus is to learn to appreciate and value the self in a healthy and balanced way. However, the downside of Taurus is expressed as an addicted receiver. Some images I have gathered from my own personal experience come from when I lived in Los Angeles. I had the opportunity to see a lot of horoscopes of guys with strong Taurus. They were usually the boyfriends of many of the women I had as clients. These women were typically dancers, models, and actresses. When I looked at the charts of their boyfriends, I found that most of them had Moon or Mars in Taurus. The most common complaint I heard from these women was how their boyfriends were gorgeous guys, but all they wanted to do was lie there. They were addicted receivers. There are four archetypal trainings that are givers and one that is a receiver. Taurus is the receiver energy, and when done in a healthy way it is a great gift to the giver to have someone totally and completely receive what the giver is giving. One example of healthy Taurus is expressed in the following image: Imagine a masseuse, who for two hours gives a massage to someone who is fully into receiving, enjoying, and appreciating the massage, without worry or concern of having to give something in return. This is a wonderful gift to the masseuse, because it completes the life force circuit. If something is given and not properly received then what is given is not fully honored; the gift is not fully realized, and the energy associated with the gift is wasted. The invaluable gift Taurus brings to the universe is the art of being a great receiver.

In contemporary western culture, special challenges exist for the male who expresses the Taurus archetype. Men are not trained to view the artistry of intimacy, aesthetics, or receiving as valid masculine qualities. Yet, to reestablish a full spectrum of authentic archetypal expressions of the masculine, Taurus qualities are as valid and as needed as the more current culturally validated expressions. Healthy and authentic Taurian masculine qualities are similar to the qualities found in the female gender, but when mixed with additional yang energies it produces an exquisite balance of giving and receiving, and of action and receptivity. No images of laziness, indulgence or sloth here. Rather, the images are men with fully developed capacities for intimacy and savoring life at it deepest levels. They are true artists and epicures. The masculine expression of the Taurus archetype is currently largely uncharted territory. It is even more uncharted territory than the situation with the feminine experience working to reclaim the Aphrodite mysteries from the current social violation. Part of reclaiming wholeness for humanity and the masculine principle is the birthing of the new Taurian masculine *Gods.*

It is common for the Pluto in Leo generation, with Taurus Moon, to have heavy Saturn or Pluto aspects to their Moon. This type of strategy sets up their life in such a way that they don't get validation for their best qualities, causing a wound that eventually must be healed. For Taurus to properly heal, they must once again be in a healthy position to be a receiver. However, I have also known numerous people with Taurus Moon that are total Taurus addicts. Kept women or men, courtesan types, and gigolos, are some examples of the addicted version of Taurus. Those who are not able to feel comfortable with their area of mastery, on the other hand, exemplify the violated or invalidated versions of Taurus. A common example of violation to the Taurus archetype is when a woman, who comes into the life tremendously comfortable and healthy with her sexuality, has Pluto square her Taurus Moon. The violation often manifests as sexual abuse from her father, or brother, or uncle, or some other male figure in her life. Some situation occurs where she experiences an early violation. She gets the message that it's not safe to be who she really is. The good news, if there is any, is the intent of this strategy is to no longer be identified with Taurus. It allows something different to be developed. Then, at some point, the wound must be healed. This is represented in our culture today by the increasing awareness of child sexual abuse issues and the process victims of this type of abuse go through to heal. The Taurus archetype must be restored so those with Taurus mastery can know who they really are. They are the masters of intimacy, and they know the full range of cellular and spiritual intimacy in the body.

TAURUS TRAINING asks two questions; *"What is the nature of intimacy, and what is the nature of aesthetics?"* Not the knowledge of aesthetics, but the physical experience, in the body, of aesthetics. It is a tantric path, where one learns to be completely into the current of life, and to increase their own life force energy. The enlightenment path for Taurus is the Garden of Eden, to fully bring spirit into matter, for the purpose of pure enjoyment. From an eastern perspective, there is actually a form of yoga known as Bhogabhumi; the path of union through pleasure. Certainly this is a Taurus mystery school! In the west, the philosophical school of Epicureanism is associated with Taurus. Taurus is the mystery school of beauty as a path to God. The great Russian artist, Nicholas Roerich, was an exponent of this path.

♊ GEMINI ♊

"The Truth? Why the truth is simply an excuse for a lack of imagination!"
Garrick-Star Trek, Deep Space Nine

The Gemini and Aries archetypes are similar in several ways. They both can share the imagery of the Puer or Puella, the eternal youth, and the female Peter Pan. The lineage for both is footloose and fancy-free. Gemini, however, is more spirit oriented. It is magical. The Gemini archetype is the troubadour minstrel, the trickster magician, the coyote, the court jester, the clown. The court jester was the only one who could tell the king the truth and not be killed for it, because the court jester was not operating out of an ego stance. Another archetypal image for Gemini is the Fool in the Tarot cards. The Fool leaps empty handed off the cliff into the void, knowing the law of gravity has no effect on him (or her) because s/he has transcended the law or gone beyond it.

Masters of the Gemini archetype are accustomed to living life *with* diplomatic license plates. They were not subject to the same rules as everyone else. This creates a considerable challenge for those who have mastered Gemini and are now here to explore a different mystery school like Capricorn or Virgo, where it is important to know what the rules are and to follow them. The transition to experiencing life *without* having diplomatic license plates is difficult to say the least. Often times, those with Gemini lineage find they are the ones who really do have to grow up and learn how to take responsibility. They are learning to be in third dimensional reality, and to deal with boundaries. Yet, the freedom place for Gemini is to be connected to an approach to life that is magical. Gemini is in its freedom when it's connected to the creative Muses, or channeling the divine comedian, or the divine Fool.

An original myth for Gemini is the imagery of a bard (or a wandering minstrel) on a circuit. This circuit includes many castles of various realms. The wandering minstrel shows up and gives a thoroughly entertaining performance. Wildly popular and much loved by all, the minstrel is freely given special privileges, like his or her own royal suite in the castle. Later that night, the bard may even entertain one of the leading ladies or gentlemen of the court in their room, then leave the next day. It was accepted and well known that wandering minstrels were never expected to stay long.

Gemini is not a mother or father energy, but it *is* sexual. In ancient Greece, there were stacks of stones everywhere called Herms. They represented the phallic projections of Hermes marking his territory. As we receded from that time and moved into patriarchy, Hermes transformed into Mercury, and Gemini transformed into something more androgynous, becoming less and less vitally sexual, and more and more pubescent or immature. The original lineage of Gemini was quite phallic and sexual. The southwest Native American imagery of Kokopeli is also sexual, musical, and a bringer of magic. He is similar in imagery to the wandering minstrel. No one would ever consider Kokopeli, as a father or husband, yet at the same time the imagery of Kokopeli is also not that of a rapist. This imagery does not include taking advantage of women or brutalizing them, but rather it is understood as a magical connection.

Like Aries, Gemini is playful, although in a different way. Aries is a rougher form of play. Aries takes itself seriously when it plays, but not Gemini. Aries is the rugged individualist, and fiercely competitive, whereas Gemini is just having fun. If Gemini is running a race they may be way out in front, easily beating everyone and then stop just short of the finish line and let everyone else win. Gemini would think this is a real hoot, because it is such an unexpected thing for someone to do. Aries would never think of doing such a thing. True Aries has a one-pointed focus to win the race, Gemini's focus is the trickster, and doing what is least expected. Gemini is also like the shape shifter, so Gemini is much less likely to provoke a confrontation, as Aries might. Being rugged, and forceful, Aries has no subtlety associated with it. Gemini, on the other hand, is the essence of subtlety.

The rehabilitation process for the Gemini archetype is to reconnect with their own creative Muse, reconnect with spirit, and reconnect with humor and freedom. For women, this has nothing whatsoever to do with the patriarchal feminine principle of the woman as wife, girlfriend, mother, or nurse. Gemini is not in the body; it is not in the organic dimension of the emotions or feelings. It is in the creative spirit.

In traditional astrology Gemini is the epitome of high-speed, efficient, mental functioning. That's the reason Gemini is considered Mercury's favorite place, because the emphasis is on left-brain, intellectual dexterity, and acumen. However, the real essence of Gemini goes beyond that, to the irrational. The trickster joke is not the foolishness that exists *before* rationality; it is the foolishness that comes *after* rationality, after the law of life has been completely fulfilled. Then the irreverent cosmic trickster humor of Gemini happens easily because Gemini has already mastered rational, linear reality. So, unless a person really knows what they are lampooning and have mastered rational, linear reality, chances are they won't genuinely be funny.

GEMINI TRAINING can be summed up in this statement: "Do what thou wilt is the whole of the law." That statement only makes sense if a person already fully knows what the law is, and has completely fulfilled it. Gemini training requires a person to know and fulfill the law, and then go beyond it to a place of complete and total freedom. It is about getting the joke, or the cosmic humor beyond linear reality. A person taking Gemini training, and in doubt about what to do next, might ask, "What would Robin Williams do now?"

How does the serious, disciplined person now signed up for Gemini training learn the Gemini lessons? The following story gives a flavor of what their experience might be: The serious person undertakes a project that requires tremendous discipline, a great deal of skill, knowledge, and courage such as climbing a particularly dangerous and treacherous mountain. When they finally reach the top of the mountain, they think they have at last successfully completed their goal. Through their perseverance, and ability to be disciplined and follow the rules, go through the rigorous training, and stay one-pointed on their task, they have accomplished something very few others ever have. However, to their amazement they are given one last instruction. Jump Off!! One of the main features of Gemini training is to fully know the laws of nature do not affect you; you are truly free from the rules. Gemini's intent is to learn to be the eternal youth, free spirit, entertainer, artist, or divine comedian, connected to the creative Muse and to ultimately achieve complete freedom.

♋ CANCER ♋

Of the twelve archetypes or trainings, four of them are giver energies. These are Cancer, Pisces, Virgo, and Capricorn. Each of these four archetypes has a different emphasis, or reasons for giving (and all of them can fall into the addicted giver trap, see Pisces for more details). Virgo directs their giving through their total dedication to the sacred work. Cancer directs their giving to their family or those they choose to nurture. Capricorn gives through taking responsibility for the community, knowing the rules, and how to keep things together. One of the main differences between Capricorn and Cancer is Capricorn acts out of a sense of responsibility and duty. Cancer acts out of love, empathy, and sensitivity.

The primary identity for the Cancer archetype comes through *responsibly nurturing* their family, their children. Cancer is a water sign along with Scorpio and Pisces. All three operate out of the feeling function, but they all have a different emphasis on how their feelings are experienced. For Cancer, the emphasis is on the ability to feel the feelings of those they are nurturing, so they can better give the love, attention, and caring that is needed. Pisces is different from Cancer because Pisces do not discriminate in whom they are giving to or whose feelings they are feeling. Cancer is clannish. For example, in China there is one law for people in your Clan, there is another law if you are Chinese, and there is still another law if you are not Chinese. Cancer loves all their children and family members unconditionally, but they have a specific definition of who their tribe is, who their family is, and who their children are. It might be so extreme as to manifest in the kind of love and caring Skin Head gang members display for each other, even though they hate everybody else. This is the shadow side of how Cancer can have strongly defined boundaries for those they choose to responsibly nurture. Pisces has no such boundaries; they have the same degree of empathic, sensitive giving for all. That's why Cancer is more of a householder position than Pisces. The householder tribes, like Cancer, Libra, and Capricorn, are the ones responsible for keeping the culture together from one generation to the next.

Within the framework of the Cancer archetype there is not an emphasis on the development of a personal identity, other than through their connection to the children and other family members. Therefore, Cancer is not an individuated training. It is a training based upon a person's connection to their progeny, or to their family.

The Cancer Goddesses are represented by all the nurturing mother Goddesses, and women primarily connected to their clan, tribe, or family. For men, the Cancer archetype is the path of responsible nurturing operating out of the feeling function. This does not show up as a valued male quality within patriarchy. Part of the work of the male mysteries is to discover what responsible nurturing is really like for men, because this is a valid male quality that must be recognized and honored. The Cancer archetype has no known Gods from the ancient pantheons that describe Cancer for men. That's why Cancer, along with other archetypes, is in the process of creating new myths that are valid and important for both men and women.

CANCER TRAINING asks: *"What is the nature of family, roots, and home?"* Those taking Cancer training are learning how to demonstrate the qualities of love and nurturing that creates safety for the children, and they are learning how to be committed to a foundation that has concern for the seven generations to follow. Cancer training involves serious, responsible giving of love to progeny or projects (seeds) until the seeds or projects reach what for them is maturity. The emerging reformulation of this archetype is to redefine family. Cancer's job is to answer the question, *"How to do family in new ways, appropriate at the turning of Ages, that are responsible, committed, nurturing, and loving?"*

♌ LEO ♌

The main lesson learned in the astrological mystery school of Leo is radical self-love, radical selfhood. A descriptive Leo statement is, *"I AM THAT I AM! I am the one who runs the energy!"* Someone who is really together with Leo can walk into a room, and know their greatest contribution to humanity is showing up. It has nothing to do with how good they are, or what they do. So even though Leo is a masculine sign, when Leo is healthy, it is opposed to the patriarchal principle that says: The Success You Achieve, and the Love You Receive, is based upon how good you are, or what you do. Leos love themselves so much they make their contribution simply by showing up. What is their contribution? Leo empowers others through their own self-confidence. This is the king/queen archetype or the leading man or woman. Those with Leo Moon have already had a shot at developing radical self-love in the past. They may have had the experience of being born into royalty. This doesn't mean they unfairly had power to be superior over other people. They were royalty because they represented the best qualities of the people. At certain times in history, literally, if you were not in a certain bloodline, you wouldn't have had the ability or the genetic encoding to experience certain things. Archetypally, a Leo Moon suggests a person has had experiences that enabled them to develop radical self-love and were in a position of leadership as a result.

Another way the Leo archetype might show up is the famous person who arrives in a limousine, automatically gets the front row, is deferred to, and is treated like the star. There is no judgment made by others as to whether they earned it or not. In fact, most people who have done Leo training, did work hard to become a leader or a star, and were then deferred to for it. Individuals coming into the life with mastery in the Leo archetype have already experienced and learned the Leo mysteries. Now, as part of the strategy to break the addiction or expectation of the past training, they are often required to experience life as one of the common people. They have to learn to be humble and have humility. They might wonder why they aren't being deferred to or treated like royalty. The circumstances of their life force them to give up their attachment to special privileges. This is not an easy thing for Leo Moon to learn.

There are two archetypal stories that describe how the addiction to the Leo archetype might be broken. These stories are intended to give a flavor of the experience, and may not reflect what a person's real experience is. However, these stories do provide a framework for how the scenarios can unfold. The first story is of Guatama Buddha, or Prince Sidhartha. He was born in the lap of luxury, silver spoon, everything going for him. His father kept him from having any experiences of what life was really like. Out of choice, Sidhartha overturned the system, so he could fully experience all of life's possibilities. He actually allowed himself to experience the entire shadow side of life by passing as one of the common people. He wanted to find out what really goes on in third dimensional reality. The second archetypal story is that of the beggar. In our culture, the beggars are judged by the right wing Republicans as a bunch of lazy bums, who could get their life together, if they just picked themselves up and did some work. A left wing Democrat immediately wishes to provide food for all of them. However, in India they say not to judge, or feel sorry for the beggars. Why? Because that beggar may have been a great and wonderful Maharaja last life, but one thing a Maharaja can never learn is humbleness, humility, and powerlessness. Therefore, he has chosen this as a concentrated experience of powerlessness, and this will be his last life.

Another aspect of the Leo archetype is one of true leadership. The Leo leader is not the leader who is the manager, or the one who control things, but is the leader who leads spontaneously from a place of selflove. It might be a person who is in charge of a project, and someone comes to them and shares their dream or idea. If the Leo leader's intuition really understands the dream and gets that it is a great idea, they will ask what is needed to fulfill the dream and then proceed to give whatever is necessary so the dream is realized. The person with the dream then feels love and appreciation for the Leo leader. This has the effect of increasing the Leo leader's own auric field. Is this an altruistic gesture on the part of the Leo leader? Not really. Leo is *not* considered a giver energy, because Leos give for their own empowerment. This is similar to the kind of empowering experience a person has when they are around someone who genuinely loves who they are.

LEO TRAINING is primarily to develop radical, radiant self-love. The philosopher Gurdjieff once said, "Self-love is humanity's greatest problem when it is vanity, but you can't get enlightened without it." At a certain stage, we do have to develop a radical sense of self worth. *I AM THAT I AM!* It is no different than the new age idea of each one of us being God. The way Leo gets enlightened is to expand their ego to the point where it is so big that it is as big as God's! This is the opposite of Pisces, because Pisces gets enlightened by having no ego whatsoever, not even a trace. If a person has Leo Rising and Mars or Venus in Pisces, the challenge is to have the Mars or Venus in Pisces serve Leo Rising. Ideally this expresses itself as the Mars or Venus in Pisces person who also has a sense of self. Mars in Pisces truly loves to serve, but with Leo Rising they don't have to have their self-identity extinguished in the process.

Leo's intent is to first empower themselves first and then to also dynamically empower others. Leo does not consciously think or consider whether they are helping others.

Rather, their intent is to increase the love they are getting from others, because it feels good to them. That is why Leo is not the same as a true giver energy. It's fun to be around someone who truly loves who they are in a healthy way. Leos increase their own auric field as they act to empower others, because they receive more and more love from the people they are empowering. This in turn increases Leo's personal power in a way that benefits everyone.

♍ VIRGO ♍

Virgo, as one of the four giver signs, gives through its absolute dedication to the sacred work. When Virgo is giving there is no personal self, no personal ego involved. They are not performing the work for their own self-aggrandizement, or for personal reward, money, fame, or wealth. For the true Virgo archetype, it is their great joy to be aware of the natural rhythms and cycles, and to then do the work necessary to keep everything together for all the rest of us. One good example from times pas, is represented by the women, the priestesses, who performed the winter solstice ceremony. The understanding, at that time, was that if the winter solstice ceremony was not performed properly, and during the correct timing, the Sun would not return. The Virgo adepts experienced joy as a result of their successful participation in that type of great ritual drama. Within the framework of the Virgo archetype personal joy, personal pleasure for self is considered indulgent and, in fact, irrelevant. Hence, all actions were performed for the benefit of the people and the community.

I believe Virgo has been radically and wrongly interpreted by patriarchy. Virgo has a reputation for being critical, nit picky. Virgo is not necessarily critical in a judgmental sense; rather it is Virgo's job to notice the pattern of life. Virgo is the energy whose presiding deity in the Native American Tradition is Spider Woman. Spider Woman spins the web of life, the web we are experiencing. The lawful structure of the web, of Maya, has a patterning to it. Virgo notices it, and co-creates with it. It is the tapestry of life. It is Virgo's job to be ceremonial with it. Virgo is also ruled by Hestia or Vesta. Among the Greeks, Hestia was the one the first prayers were offered to, because the people knew Hestia must perform the sacred ceremonies at the right time or everything would fall apart. There was no statue of Hestia, because it wasn't an ego thing, and we never saw Hestia in a beauty contest. Why? Because her job had to do with sacred function and did not include indulging in personal concerns.

Virgo is not a personal sign; it is impersonal, and complete unto itself. (Virgo doesn't have to be with anyone to know who she is.) In the old days, Virgo was often found as a Priestess in the temple, performing the sacred rituals including the ritual of the stranger. In this ritual, the stranger comes to the temple and spends one night a month, or one night a year with the Priestess. The Priestess is under vow *not* to form a personal connection with any man, yet she is honored as a Goddess. The man who comes is the supplicant.

Virgo's job is to know the patterning of life, and then be devoted and dedicated to maintaining the sacred harmony of life. If something is out of pattern, Virgo's job is to notice it and then re-establish the harmony of the pattern. How does our culture respond to Virgo? For example, a married Virgo woman says to her husband; "Gee dear, this is the thirteenth morning in a row that you haven't squeezed the toothpaste up to the top." Her husband responds by saying; "Stop attacking me!" But, she wasn't attacking him, and she wasn't about to write him off, or judge him. She was simply noticing a pattern. Little did her husband know--she was doing her sacred function by noticing the pattern. What Virgo doesn't understand is how most people are sensitive, and they take these things personally. If something is out of pattern, Virgo discriminates, and makes what appears to be a judgment without regard to what others are feeling. The evolving Virgo archetype must understand that most people do take it personally, and develop some awareness and tact about how they deliver the pronouncements of the priestess or the priest, because not everyone understands they are doing a sacred function.

The Virgo archetype has been greatly violated by patriarchal culture and there has been very little room for it to express in a healthy and vital way. For women the primary role left for them has been to get married, have babies and be priestess in the home. Even though most Virgo women have done a good job with these things, it has been at great cost to their original essence as neither getting married nor having a family was considered high on Virgo's list of priorities. Other typical Virgo roles, more recently, have been the nun, or a spinster schoolteacher, or even worse, a systems analyst for some company. They are very good systems analysts, but at an extremely high cost, because they've lost their organic pagan roots.

Being an earth sign means Virgo is healthy when it's connected to the natural rhythms and cycles of the planet. That's why Virgo is not primarily intellectual rather it is analytical. It operates out of what I call the left-brain of the Goddess. Virgo's psyche is in tune with the patterning of the universe and the Earth, and the cycles of the Moon. In the past it was the Virgo archetype that was responsible for the invention of agriculture. Archetypally, Virgo is found out in the garden, working with the earth, and channeling their energy into the earth. Since Virgo is tuned into the cycles of the Earth and the Moon they knew when to plant and when to harvest. Virgo also rules women's menstrual cycles. This means, under ideal conditions, women with strong Virgo are in a position to take three to five days a month that are just for them. They don't do what their normal responsibilities are, but instead, either symbolically or literally go to their moon lodge. They give themselves time to get into their emotional depths, into their roots, into their connection with the natural rhythms and cycles of the Earth. It is obvious that our current culture has violated the sanctity of this time. It's time now for women to take back that sacred time as best they can. A similar violation has occurred to Virgo men. However, the men at least get to be work-aholics and spend a lot of time at the office.

The question now at The Turning Of The Ages is *"How can the Virgo archetype be empowered?"* This involves becoming aware and reawakening the knowledge of what the original essence of Virgo is. It is the priestess lineage. Paired with the Scorpio archetype, both signs have energy associated with the most powerful images of the matriarchy. Those with mastery in Virgo tend to get angry when they are not honored or recognized for their work, because their memories from the past tell them they once did get honored and recognized for what they did. Those with Virgo lineage must reconnect with the sacred timings, and the patterning of the manifest world and then be ceremonial in some vital way that reconnects them to their mastery of sacred function. When Virgo is the lineage then this is done no more than one-third of the time.

VIRGO TRAINING asks the question; "What does the Priest or Priestess do now?" It is time for Virgo to develop a new approach for how to be priestess or priest in our culture, and to answer the question; *"What is the nature of the sacred work at the Turning Of The Ages?"* The challenge is to find what the sacred work is, and then to apprehend and co-create with the ongoing repatterning of the manifest world.

♎ LIBRA ♎

The Libra archetype focuses on conscious equal partnership. In the past, people who took Libra training were probably born into a culture where they had arranged marriages, or they were born into a culture where the principles of the culture worked really well generation after generation. The Confucian golden age where all relationships were in balance illustrates how this has worked. In a golden age, the right husbands are with the right wives, the right children are with the right parents, the right subjects are with the right king, the right friends are with the right friends, and the right teachers are with the right students. When all of these are in exact balance, it is a golden age, there is harmony, there is civilization, and the culture really works. This is when the phenomenon of arranged marriage works. In golden ages past relationships were not based upon romantic love or physical attraction, but they were based upon family history, class, caste, economic situations, and the astrological chart. So, by definition each person got the exact right partner.

Libra training involves becoming a master of relationship. If a person has a Libra Moon they are coming into the life already a master of relationship. Typically, there are two different scenarios they might encounter. One is they might have an attachment to, and an expectation of, associating with people who have the same standards of relating as they do. At the turning of the ages, they discover virtually no one has or understands these standards, but find instead that people are confused. What often happens is these Libra masters get trashed for their excellent relationship qualities. It is experienced as a rude awakening for Libra. However, their Ph.D. is still in right relationship. Their best traits are coming from their past mastery in relationships, but if they are addicted or attached they won't get validated for those traits. The second scenario occurs when the Libra adept unconsciously or instinctively assumes they are doing absolutely all the right things in the relationship, according to the way they were brought up, but, in fact, they are totally out of touch with what's really happening with their partner. If Libra continues to operate from the unconscious or instinctive level, they remain incapable of moving into new vital forms of relationship.

Another way of looking at Libra beyond the mysteries of partnership and relationship, is to use the imagery of Libra as a balance beam or scales. The question is what is Libra balancing? On one side of the scales is consensus reality, the rules of the game of whoever has been in charge recently! It is similar to what Christ meant in the Bible when he said, "Render unto Caesar what is Caesar's." He did not mean that you must believe in Caesar, but rather a person's life works better if they know what these principles or rules are. The other side of the scales is a person's personal truth. What is true for them irrespective of whatever consensus reality is. The mystery of Libra is to have these two sides in exact balance. Where the Libra archetype shows up in the script is where the person intends to move toward experiencing balance. So, if a person has a nontraditional lineage, moving toward the balance for them is to become more traditional, more of a householder. If a person's lineage is the traditional householder type, then moving toward the balance for them may involve developing wild individuality.

The challenge is for Libra to be fully balanced between the reality of the world as it is, or the laws as they are, and what their own beliefs are. This means one is comfortable in the world as it is, but at the same time they haven't sacrificed their own beliefs so much that all they know is what the world believes. A regressive Libra archetype is one where a person has no truth except the truth that comes through the eyes of other people. The weakness of the Libra archetype occurs when there is no self. (For example, based upon the model of soul mates or romantic love and physical attraction many people have the idea that they are fifty percent of a whole and if they could just find another person who was the other fifty percent they would then somehow be complete.) The old Libra archetype tended to define who they were by whom they were with. The greatest value of a strong Libra archetype is the *awareness* of partnership and relationship. The new emerging imagery of the Libra archetype includes the awareness of partnership and relationship, along with the autonomy and sovereignty of the individual.

On a cultural level, the Libra archetype extends the desire for conscious equal partnership to a vision of community, akin to the Arthurian round table, where representatives of all twelve mystery schools, lineages, and archetypes sit together, as spokes of a wheel in a circle, all in non-hierarchical acceptance and respect for all the authentic expressions of the human journey. In this imagery, the figure of Arthur the king fades away, being replaced by the Native American *talking stick,* where, in democratic fashion, each of the twelve has equal freedom to command the space and represent their views.

LIBRA TRAINING asks the question, *"What is the nature of partnership and relationship? What is nonhierarchical conscious equal partnership?"* In Libra training relationship itself is the path to God, or the highest spiritual path. Again, it is not a weak expression, such as defining who you are by whom you are with, but rather it is about learning conscious equal partnership. It is about taking the curriculum of relationship. A person in Libra training has as much merit, as much going for them, as those who are not in Libra training, but their challenge is to take the curriculum, to take the whole journey, to go through all the grades, to go through all the different experiences, until they achieve mastery in relationship. This is a path of constant process, constant interaction with other people, and thereby those on a Libra path refine their awareness through their interaction with a partner and with other people.

♏ SCORPIO ♏

"You never know what enough is, until you know what more than enough is." -William Blake

The water signs, Scorpio, Pisces, and Cancer, all have as the first phase of their training the necessity to feel the full range of feelings. Unique to Scorpio training is the second phase requiring total involvement in their own personal feelings and then learning to command them. Scorpio training is the exact merging of will and desire. It does not operate theoretically; it operates out of mastery of the feelings and the emotions. It is a tantric energy. I define tantric as: *The current of life itself is a path to God, or life force energy as a path to God.* The Scorpio path, six to eight thousand years ago, was associated with the path of sorcery and magic. Sorcery and magic are mysteries that deal with developing the will in order to command the earth, the water, the organic mysteries. This results in the empowering of personal energy.

Scorpio is another energy that has been greatly misunderstood and violated by patriarchy. Remember, the first requirement in Scorpio training is to be able to feel the feelings; the second requirement is to command the feelings. In our culture, feelings are not well validated. Therefore, Scorpio has often had to learn to deal with the feelings through denial, repression, suppression, and control, in the negative sense of control. Those in Scorpio school or Scorpio training are required to take Control 101 as part of their curriculum. If they don't learn control, they flunk the Scorpio curriculum. The survival lessons in Scorpio school, in part, involve learning control, but it doesn't mean be attached to the control. It means learning to bring your will in alignment with God's will. Scorpio's motto is: *I Will That My Will Be Thy Will.* Notice three wills are mentioned and two of them belong to Scorpio or the person taking Scorpio training.

The Scorpio master in today's culture does not get validation for their feeling function. That's why to this day; I have yet to meet a woman with a Scorpio Moon who does not in some way resonate with the motif of having been burned at the stake. These women feel if they really speak the truth about who they are, and about what they feel, or about what they desire, it would be unsafe or dangerous for them. Historically, a great many women in European history were killed for doing something as simple as gathering herbs. The Scorpio mysteries are women's mysteries, the mysteries of death, and rebirth. I believe Scorpio, in essence, is not secretive, but that Scorpio became secretive for survival reasons.

In addition to being forced to be secretive, Scorpio energy has been increasingly repressed and denied, because there is very little training available in the present time that validates feeling the feelings. In contrast to today's perception of Scorpio energy, one of the most popular signs in ninth century Japan must have been Scorpio. The original Zen Samurai training was not just sword fighting; profound spiritual traditions were behind it, and they were very much connected to the Scorpio mysteries. I have a feeling that while the original teachings associated with the so-called martial arts had much to do with the awareness that the true human state is beyond life and death, they as much believed in a realm that was very passionate and included the feeling function. What we see now is denial of this. Our current understanding of the martial arts includes the denial of the feelings in the eastern cultures, and is exactly the same predicament we find with Scorpio energy. For Scorpio to get its power back it must be healthy in the feelings, and then be in a state of mastery over that realm.

In the past few thousand years healthy Scorpio training has not been readily available. Scorpio learns not by reading about danger, but by experiencing it. These types of experiences let Scorpio know how they react to being on the edge. That's why Scorpio has a reputation of being a firewalker or edgewalker. When healthy Scorpio training is not available, then one makes use of what is available, such as: fast motorcycles, or taking large amounts of passion-producing drugs, or going into rough biker bars or seeking out other dangerous situations. Strong Scorpio or Pluto types tend to attract to themselves the dark side or the repressed and denied side of those around them. This is called being a shadow magnet. It doesn't mean everyone who is signed up for Scorpio training must go through these types of experiences, but they do have to have some way of feeling their feelings and then learn to command them. Other ways this may happen is by having experiences that are beyond their control that overwhelm them and force them to feel their feelings.

Another quality or avenue of expression for Scorpio is to promote or induce response in others. The joy that Scorpio has in everything they do, whether it is mental activity, physical activity, or sexual activity, is their ability to produce a response in someone else. Scorpio's job is to cause the energy to rise, producing a response in others. For example, when a Scorpio speaker is giving a talk, their objective is to get the audience turned on by being provocative. Imagery where this occurs is the revivalist minister who charges up his audience. He gets them rocking and rolling, and excited about his message. Musicians working out of Scorpio energy perform their music not only because it gives them orgasms, but because it also induces orgasms in others. The sorcerer's function is to pull out that type of a response. However, for Scorpio, the bottom line is that they personally are the ones getting off on the response they have produced in others. The down side or dark side of Scorpio is when there is no concern whatsoever about whether or not the response has negative repercussions. There are circumstances where Scorpio might successfully produce a response in a person, but essentially they were leading the other person on or ripping off their energy. Pure Scorpio doesn't include the empathy to be concerned about what the other person is actually going through, because it's directly linked to the energy itself. That's why it is best when

Pisces or Cancer is connected to Scorpio, because they bring in the elements of sensitivity, compassion, and empathy-qualities that are missing in Scorpio. Because Scorpio is pure sorcery, pure life force energy, it doesn't care if the other person is benefiting from being turned on or not. Rather Scorpio is thinking either in a conscious or unconscious way how great it is for them if the other person is turned on or responding to the energy. Which brings us to the structural similarity between Scorpio and Leo. The Leo person is also doing it for self-centered reasons, even though when it is done well or when there is not a dark side associated with it, everyone is benefiting.

A person with a Scorpio lineage has a sense or memory of having mastered the feelings and being in command and control of life force energy or producing a response, but they don't remember the training they took to gain that mastery. It is not unlike a person who has Leo as their lineage who has a sense or memory of having been the star or the leader, but they have no memory of the training they took to become the star or the leader. When a person is over identified with the Scorpio archetype, their experiences are designed to bust them of any attachment to their will or the expectation of running that kind of energy. This is indicated on the natal chart by hard aspects from Saturn or Pluto to the Moon position, and creates a wound from violation, invalidation or both. For the Scorpio adept to regain his or her power in the area of their mastery they must learn how to rehabilitate or heal their Scorpio energy without being attached or addicted to it. To help facilitate this healing process I highly recommend anyone with strong Scorpio or strong Pluto read *Descent to the Goddess*, by Sylvia Perrera, subtitled *A Woman's Path of Initiation*. This book is probably the greatest book on Scorpio/Pluto ever written, even though there is no astrology in it. It is a Jungian retelling of the myth of Inanna and Ereshkigal, a Sumerian Myth that was a precursor to what later became the myth of Pluto and Persephone in patriarchy. (The same author has written another phenomenally good book about Capricorn/Saturn, called *The Scapegoat Complex, Toward a Mythology of Guilt and Repression.*)

Scorpio is the lineage of *women's mysteries*. When it is not repressed, suppressed or denied it stands on the foundation of a sorcery lineage that combines will with desire in a healthy way, without being attached to it. This is demonstrated by the Goddesses associated with Scorpio, such as: Madame Pele, Kali, Durga, the Cretan Snake Goddess, and Hecate. (Some of the Gods associated with Scorpio are the Green Man, the King Stag, and the Horned God.) When patriarchy took the Scorpio teachings away from women, they turned it into a masculine wizard craft and wizard lore. Even the tantric teachings were originally a women's mystery that were later taken over and controlled by men. Patriarchy felt it was important to disempower women and the Scorpio teachings by preventing them from realizing they were the ones who had original mastery over the Scorpio mysteries. It is time now At The Turning Of The Ages for the Scorpio mysteries to be re-enlivened and once again empowered in an even greater, more comprehensive way, irrespective of gender.

SCORPIO TRAINING is a shamanic training and similar to the Castenada view of sorcery. In Scorpio training *life force energy is the path to God*. It is the complete descent into third dimensional reality, fully bringing spirit into matter, fully feeling the feelings and learning to command the experience, or to experience the deepest, most powerful emotional and physical realms and then to master them.

♐ SAGITTARIUS ♐

...of the gladdest moments in human life,
methinks is the departure upon
a distant journey to unknown lands.
Shaking off with one mighty effort the fetters of Habit,
the leaden weight of Routine, the cloak of many Cares,
and the slavery of Home, man feels once more happy.
The blood flows with the fast circulation of childhood...
afresh dawns the morn of life...
-Sir Richard Burton
Journal entry December 2, 1856

The essence of Sagittarius is: *The expansion of the self to the widest possible horizons.* To boldly go where no one has gone before. It is the quest for the truth. It represents adventure, but the adventure is not just for adventure's sake, but also to find a deeper spiritual truth as a result. The spiritual motif for Sagittarius is found in the vision quest.

Some mythological stories that best describe the Sagittarius archetype are: The Voyages of Odysseus, The Twelve Labors of Hercules, and, if combined with water signs elsewhere in the chart, The Quest for the Holy Grail. Sagittarius, Leo, and Aries are the three fire sign tribes. For a sense of how these three tribes vary in their training, let's look at what different kinds of motivation are behind someone from each tribe deciding to climb a mountain. If Aries decides to climb a mountain, it's because it is there and it seems like a fun thing to do. Leo, on the other hand, decides to climb the mountain because there is a film crew filming a potentially award winning documentary on mountain climbing. The reason Sagittarius climbs the mountain has to do with the quest for the meaning of life, to find God, or some greater spiritual truth. Another model that describes Sagittarius is the quest for the impossible dream. For example, undaunted by their baseball team's last place standing at the beginning of spring training, the Sagittarius team player has visions of Camelot, of going all the way and winning the series. They are the ones who dare to dream the impossible dream and often accomplish amazing things as a result.

Another imagery that gives a sense of the Sagittarius archetype finds them exhilarated and inspired while climbing a great mountain. Reaching the top of the mountain they experience a great high, and a feeling of clarity, because they have a sense of cosmic overview. They have achieved their goal, and that results in a renewal of their vision. As they blissfully survey the scenery from the mountaintop their vision catches a yet higher mountain. This brings about an additional surge of elation, because now they know the next mountain they will climb. This is when they look into the eyes of their co-travelers and say, "Isn't it incredible that we are the ones who get to do this." For Sagittarius enlightenment is not a place to get to, but a process that keeps opening up in front of them. That's why loss of vision is one of the most difficult things Sagittarius could ever face. They must have a continued renewal of vision, or they will find themselves close to a complete death of spirit. This happens anytime their sense of inspiration and vision is lost, or they are stuck in a routine for too long doing the same thing over and over. It is essential for Sagittarius to have some kind of connection to a vision that inspires them.

Mythically, Sagittarian stories are about the quest for consciousness, individuated consciousness, and freedom. They are often found on the trail as trail mates or quest mates looking for the highest truth. It is a masculine path of enlightenment, going towards spirit. Sagittarius is not a householder archetype, and chances are intimacy was limited to whomever they met on the trail, or it was just for the fun of it, or the athletics of it. That doesn't mean there was a deficiency in intimacy. What it means is, the emphasis was not on intimacy. The emphasis was on the meaning of life, the quest for the truth or the adventure itself.

The Sagittarius archetype is also known for being absolutely, bluntly honest. This stems from their serious quest for the truth. Of all the archetypes, Sagittarius is the most honest and straightforward. The only other archetype close to Sagittarius in this area is Aries. However, Aries' views tend to be black and white, and that can cause their interpretation of the truth to be inflexible. The absolute truth is not as important to Aries as it is for Sagittarius, because once Aries gets what they think is right or wrong, they are no longer concerned with finding out an additional truth. That's why Aries can easily be the fundamentalist, because when they get what they perceive is the truth, they put everything into it. As far as they are concerned it is a waste of time to think it through anymore. Unlike Sagittarius, for Aries there is *no* expansion of context.

Sagittarius, along with Aquarius, has as part of their energy the true definition of spirituality from the perspective of Shamanic Astrology, spirituality means constantly expanding context. Said another way, it means no matter where a person is in their life, their objective is to see the widest possible view, to continually keep expanding the context. The Sagittarius archetype does this more than any other.

SAGITTARIUS TRAINING is the quest for the meaning of life, the expansion of the self to the widest possible horizons, going on adventures, doing vision quests, attending spiritual growth workshops, boldly going where no one has gone before.

♑ CAPRICORN ♑

Capricorn is a giver sign, but is different from the selfless service found in Pisces, or the loving, nurturing qualities of Cancer. Capricorn is dedicated to keeping it together for everyone else, but in return for that function they receive great respect, and get to be in some position of power to better carry out their responsibilities. Within this particular archetype there is little room for personal joy or personal pleasure other than what one gets from being loved and respected for having done the job so well.

The Capricorn archetype is associated with the elders who called out the law. The Capricorn job, in any culture, is to know the rules and to be there in a responsible way for others. Some examples are the fathers, the prime ministers, the counselors and teachers. The scapegoat is a negative image that has also been associated with Capricorn. Where did the scapegoat originate? In the original Yom Kippur ritual there were two goats. One goat was killed in a ritual sacrifice and its blood used on the altar. The other goat was selected to carry the symbols, images, and icons, representing the sins of the community on its back out into the wilderness, because the goat was strong enough to survive in the harsh land and carry these symbols far away from the community. The problem was it wasn't long before the goat began to believe he was responsible for all of the problems.

The downside of the Capricorn complex manifests as the person who believes they are somehow responsible for all the world's problems, and now must do an infinite amount of atonement to help solve these problems. They tend to think they must always carry the weight for everybody. To a certain extent this is one of the positive sides of Capricorn, because someone has to know the rules, be willing to take responsibility and hold it all together. This is Capricorn's gift to humanity. In return they get respect and hold positions of power or authority when they have successfully demonstrated responsibility. The Capricorn archetype wants to get respect, have an important function, and to play the responsible management and control role. Those signed up for Capricorn school must be able to play this role to pass the required curriculum. However, if Capricorn is a person's lineage and all they are doing is taking responsibility for everyone else and counseling or teaching others, it is a deep addiction. That's when they encounter circumstances designed to move them away from their attachment to that role by making sure they don't get the respect they feel they deserve even if they do the job perfectly.

Leo and Capricorn can both show up in positions of leadership, but the type of leadership role each plays is different. It is like the difference between the king and the prime minister. Leo, as the king, rules by decree. Capricorn, as the prime minister, does all the work, takes responsibility, and is doing it for everyone else, as long as they get respect. Leo is doing it only for them selves.

CAPRICORN TRAINING is to learn *Responsible Administration Of One's Domain;* they must learn to manage and control their environment in a responsible way and to get results. This is a householder training. Emerging Capricorn, Capricorn at The Turning Of The Ages is here to receive the new information about how to do family and community. We have to reinvent family and community and Capricorn's job, along with Cancer, is to assist in this process. The emergent Capricorn has signed up to be the elder of the future.

♒ AQUARIUS ♒
All life forms should have the right
and the opportunity
to have an existence,
which is endowed with the freedom to produce
the maximum amount of probable lines of reality,
in an evolving direction by choice,
without repression of awareness,
or manipulation of physical, mental, or spiritual aspects.
-Val Valarian

Aquarius is similar to Sagittarius. Like Sagittarius, Aquarius lineage operates outside the realm of the physical and the emotional; it does *not* involve the feeling function. For example, the Aquarius archetype might show up as the Moon of a person who has had a series of lifetimes where they were purely intellectual, the ivory tower philosopher, writing books about relationships without ever having one. They may have been a theoretician about life, but never had to get their hands dirty. Expand this out to people in ashrams, people on a sattvic spiritual path, refining the awareness to higher and higher levels. These are the type of people who don't want anyone to get too close to them, because they don't want to mess up their field. One mythological explanation for Aquarius is they come from the realm of fairy, the fairy princess, or the elf. They are women and men who have not been in third dimensional reality for a long time and they have come into physical form so they can be part of this grand experiment. Hence, traditional astrology promotes the idea that Aquarius will try anything. What Aquarius is really looking for is to be able to translate this experience back into the higher chakras. Despite the fact that some men and women with an Aquarius lineage have been completely wild, and actually have tried just about everything, what they are really going for is spirit, intellect, or some higher chakra experience.

One of the best stories that work to describe Aquarius is the one that has to do with the Pleiades. The Pleiadian story says Aquarius is not from Earth; rather they come from the Pleiades or a different star system, where they have a rule (or Prime Directive) of noninterference, similar to the TV series Star Trek. For those entities wishing to make a contribution here, the only way around the Prime Directive is to incarnate here. The problem with incarnating here is the person can forget their mission, because the karma and density of this reality is so heavy and it's not their karma anyway. However, when they do incarnate here they can't help taking it on, and the reality is they may not be fully prepared for such a descent.

What Gods and Goddesses are associated with Aquarius? It's hard to find any from the known pantheons. I did, however, come up with two images that seem to work. The first image is of a male or female avatar; someone who is working on their spiritual path so intensely they have practically moved beyond the need to have a body. They are operating purely in the higher centers. The other image is the statue put up by some Chinese students in Vancouver after the Tienamen Square massacre, which was apparently a replica of a statue that had been in Tienamen Square before the massacre. The statue is of a woman holding a torch. Her face looks like Kwan Yin. The caption on the statue reads "The Goddess of Democracy." This is a marvelous emerging image for Aquarius in the feminine form. It is interesting to note the Chinese experience, when combined with freedom and egalitarian ideals, is expressed as the "Goddess of Democracy," who represents freedom, sovereignty, independence, and free will.

AQUARIUS TRAINING is associated with the attainment of cosmic consciousness, learning detachment, and the ability to disengage from the physical and emotional planes. They are going for pure spirit, or the higher chakra experience. The training includes the Aquarian Dispensation; the egalitarian belief that all human beings should have the freedom to take responsibility for their own evolutionary path.

♓ PISCES ♓

The Pisces gift to humanity is the ability to merge with another person, feel what they are feeling, and then give the person the love and understanding they really need. Like the other giver signs, Pisces does not know who they are save through what they are doing for others. Cancer and Pisces both operate out of the feeling function and both are giver signs, but Cancer has different boundaries for giving than Pisces. Pisces is the empathic, sensitive giver without any discrimination. Cancer discriminates in its giving. Cancer has universal, unconditional love for their family members, but not beyond their definition of family. Pisces, on the other hand, is transpersonal. It is not impersonal, and it is not personal. It is transpersonal. So, Pisces have the same degree of empathic sensitive giving for everyone.

In Shamanic Astrology the feminine principle is viewed as a twelve-spoked wheel, and each spoke of the wheel is presided over by a different goddess, a different story, a different set of themes. Patriarchy has managed to channel these twelve spokes into three roles, woman as mother, woman as girlfriend or wife, and woman as nurse. As valid as these three roles are, they are obviously not the entire spectrum. Some archetypes are more easily channeled into these three roles than others. Culturally, the Pisces archetype for a woman is perceived as more like the householder archetypes of Cancer or Libra, because Pisces energy is easily channeled or expressed through family and marriage. However, Pisces is not necessarily a householder energy.

When the Pisces archetype shows up as the Moon it indicates someone who has already demonstrated expansion of the heart, sensitivity, and compassion. These people tend to fall into the trap of co-dependent relationships, where they give and give and give, expecting and assuming that someday they will get a return. The irony is they have *already* experienced lifetimes where they did get a return for giving. If they think it is their job to be there for a partner, or a group, and to be a giving, loving, sensitive, person, it is a misunderstanding. It *WAS* their job. If a Pisces Moon is playing the role of giver, and not being validated for their giving, and is then upset about this, it is not a character flaw. It is simply a misunderstanding. It is common for those with a strong Pisces lineage to continue to play the role of giver. What they eventually realize is the return they receive for their giving is not commensurate with what they have given. That's when they notice something is wrong. Typically the first reaction is for them to give even more, but still nothing changes. Realizing something is definitely wrong, they conclude they are in an unfair system, and get really angry! They might even try to force a response from the person or group they have been pouring their love and giving energy into as a reaction to this realization. Expecting to get a certain return, not getting it, and then trying to force the person to give them that return is the worst downside of being the giver. This is the "giving to get" addiction born out of misunderstanding. There is no additional reward for continuing to live the Pisces path if that is a person's lineage, and the wake-up call may be to develop something else. For example, if the Pisces Moon has Scorpio Rising, they are in the current life to learn to develop a strong individuated self. The Sufis have a statement, "You can not lose your ego until you have one." Scorpio training, in this case is to develop the self, or the ego. Since Pisces training is about selfless service to others, signing up for Scorpio training requires a major shift of gears.

PISCES TRAINING is legitimately about learning to be a giver in a healthy way. When a mother has a child she doesn't have to think; "If I love my child, he/she will love me back." It is an automatic exchange that takes place. In Pisces training, there is no self, there is no ego. They learn to be there for others and to merge energy. The spiritual side of Pisces is the Boddhisattva, a person who has worked on their own individual Karma the whole way. They are liberated, but decided to stick around. They don't merge with the infinite, they don't go to the celestial realms, they don't go to the absolute, instead they stick around to be of selfless service. They don't do this as a teacher, or a guru necessarily; they are just making available to the world what they do best. This is not to say that everyone with Pisces training is an enlightened Boddhisattva, but this imagery describes what the attitude of Pisces is towards what they do. For example, Pisces is healthy when they understand they don't have to prove anything. They are just here to be of service. It represents the truly enjoyable side of being in service, the true Seeva (Hindu term for service) ideal. This is not the guilt-ridden social worker who feels they have to save the world so they can be okay. This is a person who knows that the most pleasurable and enjoyable and wonderful thing they can do is simply make available to the world what they do best. It is important for the Pisces archetype to exist beyond the patriarchal Saturn complex. There are no rewards for being the best possible giver. One just, in a graceful natural way, makes available what one does best. Since Pisces is described as the twelfth sign, and since the Pisces archetype exists just prior to the spring equinox, in many respects it does represent a completion. Just as Aries is the innocence of youth, the two-year-old going at life as if for the first time, Pisces is the full establishment of the state of no self, the absolute merging into the collective, into the universal, into the Godhead.

THE SHAMANIC ARCHETYPES OF THE PLANETS

☉ THE SUN ☉

In Shamanic Astrology, the Sun describes the type of fuel a person burns. Since the Sun is the fuel and not necessarily the emerging archetype (as described in Class 3), a person may or may not display all of the characteristic qualities associated with their Sun sign. However, the Sun does represent the intent to have the qualities of the Sun sign be an intrinsic part of who a person is in a general way, across the board. Ideally, the Sun is the fuel that drives a person, and thereby supplies the means to accomplish the intent for the current life. That's why the Sun is not necessarily a description of inherent personality traits, and is only accurate about two-fifths of the time in describing a person's basic personality. Due to the recent popularity of Sun sign astrology, the Sun sign has been credited with too much importance. The Sun stays in one sign for approximately thirty days, and is connected to the seasonal cycle. For this reason, the Sun is not as individualizing of a factor as the other personal planets. For example, the Moon changes signs every two-and-a-half days, and the Rising sign changes signs approximately every two hours. There are many symbols in the human psyche--the Sun is only one. However, the Sun is important and that's why we call the Sun the fuel.

ARIES *fuel is fiery, aggressive, playful, competitive, courageous, self-centered, willful, independent, straightforward, childlike.*

TAURUS *fuel is earthy, sensual, physical, receptive, self-centered, high aesthetic standards, love of pleasure.*

GEMINI *fuel is airy, creative, intellectual, communicative, entertaining, socially gregarious, free-spirited, comedic (funny).*

CANCER *fuel is watery, responsible, loving, nurturing, giving, family oriented, instinctual, organic, serious, parental.*

LEO *fuel is fiery, courageous, dominant, confident, self-loving, charismatic, willful, leader oriented, outgoing, and loves to be the center of attention.*

VIRGO *fuel is earthy, organic, discriminative, perceptive of the patterning of the psyche and nature, attentive to detail, devoted, giving (especially in connection to the sacred work), perfection oriented.*

LIBRA *fuel is airy, partnership oriented, civilized, just, balanced judgment, aware, social, peacemaker.*

SCORPIO *fuel is watery, intense, lives on the edge, sexual, tantric, willful, deeply and powerfully feels the feelings, runs the energy, magical, commanding.*

SAGITTARIUS *fuel is fiery, adventuresome, independent, philosophic, inspired, truth oriented, in search of the meaning of life.*

CAPRICORN *fuel is earthy, responsible, serious, administrative, management and control of one's domain, a lawgiver, law abiding, keeps it together.*

AQUARIUS *fuel is airy, the grand experimenter, intellectual, the cosmic visionary, revolutionary, detached, the universal free spirit.*

PISCES *fuel is watery, empathic, universal compassion, unconditional love, selfless service to others, giver, deep mystical vision, safe space for others.*

☽ THE MOON ☽

The Moon represents the lineage, or tribal ancestral history. The lineage is a combination of: family history, what is written in the genetic code, and past life themes; all merged together. The Moon position provides the greatest clues on an individual's chart about what the attitudes, habits, expectations and addictions are. The Moon position tells us what our greatest training has been from the past, what we are best at, where we have already earned a Ph.D.; as well as what we can become most addicted to, or over-identified with. Ideally, the area of mastery and the qualities associated with our Moon position are the foundation we stand on in this life to achieve our purpose and goals. In traditional astrology, the Moon describes the instincts, emotions, feelings, and characteristics ascribed to family and roots. When looking at the Moon position as the lineage, it is easy to understand why these traits have been traditionally attributed to the Moon position.

A person has already mastered the Mystery School the Moon position represents. They have already received rewards and recognition for accomplishments in that area. The law of the Moon states: *if you were to continue living your life based upon the accomplishments and achievements of your moon, or continue to have your identity based upon your moon; it is insufficient to your liberation.* If a person consciously or unconsciously expects the rewards to continue, the law of the Moon says; *It is insufficient to their liberation.* Typically, one of two strategies then take place to push the person into their current life intent. The first strategy is to simply remove the reward associated with the continued activities of their Moon no matter how perfectly those activities are performed. It is experienced as a box canyon and as violation or invalidation of a person's best traits and qualities. This strategy is indicated by hard aspects to the Moon from the outer planets; Saturn (invalidation), Pluto (violation), Uranus (violation or invalidation), or Neptune (wipes out the awareness of the past accomplishments and achievements). A woman with a fire or air Moon, or a man with a water or earth Moon automatically experiences violation and invalidation based on what are considered acceptable male and female roles in the current culture. The good news is these strategies usually do motivate a person to try something different. The bad news is there are wounds a person has to recover from. The second strategy is boredom. When a person is successfully continuing to do their Moon out of addiction, what happens is one day they realize they are extremely bored and decide to check out something new. The good news is there is no wounding to recover from; the bad news is the person may not be sufficiently motivated to make any changes.

When a person moves to a place where they are no longer addicted or attached to their Moon, the intent is for them to stand on the foundation of their Moon, and use their area of mastery and talents to serve the new mystery schools and the new goals. A good rule to keep in mind is: *if you are using your Moon more than one third of the time, it is an addiction.*

(For more on the Moon see Class Two)

THE RISING SIGN OR ASCENDANT

The Rising sign is the portion of the zodiac that was coming up on the eastern horizon at birth. The Rising sign and the other angles of the chart are the main factors that individualize the chart, because the angles change signs approximately every two hours and change degrees about every four minutes. The Rising sign represents the Personal Identity Project or the mystery school a person has signed up for in the current life. It is the training the person intends to undertake in the current life, and it is the "way out" or liberation point. All twelve trainings are equally valid, but each has a different intent. For example, the training for Libra Rising is to answer the question; "What is the nature of partnership and relationship?" Libra Rising's job is to discover new and better ways of doing relationship. The training for Sagittarius Rising includes answering the question; "What is the meaning of life?" Sagittarius Rising's job is to discover the meaning of life and to continually expand the self to the widest possible horizons.

The training a person has signed up for in the current life indicates the new territory they intend to investigate, learn about, and master. If the Moon is the same as the Rising sign, the intent is to participate in the process of taking that archetype into new territory, into a new dimension. Those with Moon in Cancer and Cancer Rising intend to take *Cancer training* to a whole new level of expression, a whole new dimension. *Cancer training* refers to the essence of Cancer, and not what the content of Cancer has been for the past three or four thousand years. The essence of Cancer is, what is the nature of family and roots? The content of Cancer in patriarchy has been, if a woman has any intelligence she better find a good provider, a man who can support her and her children. Prior to patriarchy we had matriarchy, and it didn't matter who the man was because it was a matrilineal situation. Now, at the turning of the ages, we are again going through a major shift in how we perceive and experience family. Cancer Rising's job is to help bring about this shift as the content of Cancer is being redefined. Indeed, the content of all the Mystery Schools is being redefined at the turning of the ages. The people who have Moon and Rising in the same sign are here to assist in the shift for that particular archetype. When the Moon and Rising sign are in the same sign, it is like "the once and future" expression of that sign.

The Rising sign is the main factor on the chart that describes the enlightenment path for an individual. The other factors are the lineage, individual characteristics, what archetype you are developing, and what set of images underlie and reveal your specific path. By definition, enlightenment is a state beyond duality, so I am not using enlightenment in that sense, but rather I am saying there are different, equally valid pathways for different people that are their fastest or most effective path to achieve an enlightened or liberated state for themselves. That's why understanding the essence of the Rising sign is an important key to understanding a person's enlightenment path.

(For more on the Rising Sign see Class Four)

☿ MERCURY ☿

Mercury represents the current life tool for how a person thinks, for how they perceive reality, for how they process the external world and then communicate their experience. Therefore, Mercury is the intended tool for the thinking process that, when properly accessed, helps to move a person in the direction of self-actualization. Each Mercury position has a different mode of operating. The four elements of fire, earth, water, and air seem to correspond to what Carl Jung described as the four different types of people. The fire element corresponds to the intuitive type, the air element corresponds to the thinking type, the water element corresponds to the feeling type, and the earth element corresponds to the sensation (or physical) type. These elements are significant as each element describes the overall approach to the method of thinking, and each sign has its own refinement. So the element and the sign of the Mercury position indicate how a person's thinking processes are intended to work most effectively.

AIRES, LEO AND SAGITTARIUS are intuitive types or right brain masculine. When Mercury is found in one of these signs, the intent is to boldly go where no one has gone before, check out new territory, and the faster they can get into the new territory the better. Most people think intuition has to do with the feeling function; it does not. Jung describes intuition as creative logos or mind, going into the unknown, and an outward activity. For the fire sign Mercury positions, human interchange is irrelevant in the communication process. In fact, they don't even seem to notice how the person they are talking to is reacting, or what's really happening with them. The fire sign Mercury's are not concerned with getting information, but rather they are concerned with getting a new or expanded vision, and experiencing being in new territory, being purely creative, and coming up with something that wasn't there before.

ARIES *is spontaneous in their thinking, rushing in where Angels fear to tread.*

LEO *calls out what they see and does a theatrical performance of being in unknown territory.*

SAGITTARIUS *is Solar Logos, boldly going into the unknown to get the new visions, and then bringing through their consciousness the new information. They are spontaneous, and philosophical.*

CAPRICORN, TAURUS, AND VIRGO are left-brain feminine. When Mercury is in one of these positions, the thinking operates out of the sensation function, the physical, the tangible, and must connect with third dimensional reality or physical form.

CAPRICORN *is aware of the entire structural reality in form, and in law, from the Godhead, to the densest entrapment of spirit in matter. It is like sacred geometry.*

TAURUS *has a reputation for being slow, but actually it is unbelievably thorough. Because of the thorough mastery of what Taurus puts their attention on, when they get something, they really get it.*

VIRGO *is associated with the left-brain of the Goddess and the feminine mysteries. It notices and has an awareness of the tapestry and patterning of the psyche. It is logical.*

SCORPIO, PISCES, AND CANCER operate out of the feeling function (right brain), and if emotionally in balance they can be unbelievably brilliant. They can perceive the subtlest shades of passion, sensitivity and feeling. Left-brain consensus reality considers these people to be irrational, and unable to think clearly; but they are not intended to be rational thinkers. Rather, the intent is to have a healthy way for expression of the mind to operate through the feelings, to be in the present moment, and to be able to merge with another person.

SCORPIO *is the "Eros of Logos." Logos is creative mind or pure mind; Eros is erotic, sexual and passionate. Thus, sexy mind.*

PISCES *mind operates through deep, empathic, compassionate feelings.*

CANCER *is like Pisces, only primarily directed to their family, tribe, group.*

AQUARIUS, GEMINI, AND LIBRA operate from the thinking function, so it is like a doubled, tripled version of thinking, intended to function best in detachment, objectivity, or cosmic overview.

AQUARIUS *is fully involved in life; but the thinking is detached, watching from the ceiling, witness consciousness, or cosmic consciousness. Key word is detachment.*

GEMINI *gathers information from everywhere with no prejudice about some information being better than any other. They are information junkies, and they love to network. Their minds function at high speed.*

LIBRA *is the most aware of consensus reality or the belief system of the majority. Social sensitivity and partnership sensitivity is strong, but it's an idea-based sensitivity, and not out of the feeling function.*

MERCURY RETROGRADE

Mercury goes retrograde for about three weeks, three times a year. The outer planets, Saturn, Uranus, Neptune, and Pluto are retrograde at least one third to one half of the time. Therefore, when the outer planets go retrograde the impact is much less than when Mercury goes retrograde. The mythology of Mercury Retrograde according to traditional astrology says: the logical, rational processes break down. Unpredictable and uncontrollable events take place. Furthermore, it is suggested a person not try to communicate, sign a contract, or expect things to work logically and rationally when Mercury is retrograde. It is a confusing time, and nothing seems to work like we expect it to during Mercury retrograde. Actually, Mercury Retrograde is nothing more than a polarity to Mercury in direct motion.

Mercury Retrograde is not good or bad, right or wrong. The polarity is right-brain, left-brain. Right-brain is not better than left-brain, and vice versa. However, our cultural prejudice says logical, rational, left-brain type thinking is consensus reality. The people who have the toughest time with Mercury Retrograde, are the ones with Mercury in air or earth signs, because these signs represent predominantly left-brain thinking. The fire and water signs represent predominantly right-brain thinking. Therefore, when Mercury goes retrograde, the polarity reversal causes the emphasis to shift from left-brain logical and rational thinking, to right-brain intuitive and emotional thinking. (See Class Four)

♀ VENUS ♀

VENUS ON A WOMAN'S CHART represents what version of the feminine principle she is working on in the current life. A woman's Venus answers Freud's famous question; "What does woman want?" In Shamanic Astrology there are twelve different answers depending on what Venus position the woman has.

ARIES *is the Wild Woman or Virgin Amazon. Amazon means her identity is based upon her accomplishments and achievements. Virgin means she is complete unto herself, she doesn't have to be with anyone to know who she is. She is a courageous defender of the cosmic order. She does what she wants; don't tell her what to do. Honor her independence, freedom, and ability to play.*

TAURUS *is associated with the "Lover." Her intent is to bring spirit fully into the physical and experience the deepest intimacy on the basis of friendship and trust. She wants to be fully honored, loved, and savored as a master of intimacy, where lovemaking is an art form.*

GEMINI *is the Eternal Youth. Her intent is to be socially gregarious and free from the rules. Honor her for her brilliant, free mind and her connection to the creative muse.*

CANCER *is the Mother Archetype. Her intent is to demonstrate responsible commitment-oriented nurturing. Honor her for her ability to nurture, responsibly give love, and be committed to the family.*

LEO *is the Amazon Queen. Her intent is to develop the highest qualities of self-love. Honor her as a leader, and a creative force.*

VIRGO *is the Virgin Priestess. Her bottom line is her dedication to the sacred work. Honor her as High Priestess in her sacred space.*

LIBRA *is associated with Partnership and Relationship. Her intent is to experience relationship as the path to God. Honor her ability to be a good partner and prioritize the relationship over self.*

SCORPIO *is the Sorceress/Witch. Her intent is to experience the most profound emotional and physical realms and then master them. Honor her ability to consciously experience and share the deepest emotions of sexuality. She can experience the current of life force energy as the path to God like nobody can.*

SAGITTARIUS *is the vision quest Amazon. Her intent is to experience the quest for the meaning of life. Honor her quest and independence.*

CAPRICORN *is the Matriarch herself. She wants to be honored and respected for her responsible mastery of her domain. Her intent is to learn responsible administration of her domain.*

AQUARIUS *is the Female Avatar. Her intent is to attain Cosmic Consciousness, free from the entanglements of the physical and emotional planes. Honor her for her mind and her spiritual path.*

PISCES *is the Empathic Woman. Her intent is to live a life of compassion and service for all sentient beings. Honor her ability to be truly a safe space of unconditional compassion and love.*

VENUS ON A MAN'S CHART represents what qualities of the feminine principle he is most attracted to. Similar to Jung's anima, Venus is associated with the "magical feminine." These are the qualities of the feminine the man must develop within himself in order to get the sacred marriage. The sacred marriage for a man is when he walks with the qualities of his inner woman on his arm at all times, regardless of whom he is with, or whether he is with anyone at all.

(For more on Venus see Class Three)

INVOCATION TO THE GODDESS
Visions Of the Full Spectrum Of Femininity
These invocations are by Debra Giamario

These Goddesses can be honored in scared community fire circles, song and dance, as you take your place on the wheel.

ARIES: I am warrior woman. I defend you in battle against the dark lords, the greedy, and those exploiting Mother Earth. I will fight to protect the Cosmic Order. *I Am Goddess Of Victorious Triumph!*

TAURUS: I am your initiator into the joys of sensual pleasures and intimacy. This is the garden planet of earthly delights and beauty. Relax. Breathe. Slow down, and smell the flowers. What's your hurry? *Let's Get Comfortable So We Can Savor And Enjoy The Present Moment!*

GEMINI: I am the wandering minstrel, storyteller, bringer of news and information. I am creative, playful, and mischievous. I often channel the divine comedienne. I am the trickster coyote, the shape shifter. *Catch Me If You Can!*

CANCER: I love my home planet; it is my sweet retreat. I can responsibly commit to family, tribe, or community projects. Do you need anything? I'll take care of you. I am nurturing and kind. I let the children play and keep them safe. *I Am A Feeler, Let Me Come To Your Emotional Rescue!*

LEO: I am the super star. I light up the stage with my confidence and radiant self-love. I am a leader who empowers others. *Let's Walk Like Royalty And Shine Like The Sun*!

VIRGO: Please honor my sacred space and my sacred timings. I am a sovereign priestess making my contribution. Fascinated by my sacred work, I am doing what I was born to do. *How About You?*

LIBRA: I like my partnerships to be with conscious equals. I am "hostess with the mostess" and a powerful helpmate to my husband. Loving harmony, I am a peacemaker, a negotiator. "I get by with a little help from my friends." *My friends are magic!*

SCORPIO: I am mistress of magic, your enchantress, a siren. Come lose yourself in the realms of emotion, desire and passion. I'll take you there. You may feel me vibrate you out of the water, because I am temptation. *You Want Me!*

SAGITTARIUS: "Come fly with me." I'll be your trailmate and give you freedom to pursue your path. I "boldly go where no one has gone before." I love the outdoors, where I receive my finest vision. As an explorer of human consciousness, I am philosopher and humanitarian. *Explore With Me!*

CAPRICORN: I seek to be a pillar of the community and bring honor to my family. My role is counselor, elder, and leader. I am a good provider, businessperson, and a wise manager of my domain. I care about preserving the planet, and resources for the next seven generations to come. *Show Me Respect And I Will Do A Good Job For You!*

AQUARIUS: As cosmic revolutionary I seek to improve the human condition. I teach self-reliance. My freedom is my greatest treasure. People think I am aloof and cool headed. I need space to spread my wings in the celestial realms of bliss. *Let me lift you to the mountain to See With The "Birds Eye View" The Big Picture, and Hear "The Big Music!"*

PISCES: I sacrifice myself in service to others. I am empathic to what you are feeling and a safe space for your emotions. I allow you to be who you are/where you are, for my ecstasy is in rapture with the divine. *Swim The "Sea Of Love" And Compassion With Me*!

♂ MARS ♂

MARS ON A MAN'S CHART represents what version of the masculine principle he is working on in the current life. Carl Jung's definition of masculinity is; "To know your sword and to know how to use it." The Mars position on a man's chart describes the type of sword the man intends to experience in the current life. The anger, rage, and grief most men experience today is the result of not having a healthy expression for their Mars.

ARIES *is The Rugged Individualist. His intent is to learn childlike innocence, trust and courage, and to have fun. His sword quality is spontaneous, aggressive play.*

TAURUS *is the "Lover." His intent is to bring spirit fully into the physical and sensual, and to establish the deepest intimacy on the basis of friendship and trust. His sword quality is comprehensive sexuality, and love making as an art form.*

GEMINI *is the Entertainer and Eternal Youth. His intent is to learn to be free from the rules or laws. "Do what thou wilt is the whole of the law," applies to Gemini. His sword quality is freedom of mind.*

CANCER *is the "Good Father." His intent is to demonstrate qualities of love and nurturing so it is safe for the children, and to be committed to a healthy foundation for the seven generations to follow. His sword quality is to nurture.*

LEO *is the "King" Archetype. His intent is to develop the highest qualities of self-love and to fulfill the mantra, "I will, my will, be thy will." His sword quality is courageous will, individuated self, and self-love.*

VIRGO *is the Priest. His intent is to find the sacred work, and to apprehend and then co-create with the patterning of the manifest world. His sword quality is his dedication to the sacred.*

LIBRA *is the Husband or Partner. His intent is to experience relationship as a path to God and to fulfill the quest for the soul mate. His sword quality is relatedness.*

SCORPIO *is the Sorcerer/Shaman. His intent is to experience the deepest and most powerful emotional and physical realms and then to master them. His mantra, shared by Leo, is; "I will, my will, be thy will." His sword quality is conscious sexuality.*

SAGITTARIUS *is the Heroic adventurer, as in the Hero's quest. His intent is to experience the quest for consciousness and the discovery of the meaning of life, and to boldly go where no one has gone before. His sword quality is inspiration and enthusiasm for the quest.*

CAPRICORN *is the Elder or Lawgiver. His intent is to bring spirit into matter so as to fully comprehend and then apply the operating manual of life. His sword quality is management and control, and the responsible administration of his domain.*

AQUARIUS *is the Scientist or Cosmic Visionary. His intent is the attainment of Cosmic Consciousness. His sword quality is detachment and pure spirit.*

PISCES *is the Empath. His intent is to live a life of compassion and service to all sentient beings. His sword quality is universal compassion and unconditional, transpersonal love.*

MARS ON A WOMAN'S CHART represents the qualities of the masculine a woman is most attracted to. Similar to Jung's animus, Mars is associated with the "magical masculine." These are the qualities a woman must develop inside herself to get the sacred marriage. The sacred marriage is when she walks with the qualities of her inner masculine on her arm at all times, regardless of whom she is with, or whether she is with anyone at all. (For more on Mars see Class Three)

INVOCATION TO THE GOD
Reflections On The Full Spectrum Of Masculinity

These may be spoken aloud, acted out, put to music, or meditated upon.

ARIES: I am willful. I am unstoppable. I am ruthless and relentless. I am the warrior protector of the cosmic order. *Step Aside!*

TAURUS: I am sensual. I am receptive. I crave physical stimulation. I know what's good. I am your eternal lover. *Stroke Me!*

GEMINI: I am trickster. I am shape shifter. I am thief. I am the eternal youth and your ever-changing contrary. *Look Out Behind You!*

CANCER: I am your provider. I am there for you. I see to your safety. I nurture your children. *I Overwhelmingly Love You!*

LEO: I am the King. I am the universe's ultimate leading man. I radiate my magnificence and empower everyone around me. *I Totally Love Myself!*

VIRGO: I am priest. To my sacred work, I am totally dedicated. I serve the Goddess in all her forms. *Nothing Can Deflect My Focus!*

LIBRA: I am your husband. I am your conscious partner. I see all sides. I bring peace and hope that all have their needs met. *In Your Highest Visions, I Am At Your Side!*

SCORPIO: I am wildness. I am desire. I am ecstasy. I am the green man and horned God. I am sought in the oak grove. I am Pan, driven by passion. *No One Runs Life Force Energy Like Me!*

SAGITTARIUS: I quest for the meaning of life. I heroically seek the truth. I inspire your spirit. *I Will Expand Your Consciousness To Its Widest Possible Horizons!*

CAPRICORN: I am your elder and teacher. I am your father. I am the wise old man. I know the rules. I will take responsibility. *I Will Be Respected!*

AQUARIUS: I am completely free. I am the eagle who perceives the big picture with crystal clarity. I am a cosmic revolutionary. I question authority and encourage new experiments. *I Surround You With Light And Unconditional Love!*

PISCES: I seek mystical union. I feel pleasure in compassionate service. I feel what you feel. I surrender to the will of God. *I Die So That I May Be Reborn!*

♃ JUPITER ♃

In traditional astrology Jupiter is often described as a benevolent planet and as the symbol of expansion. Whatever Jupiter impacts it expands. This is not always benevolent or "good." Jupiter's sign describes the rite of initiation, or the type of initiation ceremony, or the specific type of action most useful in assisting a person to reach their goals.

Jupiter's purpose is to serve the angles of the chart (the Rising sign, the Midheaven and their opposite points) and represents the motif, the underlying theme structure and the kinds of experiences that a person must have to achieve the goal of their enlightenment path. These experiences are the direct stepping-stones to the fulfillment and mastery of a person's chosen mystery schools. To illustrate how this works let's look at Jupiter and how it applies to the Rising sign. If a person has Leo Rising the intent is to develop radical, radiant self-love. If they have Jupiter in Pisces the fastest path for development of radiant self-love is through selfless service to others. If Jupiter is in Virgo, the fastest path to developing radical self-love is through dedication to the sacred work.

A good way to work with Jupiter is to use the following phrase. "The quest for _____." Fill in the blank with the motif of the archetype or sign of Jupiter.

ARIES *The quest for aggressive play, for rugged individualism, for new experiences for the fun of it.*
TAURUS *The quest for sensual and tantric pleasure for savoring the aesthetics of life, for appreciating the artistry of intimacy, for learning how to receive.*
GEMINI *The quest for the creative muse, for the eternal youth, for the cosmic joke, for the reality beyond rationality*
CANCER *The quest for home and roots, for something to believe in, for a responsible and committed experience of nurturing.*
LEO *The quest for radical, radiant self-love, for a strong will, for the self-confidence to be a leading player on the stage of life.*
VIRGO *The quest for the sacred work, for co-creation with sacred patterning of life, for participation with the rhythms and cycles of the organic world.*
LIBRA *the quest for non-hierarchical conscious equal partnership, for relationship as a path to God, for living in balance between individual self-knowledge and consensus reality.*
SCORPIO *The quest for complete experience of life force energy and for training in command of life force, for Eros and sexuality as an enlightenment path, for development of an individualized will in concert with a full response to desire.*
SAGITTARIUS *The quest for truth and the meaning of life, for the expansion of the self to the widest possible horizons, the quest for the "quest'" and for continual renewal of vision.*
CAPRICORN *The quest for the rules and the principles of the operating manual of the universe, for responsible administration of one's domain using the rules and principles, and to be an emerging elder.*
AQUARIUS *the quest for detachment and cosmic overview, for visionary eccentricity and idiosyncratic avant-gardism, for cosmic consciousness.*
PISCES *the quest for empathic service, for devotional surrender, for the Boddhisattva ideal, for mystical union, for the visionary dream.* (For more on Jupiter see Class Four)

♄ SATURN ♄

Traditionally, Saturn is thought of as something negative, not looked forward to, representing: bondage, limitation, heavy dues paying, rolling the stone up the hill only to have it come crashing back down, not being okay just the way you are. This is how the content of Saturn has been expressed in our patriarchal society. However, this is not what the true essence of Saturn is. If we go back 6,000 years Saturn doesn't even begin to resemble patriarchy, or a father principle that much. The essence of Saturn is connected to man-made law or humanity's law. In Saturn's universe, moral and ethical judgments are made about right or wrong action. That's why the God image for Saturn is the Being with the rules, or the rules themselves. Saturn represents the operating manual, and the rules associated with the ruling culture of the time. Any time something comes into form, it has rules and laws. People with strong Saturn on their horoscope absolutely know if they attempt to circumvent the law, they aren't going to get away with it. There are people who are not heavily influenced by Saturn, and can run stop signs every day, never report anything to the IRS, bend all the rules, and get away with it. That is, until they hit a Saturn cycle then they can't get away with anything. Instead, they get a crashing dose of reality. Although Saturn represents the operating manual, or the law, it doesn't say specifically what the content of the law has to be. That can, and has changed collectively throughout history.

No one escapes encounters with Saturn cycles. Every twenty-nine to thirty years Saturn makes a complete transit around the natal chart. This is referred to as the Saturn return, and is considered true astrological adulthood, a true maturity point. This is often a time when people make the biggest decisions of their lives, get married, get divorced, change careers and so on. A person has to tell the truth about their life, about what works and what doesn't work. Then they must be willing to discard or change what doesn't work. Strong Saturn, or a Saturn cycle, forces a person to pay attention, to grow up in that area of the chart, and take responsibility for being informed.

If a person is focused, takes responsibility, and is paying attention during a Saturn cycle it's a time when things can work magnificently well, and hard work pays off! Saturn cycles require a person to make a significant change, to take responsibility, and make decisions about what does or doesn't work in their life. These decisions set up the next seven to fourteen years. That's why it is beneficial to know when you are in a Saturn cycle, so you can consciously choose to participate with the intent of the cycle. The encounter with the reputation of the difficulty of a Saturn cycle happens when a person tries to avoid it by going unconscious, partying their way through, or other forms of escapism.

Healthy Saturn is necessary in any system. Saturn is responsible for structure and form; without the principle of Saturn, the experience might be likened to always being on a large dose of LSD. Saturn is not good or bad; it's simply the rules. The best strategy is to learn to work with Saturn.

THE SATURN COMPLEX

Hard aspects to Saturn, such as squares, oppositions, or conjunctions with the personal planets, indicate a Saturn complex. One way a Saturn complex is experienced comes from a feeling beginning at the moment birth, an awareness that things are not okay just the way they are. This often manifests as a person who is motivated, driven, and ambitious. They have high standards, and feel they have to prove something. If a person has an especially difficult Saturn complex, they will be driven to be a perfectionist; in order to prove something to the "fathers," the authority figures, or to the world. About one in five people have such a difficult Saturn complex on their natal chart, but virtually every human being born in patriarchy is subject to this feeling to some degree. For those people who are driven, motivated, and have high standards, these are simply qualities that are part of who they are, no different than having red hair and green eyes. However, these qualities become a neurosis if the drivenness is connected to *guilt, atonement, or original sin*, or any permutations of these three. These three things are our culture's primary motivational strategy, and it has motivated a lot of people. Even if we look at the roots of this strategy and notice there is no truth to it, or the truth of it is irrelevant, numerous people are still wired at a very deep level with this one. *Original sin* is the belief we are somehow fundamentally flawed when we are born, and how good we are determines the number of "good" things that happen in our life. This is a neurosis. If what drives a person is *guilt*, or the belief they screwed up in the past and they now have to *atone* for it; it is a neurosis. Another neurosis not connected to guilt, atonement, or original sin is the belief that if a person achieves something great, if they are really good at something, if they are able to please the fathers on a really high level, and can attain perfection; they will receive an additional reward, or a pay-out occurs at that point. The joke is, if a person has a Saturn complex, *there is* no *additional reward*. It is a box canyon. There is no additional payoff!

What is the purpose or intent of a Saturn complex if there is no additional payoff? It is designed to take a person into new territory, to break them through the belief that knowing all the rules, or doing something exactly right, or being the perfectionist to the nth level is what produces enlightenment or the desired reward. The Saturn complex is designed to teach that limitation sometimes has value. The affirmation or mantra for understanding the Saturn complex is *perfection itself isn't good enough.* This is the lesson Saturn teaches us. The inside joke with Saturn is if you are a perfectionist, and want to prove something, you better enjoy what you are doing, because there are no additional rewards. When a person is doing what they are doing because it seems like a good thing to do for the moment, or because it is fun, with no expectation of an additional reward, then they are not operating out of neurosis. The action is an end in itself and not a means to an end. This is the most intelligent way to handle a Saturn complex. Ultimately, Saturn teaches us to love ourselves and not look for validation from external sources.

(For more on Saturn and the Saturn Complex see Class Five)

♅ URANUS ♅

Uranus is associated with a spirit principle. It's not in the body; it's not in form. It's not a "feminine" planet. Therefore, it has to do with principles that stand outside the universe of earth and water. People with hard aspects to Uranus already know what it is like to be different than "normal"-normal meaning average. Instead, they tend to be a maverick, and have numerous unpredictable, unplannable, unknowable, and unexpected experiences. These events force them to learn to roll with the punches, and accept their uniqueness. Trouble is sure to come when they try to be "normal." The best way for a person to participate with Uranus strategy is to give them permission to be unique and to change.

The intent of a Uranus cycle is to produce change. The mechanism Uranus uses to bring about change is, *Whatever It Takes*! Uranus' job is to monitor a person's life and to notice any patterns that have been in place too long. They may be successful patterns or not. What Uranus notices is when a person is in a rut and it's time for a change to take place. A Uranus cycle brings unexpected, unplannable, uncontrollable events that deviate us from the course we thought we were pursuing. The events that take place in a Uranus cycle can be marvelously wonderful or devastatingly difficult depending upon what is needed to produce the necessary changes. Like a Pluto cycle, Uranus operates by producing circumstances that a person has no idea are going to happen before they happen. These events are unexpected and unpredictable. However, this is not a time to try and make changes or to solidify something in form. Rather it is a time to go with the flow of what is happening, and allow the changes to occur. If a person is not attached and not trying to hold on, then the Uranus cycle is often experienced as a time of excitement and adventure. Ultimately, the Uranus principle is not about producing situations of difficulty and disaster. Difficulty and disaster happen when there is resistance to the changes that need to take place.

To participate with a Uranus cycle, give yourself permission to be in it, and follow this simple strategy.

1. Roll With The Punches

2. Trust You Are Being Taken Where You Most Need To Go

3. Approach Everything With An Open Hand (And Mind!)

4. No Clinging Or Holding On To Anything

If a person resists change during a Uranus cycle it becomes necessary for the events to become even more melodramatic to produce the change. The following lyric from a Jefferson Airplane song popular in the late 1960's describes how to best approach Uranus cycles. *"I said to the wind as it took me away, this is where I wanted to go today."*

(For more on Uranus see class Five)

Ψ NEPTUNE Ψ

In traditional astrology, Neptune is thought of as idealistic, intuitive, visionary. In Shamanic Astrology, Neptune brings in the new visions and the new dreams, but it operates through the creative use of confusion, representing what is good about an identity crisis. In his first book, Carlos Castenada is taught that the third roadblock to enlightenment, or becoming a man of knowledge, is *clarity*. Neptune cycles are intended antidotes for clarity, because if a person really thinks they know how it all is, they aren't open to new ideas, new visions, new ways of looking at life. That's why the best strategy for participating with a Neptune cycle is to give yourself permission to not have any clarity, to not know.

When in a Neptune cycle, or dealing with a Neptune complex, it is important to understand that not knowing, not having all the answers, and feeling confused is precisely the intent. Giving yourself permission in a Neptune cycle to not know anything, to pour the water out of the glass, to be empty, places you in a position to receive new visionary input. The intent of a Neptune cycle is to produce the necessary conditions for receiving the new vision and the new dreams. How can that happen if your glass is full? How can that happen if you already think you know who you are? Neptune is symbolic of the vision quest, when a person goes into the wilderness and admits they don't know anything. Even the chief of the tribe and the medicine man went out and declared they knew nothing and cried for a vision. Unfortunately, we live in a world that demands a person report in daily for duty, giving their bottom line definition of who they are, where they are going, their bank account, their relationship, their function, and their duty. During a Neptune cycle, no matter how visionary and talented a person normally is, this is a problem, because they feel confused and no matter how hard they try, they just can't figure out what to do.

Neptune cycles can happen at any time in a person's life, but there is also a generational Neptune cycle that occurs around age forty for everyone. The best strategy for dealing with a Neptune cycle is to be open, allow into your life the dreams that you have never dreamt before. Realign with the original life dreams. Experiment with the state of the empty glass, so there is a space for new water to go into the glass. In the beginning or middle of a Neptune cycle, a person might receive a wonderful vision, but it is not the time to act on it yet. It is still in process. It is still a part of the initiation. For example, say a person's biggest issue in life is finding the magical relationship. It is possible, in a Neptune cycle, for the person of their dreams to show up. However, this is not the time to act on it, because it is likely that water will also empty out of the glass. It is very hard to concretize anything during a Neptune cycle. It is time to give yourself permission to enjoy the transcendent, the mystical. It is a good time for someone to go on a long meditation retreat, or to take a sabbatical. At the end of the Neptune cycle, if the person has successfully participated with the cycle, renewed vision and clarity return, and they are in alignment with the original life dreams.

(For more on Neptune see class Five

♇ PLUTO ♇

The ultimate purpose of a Pluto initiation is empowerment. However, it often works through a reverse process. The first phase of a Pluto initiation is usually a feeling of *powerlessness*. A main feature of every Pluto initiation is; *Something Will Happen That You Don't Know Is Going To Happen Before It Happens.* This type of initiation is different from what has been popularized by many New Age groups that teach the development of spiritual techniques that allow us to detach, see the cosmic overview, and see the beauty of the divine plan unfolding in front of us. Pluto initiations are in alignment with a much older spiritual tradition described by the dark night of the soul, the forty days in the wilderness, and the descent into the lower world.

A Pluto initiation cannot be prepared for, except by giving yourself permission to go through it and to know it is not ordinary reality. I suggest making a list of what you fear is the worst that could happen, what your deepest fears are, what is your own shadow side, what has been unrecognized within you. Participating with this process provides the possibility that these fears may not have to be literalized, because you have called them out. I have found, however, that what usually happens in a Pluto cycle is something that didn't make the list. Numerous spiritual traditions speak of the necessity of the dark night of the soul, and say that the intensity of the experience is directly proportional to your level of attainment. The closer you get to your goals, the more intense the fear is when the descent takes place. The point is, in a Pluto cycle, something completely overwhelming occurs. You get to find out, through the reversal process, what is most important to you. You can't get out of it. It is *the Acute Perception Of What Is Missing In Your Life,* be it career related, relationship related, health related, life purpose related and so on. You are powerless to do anything. You must experience it and feel your feelings in connection with the experiences.

In the second phase of a Pluto initiation the energy changes, and the universe calls your bluff. *You get what it is you say you have always wanted.* This is still not ordinary time and can call out even deeper fears. Fear of success is often greater than the fear of failure.

In phase one, the strategy is to deal with the heaviness on the level of the heaviness. If you feel weak and unable to get out of bed, if you feel drained, depressed, or exhausted, give yourself permission to feel what you are feeling. Stay in bed, and dialogue with whatever force is keeping you there. Ask it what it wants of you. Jung once said, "In a culture that has demythologized itself, it doesn't mean the Gods and Goddesses do not still exist." Some of them, like the ones associated with Pluto, can only get our attention when we are depressed, ill, or in a place of acute powerlessness. So dialogue with them. When John Lennon was in a Pluto cycle he said, "I feel so suicidal, I even hate my rock and roll." This is a time when what you do no longer makes any sense. About the only type of therapies that work during a Pluto initiation are: emotional release work, holotropic breathwork, Riechian work, or any other non-cognitive processes that allow you to get your feelings out; since a fundamental requirement of a Pluto cycle is having to feel what you are feeling.

The mythological story of Pluto and Persephone describes a Pluto initiation. Another story that describes this is about Lord Vishnu meditating on top of a mountain. He is so pure and he is so high and he is so clear, that he believes he is the creator of the universe. This has been going on for many lifetimes. Then one day, seemingly no different than any other, Kali, or Durga, or some other equally heavy Goddess knocks on his door and says; "Hey, Vishnu, you haven't taken my teaching yet!" Then he is plunged into his emotions, he is pulled into his sexuality, he is pulled into third dimensional reality, and he finds he must feel his feelings; he must fully experience third dimensional reality.

This story also suggests what happens in stage three of a Pluto process. In stage three you must fully embrace the energy. The key factor of any Pluto initiation is the energetics of it. It is non-cognitive. You must feel your feelings and you must feel the energy, become aware of the life force energy and embrace it; once you do that it begins to shift. Then we reach the point originally intended by the Pluto cycle-- empowerment.

Another way of remembering what a Pluto cycle is about is in the following imagery. At the beginning of your Pluto cycle the Gods and Goddesses of your fate knock on your door to let you know it is time. It is time to be everything you can be; it is time to run on all cylinders. If you say, "Hold it, wait, I'm not ready." They say; "Sorry, but it is time. It is time you face your deepest fears, the fears that are blocking your experience of running on all cylinders." Then the initiation begins. A Pluto cycle cannot be ignored; it must be taken seriously.

The other side of a Pluto cycle is usually quite amazing. You get to experience what it is you have always wanted and it is now real life, so long as you have truly embraced the energy, faced your fears, and totally felt your feelings, and incorporated your shadow side.

(For more on Pluto see class Five)

♌ THE LUNAR NODES ☊

The Lunar Nodes are seemingly an abstract concept because they are not planets, but rather the intersection of two planes. Due to the wobble and tilt of the Earth our Moon has an eccentric orbit causing it to cross North and South of the ecliptic. The ecliptic is the plane of our Solar System, and the path the Sun, Moon, and other planets travel along. The North Node (♌) and the South Node (☊) of the Moon are always found in opposition to each other and together they form the Nodal Axis. In Shamanic Astrology *the Nodal axis is a time track* with the South Node representing the origination point and the North Node representing the destination point. We all have our own personal time track consisting of several factors including; past lives, family history, and what is written in the genetic code, or cellular encoding.

The Nodes cannot be seen in the sky because they are the abstract crossing of lines. Yet, the ancient astrologers, particularly in the culture of India, considered the Nodes to be incredibly important. To them, the Nodes had a level of importance that we might equate to Saturn and Jupiter. How could something so abstract have so much significance, especially since ancient cultures were observationally based? The answer is because the cycles of the Nodes are what produces eclipses. From the experiential view, the eclipses and the Nodes are the same thing. Every 18.6 years the same eclipse happens. The knowledge of the path of the Moon crossing the ecliptic is what allowed ancient people to make eclipse predictions. Eclipses are visually stunning events that occur in the sky. They are certainly more impressive than a planetary conjunction. Only two other events are possibly more striking than an eclipse. One is a great comet and the other is a super nova. However, these are rare and do not usually happen in predictable cycles. There are some exceptions like Haley's comet, but most comets are not predictable. In cultures based upon noticing what happens in the night sky, the Lunar Nodes became known visually as indicators of the eclipse cycles.

One feature of patriarchal civilization has been to assign the Nodes with a dualistic meaning. Traditionally, the North Node was considered good and the South Node was considered bad; or the North Node had a feature of Jupiter, and the South Node had a feature of Saturn. Shamanic Astrology is designed to move away from this dualism, or the good/bad approach. The North Node is not good; the South Node is not bad. Rather, if we look at it as a time track the good/bad problem is solved. In Shamanic Astrology the Nodes represent a 26,000 year time track. Each human being has a personal 26,000 year time track, that also relates to the collective 26,000 year time track. The 26,000 year cycle is the longest cycle perceivable by human senses (see A Shamanic Look At The Turning Of The Ages on page 5?). As suggested earlier, if we are near the end of the 26,000 year time track, then we are very close to the destination point of that time track and very far from the origination point.

In the old days, people kept track of time by doing horizon calendars. This was done by looking at notches on a hill, or tracking the path of the Sun or the Moon using stone circles. Tracking the Sun was easy. The ancients put up a stone, stood behind it and watched the sunsets and sunrises. Every year, in a predictable way, on certain dates, the Sun went precisely behind the same stone or the same notch on the hill. Thus, the Sun was predictable. However, the Moon was and is a different story. For example, if a person goes out on their birthday every year, and watches where the Moon is rising or setting, they would have to wait nineteen years before the Moon would come up at exactly the same point it was when they were born. That is the way in which we "Tame the Moon." The taming of the Moon is catching it on the nineteenth year, or the thirty-eighth year, or the fifty-seventh year. Looking at cycles this way, explains why, for most cultures, the Sun is a masculine symbol and the Moon is a feminine symbol. The Sun is linear, logical, predictable, straightforward; it does the same thing every year. However, it takes nineteen years for the Moon to do the same thing.

The North Node of the Moon returns to its original, exact zodiacal place for the first time in a person's life around age eighteen and a half, up to the nineteenth year. It happens again, sometime around the thirty-seventh birthday up to the thirty-eighth year. The next occurrence begins sometime before the fifty-sixth birthday, and ends exactly on the fifty-seventh birthday. There is a fourth window beginning around age seventy-four and ending at age seventy-six. These windows present a person with the opportunity to realign with the original life dreams. This is called a Nodal Return Cycle. There is also a Nodal Reversal Return cycle, where the transiting North Node aligns with the South Node. Both cycles are essentially the same thing, and both present an opportunity to realign with the original life dreams. The following statement used as a meditation, prayer, mantra, affirmation, or whatever, during a Nodal window helps a person to get in tune with this cycle. *If magic were to happen in my life, where, how, and with whom, would I like it to take place!* This is a magical time when the doors are open. A person must consciously participate with the cycle to gain its maximum benefits. (This is totally <u>unlike</u> a Uranus Cycle, Pluto Cycle, or a Saturn Cycle where the events that occur force a person to change, and they can't get out of it.) There are times in life when a person can tell the story of who they are and what they want to do and nobody has a clue what they are talking about. Then there are other times, when the doors are open, the person hardly has to say anything and people absolutely know who they really are and what their vision is. A Nodal window is when this is most likely to happen.

To illustrate this point let's look at a person who works as a waiter. They love being a waiter, and it is the most fun job they have ever done. What might happen during a nodal window? If they were to knock on the door of the one restaurant they have always most wanted to work at, the owner would greet them in amazement, because she just lost her head waiter and standing in front of her is exactly the kind of person she was looking for. *In a Nodal window, if what a person is doing is in alignment with their original life dreams, doing what they do works easily.*

"MAGIC" happens in our lives when three things are in exact alignment. First, a person has their tools together. Second, the timing is right. Third, the attention is on something that is part of the original life dream. If any one of these three things is not there, at best we must be patient, especially if what is missing is the timing. For example, if a person has all their tools together and what they want is in alignment with the original life dream, but it is the wrong timing chances are not much will happen. Things will tend to go wrong. Another scenario is when a person has their tools together and it is the right timing, but what they want is not in alignment with their original life purpose. Then very strange things might happen. However, if the timing is right, and they absolutely want the right thing, but they don't have their tools together, they still won't be able to achieve the goal. This can be very disconcerting. This sometimes happens in the area of relationship. A person knows exactly what kind of partner they want to be with, and it feels like a marriage cycle, but they haven't developed themselves enough. Thus, the person who might be their "ideal partner" doesn't even notice them. However, when all three factors, tools, timing, and being in alignment with the original life dreams, are working together, what happens can be remarkable, even magical.

The tools refer not only to the talents a person has that need to be utilized and refined, but their conscious awareness of those talents. One example is a person who has on their original life script the intent to be a rugged explorer, or mountain climber; and they spend twenty years in sedentary existence, so when they hit the window that presents them with the opportunity to do the quest for Shambala in the Gobi desert, they can't do it because their body weighs three-hundred pounds and they can barely walk from one room to another. Obviously, their tools are not together. A common scenario of a person not having their tools together occurs when their life purpose requires the use of a highly developed detached intelligence. (This is indicated by Mercury in Aquarius or having access to an Aquarius Moon, or a woman having Venus in Sag or Aquarius. It will show up on the chart as something having to do with cosmic overview, or an intelligent quest for the truth via a philosophical mind.) However, they live in a family or culture that has beaten down their intelligence, so they actually believe they aren't very intelligent. Then their tools are not together, because they still have to do the healing work to rehabilitate the wounded tool.

THE NODES AND THEIR HOUSE POSITIONS

The house position of the Nodes has higher priority than the sign position of the Nodes. The reason is this: a Node stays in a sign for about a year and a half. The Nodes have a cycle of 18.6 years. The longer a cycle is, the less important the sign position is and the more important the house position is. That's why the house position of Jupiter and Saturn is more important than the sign position; this is also true of the Nodes. The house position changes every two hours. It is not possible to know the house position of the Nodes unless the exact birth time is known. That's why the house position of the Nodes is far more individualizing than the sign position of the Nodes. The sign position is a general factor; the house position is a specific factor determined by birth time.

☽ THE MOON AND THE SOUTH NODE ☋

The Moon position indicates what tribe or mystery school a person has come from, what a person's training has been in the past. The house position of the South Node indicates what job that person had in their tribe, or what their specialty was in their tribe.

The following are some examples of how the Moon works with the South Node:

CANCER MOON, SOUTH NODE IN THE THIRD HOUSE

This is the Gemini job in the Cancer tribe. The Gemini job in the Cancer tribe represents a paradox of archetypes. Key to Cancer training is responsible nurturing. Key to Gemini training is freedom. The Gemini job in the Cancer tribe would look something like the one who ran the newspaper, or was a writer, or a teacher, or an artist, or an entertainer, or was involved with communication in some form. Whatever the job, it was more mentally oriented than the average Cancer.

MOON IN AQUARIUS, SOUTH NODE IN THE FOURTH HOUSE

This is the Cancer job in the Aquarius tribe. The focus of the training was Aquarius, learning detachment, cosmic overview, and so on. However, the job this person had was to perpetuate the tribe by bringing in the children and taking care of the family. In addition to the Aquarius training, they would have learned to do responsible nurturing and to be committed to a "seed" until it reached maturity.

SCORPIO MOON, SOUTH NODE IN THE FIFTH HOUSE

This is the Leo job in the Scorpio tribe. The Leo job indicates a person who was the most creative, and the most expressive person in the tribe. They had the most fun. They had some particular ability, such as playing a musical instrument, or being a dancer. The Leo job was not as intense, or as heavy, deep, and serious as many of the other Scorpio jobs.

VIRGO MOON SOUTH NODE IN THE SIXTH HOUSE

This is the Virgo job in the Virgo tribe. It is like being a triple Virgo. This person was absolutely, totally dedicated to the sacred work. There was no personal or householder version of the sacred work occurring. It was giving service to what was believed to be the most sacred. A Priest or Priestess, a Nun or Monk are archetypal examples. This combination implies an extreme path of renunciation.

CAPRICORN MOON, SOUTH NODE IN THE EIGHTH HOUSE

This is the Scorpio job in the Capricorn tribe. One of the main features of Capricorn is learning management and control and to responsibly administrate one's domain. One of the main features of Scorpio is command and control. This combination demanded a great deal of respect. The Scorpio job in the Capricorn tribe indicates a person who had a tremendous amount of authority, control, and power. They also had the ability to know the law and the rules, and to be deeply intense and serious. However, since this is where the past mastery is, it is important to know the liberation formula for this combination, which is to know you will always be a serious person, but not to take yourself seriously.

CANCER MOON, SOUTH NODE IN THE NINTH HOUSE

This is the Sagittarius job in the Cancer tribe. This is another example of very diverse imagery. The Sag job is to continually be in search of the truth and the meaning of life. They were the philosophers or explorers of the tribe, and continually stretched the tendency Cancer has to be clannish, provincial, and limited to the group.

PISCES MOON, SOUTH NODE IN THE TENTH

This is the Capricorn job in the Pisces tribe. The Capricorn job is to be the Leader or the Prime Minister of the tribe. They are the ones who take responsibility for the tribe. If things went wrong in their tribe, they took the weight or burden of responsibility. They were the ones that kept it all together and learned how to responsibly administrate their domain. This is a double-giver combination.

☊ THE NORTH NODE AND THE RISING SIGN ♈S

The Rising Sign is the tribe or mystery school a person has signed up for in the current life. The house position of the North Node indicates what job or specialty in that tribe the person intends to learn about.

Some examples of how the Rising sign works with the North Node are as follows:

AQUARIUS RISING AND NORTH NODE IN THE FIRST HOUSE

This is the Aries job in the Aquarius tribe. It is an example of the most rugged individualist amongst the Aquarians. The one who says; "I do what I want and I will do it in my own way."

SCORPIO RISING, NORTH NODE IN THE FIRST HOUSE

This is the most individualistic self-centered, or centered on self, training. The word self-centered here is not a negative judgment. This combination indicates that the development of the individuated self is the most important aspect to be worked on in the current life. If the North Node is in the first house, the South Node is in the seventh house, which means the person is coming into the life an expert at bonding. They already know how to identify who they are by whom they are with. The thing they don't know how to do is be a total, complete, and whole individuated self. Scorpio Rising, North Node in the first says their intent is to learn to be an autonomous, sovereign individual, identifying who they are by their own accomplishments and achievements.

CANCER RISING NORTH NODE IN THE SECOND HOUSE

This is the Taurus job in the Cancer tribe. The second house has to do with self worth, the solidity of the personal identity, being in the body, having a grounded being or solid form. The Taurus job in the Cancer tribe means, of all the people in the Cancer tribe, they have to learn to be in their body. This is not generally Cancer's specialty. Being in the Cancer tribe means the energy is primarily going to nurturing those who are dependent on you. North Node in the second means you learn how to do that and receive physical pleasure from it at the same time.

AQUARIUS RISING, NORTH NODE IN THE SEVENTH HOUSE

This is the Libra job in the Aquarius tribe. It is the version of Aquarius that intends to bond with a partner. Their main essence is more householder than what is normally associated with Aquarius.

GEMINI RISING, NORTH NODE IN THE ELEVENTH HOUSE

This is the Aquarius job in the Gemini tribe. This combination is primarily about the mind, spirit, higher chakras, and complete freedom. The Aquarius job brings in the element of cosmic revolutionary or visionary. They are the scientist or grand experimenter with a detached cosmic overview for the purpose of going for higher and higher levels of consciousness.

SCORPIO RISING, WITH NORTH NODE IN THE TWELFTH HOUSE

This is the Pisces job in the Scorpio tribe. Everyone in the Scorpio tribe must learn command of the feeling function. To totally feel the feelings on the deepest level and then command the experience. The Pisces job means what they learn, what they master, is a gift to the world. North Node in the twelfth, or Pisces Rising, says the person is here to be of service, because of the joy and fun they experience in making available to the world what they do well. In this case, with Scorpio Rising and North Node in the twelfth, what they do well is command the feeling function.

HOW THE PLANETS AFFECT THE NODES

First of all Shamanic Astrology does not recognize sextiles, trines or squares to the Nodal Axis, the Midheaven, or Ascendant. It does recognize sextiles and trines to planets, but not to intersections on a plane. As explained earlier, the Nodal axis is like a wave function, therefore, an aspect from a planet to a point in space, of either sixty degrees (sextile), ninety degrees (square), or one hundred and twenty degrees (trine) seems to be an ambiguous concept. However, experience shows that conjunctions and oppositions of the planets, and/or the angles, are important when looking at the Nodal axis. For example, if a planet is conjunct the North Node, the symbol of that planet and what it represents in the psyche, is the main factor intended to be incorporated into the current life path.

PLUTO CONJUNCT THE NORTH NODE is a demanding position to have, because it is a relentless, ruthless, demanding confrontation with the shadow side. Remember, the shadow refers to what has been repressed or denied, as well as our deepest fears. Therefore, Pluto conjunct the North Node describes and intent to go deeply into the most hidden recesses of the psyche, to encounter and integrate the shadow for personal empowerment of the intended destiny.

NORTH NODE/SATURN forces a person to get, at some point in their life, what they are here to take responsibility for in their world. They must have a duty or responsibility, and must learn responsible administration of their domain.

NORTH NODE CONJUNCT URANUS means a person must use their ability to incorporate into their life their extreme uniqueness, the ways in which they are "different from normal," their ability to be avant-garde. Blend all the imagery we have done from Aquarius and Uranus, and those are qualities that must be incorporated into the destination. For example, if a person has a son with North Node conjunct Uranus, who is completely identified with consensus reality, is just doing what his father did, or is doing what the culture says he is supposed to do, then he is not incorporating Uranus. Bringing Uranus in is learning to be comfortable with being different from other people. People with strong Uranus are the ones that stand out; they are different than normal, where normal is defined as average.

MARS CONJUNCT THE NORTH NODE on a man's chart challenges them to bring that version of the masculine into their life. For example, Mars in Sagittarius deals with the vision quest, boldly going where no one has gone before, expanding the self to the widest possible horizons, and integrating into his experience the quest for the truth and the meaning of life. These may be the very things he is most afraid of doing, particularly if his lineage was of an entirely different archetype. Remember that these positions are statements of "intent."

MERCURY CONJUNCT THE NORTH NODE and how it works depends upon what sign Mercury is in. Mercury is the symbol for how a person thinks, what kind of mental equipment they have. Mercury in Pisces conjunct the North Node indicates a person must integrate the Pisces ability to be completely empathic and feel the feelings of others, or merge into their thinking and their life. The planetary placement conjunct the North Node suggests an extremely strong imperative to have this planet as the leading edge of life purpose.

Natal planets conjunct the South Node create a paradox. On one hand, it is a person's best quality, representing the thing they totally know how to do from the past, and on the other hand, it is the thing they can become addicted to and over identified with.

MERCURY CONJUNCT THE SOUTH NODE again depends upon the sign position of Mercury. For example, the talent and the addiction of Mercury in Pisces is the ability to merge. The problem is they might merge so much they are not in touch with who they are and then are unable to stand separately. I don't know the statistics on this, but it is amazing how many people do have Mercury conjunct the South Node, and it is such a telling symbol. This applies to any other planetary conjunction with the South Node.

TRANSITS TO THE NODES

A Nodal transit does not necessarily mean something amazing is going to happen. It is, however, unlike a Uranus or Saturn transit where a person can't get out of it. When a planet transits the North Node the most important thing is to have awareness that the transit is happening. During a Nodal window transit a person might receive a vision, or a dream, something expansive, something amazing coming in, that gives the person definite clues about their destination.

Jupiter hitting the North Node is similar to Uranus on the North Node. For example, a person might walk by their bookcase and a book falls off the shelf. The book is exactly what they need to read at that moment. A person might hear unexpectedly from a friend they haven't connected with for a long time. When something like that happens during this window, pay attention! It is real. It has a connection to the destination point. People who have clear and vivid night dreams, may have a dream that feels prophetic, and it turns out to be nothing. However, during one of these transits to the North Node, if a dream comes through that seems prophetic, pay attention! It is very likely it's real!

If a planet hits the North Node it is an initiation window that is bringing a gift with reference to the destination point. For example, *if a man has Venus transiting his North Node*, at the very least, someone will emerge who is a positive anima figure, or a sacred marriage experience may come in where they get an opportunity to develop their own anima. They might connect with creativity, or something that inspires their soul. If *Mars transits the North Node on a man's chart,* then the gift is from the male principle; there is a trigger of awareness at that point. If *Pluto is transiting the North Node* an experience occurs that encourages the person to look at what is hidden, face their deepest fears, look into the core and the roots of who they are. *Neptune transiting the North Node* is a time when a person can be truly visionary. Neptune hitting the North Node is a great time to go on a vision quest, or go be with a favorite teacher, or go someplace where you can give yourself total permission to be open.

One of the most visionary cycles is the *North Node hitting an angle*. It is important to be consciously aware of this cycle, especially if it is not supported by other transits. Otherwise there may not be sufficient motivation to take advantage of the opportunities presented by the window. The angles of the chart are the mystery schools of a person's life. Whenever the Nodal axis corresponds to an angle of the chart, the life purpose issues line up with the time track. This happens every eighteen to nineteen years. When the North Node hits the ascendant, it is a time to realign with the Personal Identity Project. When the North Node hits the seventh house, the Partnership Project is activated. The North Node hitting the Midheaven brings a fantastic alignment with Right Livelihood, or contribution.

Transiting North Node hitting the Natal South Node is a Nodal reversal. Remember, when looking at the Nodes, it includes the whole axis, both North and South Nodes. When looking at the North Node, the South Node is automatically included. When the transiting North Node hits the Natal South Node, the intent of the cycle is to provide an opportunity for incorporating the destination point with the origination point. It's a time to harvest the benefits of the past. When the transiting North Node hits the Natal North Node, it is purely visionary, going toward the destination point. However, when the North Node hits the South Node it's a marvelous connecting of the past with reference to the future, magical repolarization, setting up a new nineteen-year cycle.

THE NODES IN CHART COMPARISON

The most potent ingredient I have found in comparing charts to determine if there are strong connections between charts is the Nodes. For example, if the South Node is conjunct personal planets on another chart, it is safe to use the imagery of past life connection. I am not claiming they really were with that person, but telling the story that way works. It might as well be true. It is not necessary for any work with past life material to be literal, instead it is creating personal mythology, stories from the past that underlie who we are. A very juicy, potent connection is *South Node/Venus*. It is like a past life intimacy connection. When a person meets someone they have that connection with, they already know each other. They never have to prove anything, because they already know how to be with each other; it's as if they were lovers in the past. There is a rapport, a similarity of energy. It does not mean they have to literalize the connection in this life. Shamanic Astrology is not intended as a tool for determining who should and shouldn't be together. The fact that two people come together to form a personal connection is part of the great mystery, but once people do come together, Shamanic Astrology is a powerful tool for figuring out what the issues are and how best to work with them.

The *South Node conjunct the Moon* has the flavor of past life family. These people are from the same family unit. In a more general way, this shows up with *South Node conjuncting the Sun*. With the Moon conjuncting the South Node there is never ambiguity, it is definitely an old family unit. *South Node conjuncting Mercury*, represents deep communication and understanding from the past. *Neptune conjuncting South Node*, suggests the person with Neptune was an inspiration, in the past, to the other person and helped to expand their mind in some way. *South Node conjunct Saturn, or South Node conjunct Pluto*, are two of the most powerful connections two people can have. If a person has Saturn on your South Node, they had some kind of authority over you in the past. Maybe as a parent, or a teacher, or an authority figure. Pluto is similar. Pluto conjunct the South Node represents someone who had power over you. The positive version of that is a spiritual teacher; the type that took you deeper than you had ever gone before. The negative side is someone who represents the descent into the lower world. The person with Pluto is affecting the person with the South Node.

NORTH NODE CONJUNCT ANY PLANET indicates future karma, or it represents a person associated with your destination point. For example, I have North Node in Taurus in the seventh house; my wife has Jupiter in Taurus conjunct that. She is the Jupiter effect that comes in as a blessing or gift from the universe. If a person has *North Node conjunct someone else's Venus*, there is an affinity, a beauty, a connection between the two people that feels good for the future in some way. *A Woman's Mars conjunct a man's North Node* means that the version of the masculine principle that the man represents is something she needs to learn about and incorporate into her life. Her ability to relate to him out of the place of the sacred marriage by taking responsibility for her Mars is instrumental for him in reaching his destination.

THE SUN CONJUNCT THE NORTH NODE, is a good all around general purpose connection. It feels good to be with that person, either as a friend, or someone to work with, or for a more close personal relationship. Such a person is somehow associated with a person's destination point and it feels good. *North Node conjuncting the Ascendant* is pure potentiality; it is visionary, but requires awareness of it to make the best use of the connection. For example, if a person has twenty-three degrees Libra Rising and they meet someone who's North Node is twenty-three degrees Libra they have amazing future possibilities. They are both on the same journey in many respects, even though they do not have to take that journey together. However, I have done a number of chart comparisons of people who according to the traditional, classical rules of synergy, had terrible aspects between their charts (such as Saturn/Venus or Pluto aspects, or other difficult aspects), but one of them had their North Node conjuncting the other person's Rising sign. Amazingly, these relationships were working and were worth working on. This is not always the case with North Node conjuncting the Ascendant but it can work that way. *Saturn or Pluto conjuncting your North Node* represents a teacher of some kind, someone that will teach you something new. *Pluto on the North Node* is similar to the Pluto cycle, where no matter how strong you are; you wind up going into something that is totally beyond your control. It is more powerful than you are; it has power or authority over you, but that can be something very positive in the long run. *Uranus hitting the North Node* is similar to a Uranus cycle, so the best response is to use Uranus strategy. Be open to any changes taking place. Roll with the punches. Trust that if you do, you will go in the direction you need to go in. Approach everything with an open hand, no attachments.

What happens when two people have their *North Nodes Conjunct*, but they are not born in the same birth year? Have you ever noticed in families that sometimes a child will have the same North Node as the Mother? This happens when a Mother has a child when she is about nineteen or if she has one when she is thirty-seven. It seems people with the same North Node are a karmic family, but in a different category than being in the same tribe. They are a group of people working on the same goals, although they may have different personalities, talents, and tools. It is a karmic grouping. This also applies to the Nodal Reversal. For example, a person with North Node in Sagittarius at twenty-five degrees, meeting someone who has North Node in Gemini at twenty-five degrees, may not have anything else in common, but the Nodal connection means they are working towards the same archetypal goals.

FORMULA FOR SORTING OUT THE RELATIONSHIP PUZZLE

Moon + Woman's Venus + Man's Mars + Ascendant/Descendant =
A Conscious Approach To Choice About Relationships
Knowledge = Power and Potential For Success

MOON POSITION and SOUTH NODE (concerning relationship material):

> Your tribal ancestral history/Who you were in relationship in the past
> Your job in that tribe/How you related in the past
> Habits, Expectations, Attitudes, Addictions

Useful Application:

> The Moon and South Node positions indicate what level of experience you or your partner had with relationship in the past. You may have had a lot of experience being in a committed and intimate relationship in the past (i.e. Libra Moon). Your partner may have been footloose and fancy free (i.e. Aries Moon). You can save yourself a lot of grief by knowing nobody is doing anything wrong. It is a learning process for both partners.

> If you know the Moon position of your partner and your relationship, or your partner, is out of balance, give them strokes for their Moon (i.e. Capricorn Moon-give them something responsible to do and then tell them they did a good job! Or Libra Moon-tell them what a good partner they are-bend the truth a little if you have to).

A WOMAN'S VENUS OR A MAN'S MARS:

> Current life intimacy intention/How you want to be honored or treated as a Woman or Man
> A Woman's feminine identity, a Man's masculine identity

Useful Application:

> If a man knows a woman's Venus, he has an important key to help her feel safe for intimacy. (i.e. Venus in Aries-let her play, give her lots of space. Don't try to confine her or govern over her, let her come to you. Honor her for her independence and accomplishments. Don't try to make her play the typical domesticated female role, she's got a fiery wild woman inside.)

> If a woman knows a man's Mars, she'll know his sword, where his virility lies, his sense of manhood, what he most gets off on. (i.e. Mars in Cancer--wants to be honored for his ability to be nurturing, to demonstrate commitment, to be a good father, or to take care of her. When he is appreciated for his well developed feeling function and ability to be a safe space for her, he feels like he is fulfilling his current life intention for masculinity.)

the secret for successfully honoring your partner:

> For a Woman-Honor her for her Moon 1/3 of the time and her Venus 2/3 of the time
> For a Man-Honor him for his Moon 1/3 of the time and his Mars 2/3 of the time

A WOMAN'S MARS OR A MAN'S VENUS:

> What we are attracted to in a man or woman (what turns us on)
> Who our inner partner is, the inner woman (anima) or the inner man (animus)
> Who we are polarized with internally
> What constitutes the Sacred Marriage

Useful Application:

> These are the qualities (or who) we are attracted to in the opposite sex. This is not always the best person for us to be in relationship with, yet we may attract this kind of person and project our relationship agenda onto them. (i.e. A man with Venus in Virgo is attracted to the "Virgin Priestess", a sovereign woman who is one unto herself and committed to a "Sacred Work" A woman with Mars in Leo is attracted to a "Leading Man" who runs the energy, is always center stage and is totally in love with himself.) The solution is to develop the qualities of the inner man or inner woman within ourselves. When we locate the inner partner within, or marry, the inner partner internally, walking through life with that person at our side at all times, then we are free to attract and be with an appropriate external partner. We complete the Yin/Yang within ourselves.

ASCENDANT and DESCENDANT (1st and 7th House Cusps/East-West points)

> Current life Relationship/Partnership intent
> Bottom line about why we would even want to be in a Relationship
> The descendant is the doorway into the Mystery School of the current life Partnership project.

Useful Application:

> When all the cards are on the table couples can make a conscious, informed, and realistic choice about the kind of relationship they want and with whom. Know what your priority and intention, is. You no longer need to waste a lot of years in illusion and hoping the other person will change. For example, someone with Cancer/Capricorn as their relationship axis: householder, committed responsible, family and community oriented, and feeling oriented. Their partner's relationship axis is Gemini/Sagittarius: non-householder, on the trail, questing for the truth, and intuitive function takes precedence over the feeling function. They love each other. They have a lot of challenges around space and freedom, commitment and life together because they each want different things and have different intentions. They both desire to be together No MATTER WHAT and are committed to working it out creatively. They now know more about what the other needs and what their intention for relationship is, therefore they can create a conscious relationship that works based on being informed.

THE RELATIONSHIP AXIS
OR THE FIRST AND SEVENTH HOUSE AXIS

The relationship axis answers the questions: Why in the world would you even want to be in a relationship? What is the current life relationship intent? What is a person's bottom line for the type of experience they desire in a relationship?

The culture we were born into has only two recognized relationship models. One is the family model, where the reason people get married is to bring a family in for the continuity of the generations to follow, and until death do us part. The other model is based on romantic imagery, the quest for the soul mate, couple consciousness, finding "the one." We tend to believe if we could find the right partner, everything would be magical and great. There are, as I will show, other valid options besides these two.

The relationship axis is determined by what Rising sign a person has. For example, if a person has Leo Rising, they are on the Leo/Aquarius axis. If a person has Aries Rising, they are on the Aries/Libra axis and so on. The relationship axis is one of the most important parts of the chart. The Rising Sign represents the Personal Identity Project. The Seventh House point represents the Partnership Project, or what doorway a person goes through to experience partnership. Hence, the relationship between the first and seventh house is what is called the relationship axis.

♉/♏ TAURUS/SCORPIO AXIS

This is the path of the "Sacred Consort," or tantra. The bottom line is, *life force energy itself*. This path has do with sexuality and life force energy. Those on the Taurus/Scorpio axis know if they are in the right relationship, if their batteries are getting charged or if there is an increase in life force energy. If they are not having this experience in connection with their relationship they are probably in the wrong one. Taurus/Scorpio is not a giver place. It is not a place where one is drained at the end. The relationship intent is to fully experience the current of life with the partner, to be fully into the current of life, or on the tantric path. If a person has Taurus or Scorpio Moon, it represents the relationship intent in the past, and is not necessarily the relationship intent for the current life, unless they have Taurus or Scorpio Rising.

If one or both partners in a marriage are on the Taurus/Scorpio axis it is essential to the health of the marriage that they have an energizing sex life, and are experiencing an increase in life force energy in connection with each other. Even if the marriage is working nicely on many other levels, such as a strong commitment to each other, many of the same intellectual interests, financial security and an ability to get along on day-to-day matters, if the sex isn't good anymore, and they aren't working on it, the commitment to the marriage has been broken. Waiting several years to do something about it is far above and beyond the call of duty, because the reason these two people are in a relationship is to profoundly experience life force energy. The purpose of marriage on this axis is to experience the tantric path through the methodology or modality of primary partnership.

When looking at the issue of sexuality, it seems human beings can be divided up into three categories, about one third each. This is not an exact division, nor does it have to do with gender, but this example helps to illustrate how the different paths of relationship can manifest. One third of human beings are naturally pair bonders for life, or would like to be. Another one third of human beings are into serial monogamy. Serial monogamy is when someone can only be fully intimate with one person at a time, but they tend to have a series of relationships. In these speeded up times, an intimate relationship may last only two weeks, but the reality is they are not comfortable being with more than one person at a time. Lastly, we have the one third of human beings that are fully capable of being intimate with more than one person at a time. In this category a person could be an insensitive, exploitive, promiscuous person, or they could be a person with a great deal of integrity, intending that every connection they have is a healing situation, or they are involved with several other partners, who like themselves, are wanting to experience divinity by sharing their life force energy. All the categories can be done well, or done poorly.

The Taurus/Scorpio path can express in all three categories, but usually does *not* show up as a pair bonder primary partnership. However, if someone has a Libra Moon, they have a past life history that was a pair bonder for life. If the Libra Moon now has the Taurus/Scorpio axis they will probably want to explore the tantric realms within the context of a pair bonding situation, and take the life force energy to its highest expression with their partner. Conversely, if someone has an Aries Moon, Gemini Sun, Scorpio Rising, and Taurus on the seventh, it is extremely unlikely they will choose marriage to one person. The more likely situation, in a positive expression, is for them to become the tantra teacher, or the tantrika, or the person who has lots of connections done well. Thus, we can see how a person chooses to express their relationship axis is dependent upon other factors on the natal chart.

♊/♐ GEMINI/SAGITTARIUS AXIS

Sagittarius/Gemini does not look like the traditional couple situation. Gemini Rising or Sagittarius Rising is the path of the quest mate or the trail mate. They desire to be with someone who is there to support them in their spiritual quest. Ideally, each partner supports the other partner's own independent quest for the truth. For example, on this path they might be out riding the trail, and every other night sharing the same tent. In today's society this might show up as two people with independent careers on separate coasts and they get together on the weekends. The bottom line on this path is that there is a lot of space and freedom. How does one on this path know if they are in the right relationship? Ideally, the relationship gives them the feeling of a sense of space, a sense of freedom, and that their own priority, which is the quest for the truth, is honored. It is plain to see that traditionally this is a relationship path not previously recognized or honored by consensus reality.

♓/♍ PISCES/VIRGO AXIS

This is the path of the helpmate. The bottom line for Pisces/Virgo is finding someone who is equally dedicated to the sacred work. If a person is on the Virgo/Pisces axis and they are in a relationship they are obsessed with, to the point that the other person is all they think about, to the detriment of "the work;" it is the wrong relationship. The point of the Pisces/Virgo axis is to have a partner that is equally dedicated to the work. The partner doesn't have to do the same work, but they must have the same attitude about "the work."

Jung defines the work, as when a person gets up in the morning, and they absolutely know what they are doing is what they were born to do. When a person knows what the work is for them, it is far more important than fame, position, money, security, or any of the rest of it. People who survive AIDS are the ones who know what the work is for them, because they have a sense of purpose; they know what they are contributing. The work is more important than the relationship itself. Any relationship that distracts Pisces/Virgo from knowledge of the work is an inappropriate relationship. Ideally, the relationship supports the work, and the work they are doing is something they really love to do.

♎/♈ LIBRA/ARIES AXIS

On the Aries/Libra axis, *relationship is the path to God*. This has been referred to as the search for the soul mate, or couple consciousness, and was expressed in the idea that if a person could just find the right partner, they would live a happy and fulfilled life. Images such as riding off into the sunset and living happily ever after have fed this concept. More accurately and realistically Aries/Libra is the creative engagement of partnership. It is through the interaction with the partner that assists Aries/Libra in learning more about who they are. The Aries/Libra axis is designed to do the most processing with their partner. That means it is just as good to have a huge argument as to have everything in happiness and bliss, because that is part of the learning process.

Libra Rising comes into the life to take the training of partnership and relationship. The joke on Libra Rising is, they present themselves to the world as being really interested in conscious relationship, but they automatically draw Aries on the seventh house. The joke is the type of partner most likely to come in, is the type least likely to be interested in processing the relationship. The Aries type is the independent free spirit; the man or woman who knows who they are. Then we might logically ask, why would a person ostensibly interested in relationship draw the type that isn't? Ultimately, this is how the Libra Rising person learns. If they drew someone who was already knowledgeable about relationship, there wouldn't be a learning process.

For Libra/Aries the most potent path to learn more about one's self is through conscious equal partnership. It doesn't mean the Libra/Aries person is home free when they find a partner. What it does mean is, through constant creative interchanges with equals, they learn more about themselves. Another way of saying it is: *The partner is the mantra.* In meditation, the instruction is, if you are off the mantra, go back to the mantra. For the

Libra/Aries path, if you are off the partner, go back to the partner. It is a process of constantly refining the awareness through interaction with a partner.

Even though the relationship intent is the same for Aries Rising and Libra Rising, there is still a slight difference between them. Totally separate from relationship, the mystery school of Aries Rising is to go at life as if doing it for the first time. It is what Christ meant when he said, "To enter the kingdom of heaven, you must enter as a small child." Learning about trust, innocence, and courage, is the Aries path. However, on the relationship path the intent for Aries and Libra Rising is the same. The bottom line for partnership on this path is the relationship itself is the path to God.

♋/♑ CANCER/CAPRICORN AXIS

Throughout the ages, the Cancer/Capricorn path is the one most concerned with the seven generations to follow, and bringing a family in. Traditionally, it is a family path and a conservative path. However, now at the Turning Of The Ages, those with Cancer/Capricorn Rising are challenged to be revolutionaries and conservatives simultaneously. The challenge to be revolutionary is in the sense of totally disconnecting from what the previous culture believed was the content of family and community, but at the same time strengthen the commitment to nurture and care for the family in new and healthier ways. Cancer/Capricorn also has a strong desire to become a responsible pillar of the community. A deep sense of caring and commitment to accomplish the goal of nurturing a family, and the community, is the primary purpose of the relationship on this path. If someone has Cancer or Capricorn rising today, it doesn't necessarily mean they are to be just a mother or father and take care of a family. They are the ones on the front lines in discovering new, healthier ways to create family and community. One key factor in accomplishing this goal is to find something to believe in and then be committed to it.

Capricorn Rising is here to participate in the creation of a new operating manual, and to be the emerging elders of a community. Cancer Rising is here to figure out what the new content of family will look like in the next age. Their job is to discover entirely new ways of creating family and roots. It means defining who your real family is, and being committed to them. The definition of nurturing and commitment from the perspective of Cancer, is to be committed to caring for the seed until it grows to what for it is maturity. It could be a literal child, or it could be anything else that takes a seed form. The Pluto in Cancer generation, from 1912 to 1939, had marvelous ideals about family, security, commitment, and the seven generations to follow, but an all too common trait of that generation was Cancer overkill. The problem for many with Pluto in Cancer is they never let go, and the initiations to separate the children from the parents never took place. The downside, or immature version of Cancer is found in the example of the mother who has a child and abandons it. Somewhere between complete abandonment and over possessiveness is Cancer balance, or commitment to the seed until it grows to maturity and then letting it go. If there is anything this culture currently needs, it's revision on a deep core level of how to do family.

Where in this world is it safe to not know anything? Where is it safe to be a child? I am defining child as when a person comes into the life not knowing anything. Even an enlightened master who decides to incarnate again comes in initially not remembering his past, not knowing anything. Most people don't think about this, but when they incarnate, there is just as much a surrender and a letting go, as there is when they die. When people die they have to give it all up; same thing happens when they incarnate, they have to give it all up. At birth, a person cannot remember their pedigree, or their high attainments. They have to let go of it and come in innocent as a child. In today's world the big question is where is it safe for the children? There is a growing awareness of the extreme dysfunctionalism of the family in our culture. Therefore, the grand project is to revise what family is, and to make it safe, at the Turning Of The Ages, for all children.

Many of us have been involved in some kind of a consciousness group, or New Age group. Almost without exception, it's not long before we discover even those groups are not safe places; it's not long before we discover what the agenda is. What I am proposing is a complete overhauling, down to the bottom line, about how to make a safe space for the children, including the inner child of adults. There are not any real experts on this at the turning of the ages. At the ending of an age, or the Turning Of The Ages, the old operating manual is being replaced, and it is all up for grabs.

The Cancer/Capricorn axis has as it's relationship intent to participate in a whole new formulation of what it is to be a householder. This axis includes taking on the responsibility of envisioning a totally new family and community structure and then to be committed to bringing it into a successful and thriving form for the generations to follow.

♌/♒ LEO/AQUARIUS AXIS

This is the most radical axis of the six. The healthy Leo/Aquarius says to their prospective partner, "I am really fine on my own and I don't need you." And the prospective partner says, "Yes, I know, and I am really fine on my own, and I don't need you either." Then at that moment a spark ignites between them and they say, "But wouldn't it be amazing if we chose to have this dynamic dance, because we can do it out of complete freedom and choice." They both recognize each other as masters; each perfectly capable of handling their own lives, but they choose to be together because they have found the most powerful empowering person they could find. Healthy Leo/Aquarius has as their bottom line intent for relationship to empower and promote each other's uniqueness and individuality. This is a path absolutely designed to break apart old versions of codependency or couple consciousness. The new emerging abstract horoscope for humanity has Aquarius Rising and Leo on the seventh house which means the new emerging paradigm for all relationship paths is Leo/Aquarius regardless of what a person's actual relationship path is. People with Leo or Aquarius Rising have two ways to approach the relationship issue, depending on their previous addictions, and depending on where they are coming from in their past life themes. This path is often scary until it is understood and the person gets to a place where they have a sense of harmony and balance. This means they have a sense of self-worth and self-love, and do not need a partner to validate who they are. If the Leo/Aquarius Rising person is into old style relationship, they will continue to choose to be in relationships with people who bust them of those addictions. If they are not addicted to old-style relationships, then often their job is to attract people into their lives who are, and then bust them. The other path is the one previously mentioned when two fully realized masters choose to participate in a relationship together.

There is no rule here that says one axis cannot be with another one; although some are more logically designed to get along together than others. This is why it is so important to know what the relationship intent is. When a person has the Cancer/Capricorn axis and they are with someone who has the Sagittarius/Gemini axis, important negotiations need to occur for that combination to work. Otherwise they each wind up projecting their agenda onto the other person, creating frustration for both partners. In some cases, a relationship not working is the greatest thing that can happen, because it gives rise to the necessity to do the sacred marriage. This is something we all have to do eventually anyway because, ultimately, there isn't anyone else out there. Experiencing the lack of a relationship is one way to get the sacred marriage teachings. The relationship axis gives us very important clues about what our true intent for relationship is, and this information is invaluable for determining our true goals and desires in regard to the intimate relationships in our lives.

HOW TO DO COUNSELING USING THE PRINCIPLES OF
SHAMANIC ASTROLOGY
Class One
INTRODUCTION TO THE SCRIPT

The five classes in this series are designed to teach a person how to zero in on the most important factors on the horoscope, such as what the issues are and what the life purpose is. My intent is to go beyond the confines of the traditional astrological systems. This approach is designed to inform people who don't know anything about astrology, as well as astrologers, about the mysteries of life purpose, the most important addictive patterns in their lives, and the places where they are stuck. Shamanic Astrology does this quickly and in a way that is conducive to a person's own personal growth and path.

Over a nearly 30 year period of doing astrology I have discovered the most important aspects in the horoscope to get to the bottom line as fast as possible. We will weave together a lot of different things in these classes. This is a preview of what we will be covering, and is more philosophical than any of the other classes. We will describe the basic principles of Shamanic Astrology, and how to use these principles from a counseling perspective. We will introduce the script and go into detail on each portion of the script. We will look at the basic archetypes of the signs and the specific archetypes of the masculine and the feminine principle. Then we will look at how these archetypes plug into the script. Class two deals with lineage, addiction patterns, and getting one's power back. This is the portion of the chart that has to do with the past. The Moon and the South Node represent this area of the chart. The third class deals with the relationship material, and how to pick out the main themes of the horoscope associated with relationship issues. The fourth class focuses on the tools and equipment of the Sun, Mercury, and Jupiter, and covers some of the karmic links and Right Livelihood. The fifth class goes into the outer planetary aspects as the indicators of the initiations and strategies designed to move us towards our life purpose.

For those who are not familiar with astrology, the first couple of classes may seem difficult, because the material is psychologically complex. However, it is also amazingly simple once you understand the key factors. Most of my work as an astrologer has focused on cracking the code of how astrology can be most useful at this time in history. Shamanic Astrology attempts to take into account the reality of where we are as a culture and a planet, and where we are in the overall cycles. Using this approach is the fastest way to bring in a more dynamic or magical aspect.

I use the term Shamanic Astrology, even though I realize it could be considered a pretentious term. Shamanic Astrology is experiential, partly based upon what is actually happening in the sky when a person is born and upon what people really experience in their lives. In the old days if someone used the word shamanic or claimed to be a shaman, a person had the right to ask them when they died. A shaman was a person who had been to the other side or had survived death. Today, the term shaman still implies some level of death and rebirth, of going totally beyond where a person thought their identity was. It could be on a psychological, physical, or spiritual level, or on all levels. The shamanic death experience, or experience of going beyond, happens in an aspect or area of a person's life where they are completely attached to believing things are a certain way. Then an event occurs, and they have to let go of their belief, totally. The best and most effective counselors today are the ones who have been at the core, or at the effect of the same issues they are now helping counsel others. The best alcohol and drug counselors are the ones who are recovering from these addictions themselves. The best relationship counselors are the ones who have had the most difficult experiences in relationships. The same goes for codependency issues, those who have been in it and through it are the ones who know the most about it. They know the journey, because they have personally experienced it. That's why, ultimately, this version of astrology works best when we are bringing our own experience into it. It is not an abstract, detached approach.

I am a Libra Sun and Libra Rising. For that reason there was a long time in my life I was afraid someone might leap up from the audience during one of my relationship talks or workshops, and ask why they should believe me, where was my wife, or how well was I doing with relationship, what made me an expert on relationships? My life pattern has been about taking the curriculum on relationships; so most of the mistakes that could be made with relationships, I made. I knew what I had been through and the mistakes I had made qualified me to talk to others about what I had learned. This fits in with the old model of being a shaman, because the shamans were the ones who had a wound, and had survived the death experience, and became healers as a result. Our culture is now discovering, in as fast a way as possible, where our wounds are, and many are becoming healers in the process.

I am offering a model for counseling. This also works for those who are already astrologers and want to deepen their skills. This series of classes also makes available the basic principles of Shamanic Astrology to counselors and healers in all areas. Those using Jungian psychology, or holotropic breathwork, or body work, can benefit from the shamanic principles of astrology, because it zeros in on what the most important issues are for an individual, and knowing the client's bottom line helps to speed up the healer's work. This dramatically increases the effectiveness of what a person is already doing. The old model of therapy was to get people addicted to the therapy and then the therapist worked with them for ten to twenty years. Shamanic Astrology makes the need for that approach obsolete.

When we tune into the archetypal principles of Shamanic Astrology, the end result eliminates the need to do interpretation. Astrologers as we know them today will change, being called upon primarily to set up the initiation sequences. People will consult astrologers about what initiation cycles they are in, and how best to participate with those cycles; thus astrologers will become more of a ceremonial aid for people, and less into predicting or interpreting. Then each person can individually tune into what the meaning of an initiation cycle is for them. For me, having people always asking what does it mean gets old? Ideally, if we are really doing the work correctly, we share these principles in such a way that people can get the meaning on their own. This is not about convincing everyone to look at astrology this way, or set up a movement or organization. Ultimately, I feel the value of this approach comes from each person's own experience and direct communication with it.

When someone is learning the Tarot there comes a point when it actually hurts the practice to continue to read more books, while attempting to tune into the cards based on a memorized meaning or something learned from a book. Rather, once the form or the basic meaning of the cards is learned, it is best to let them begin to speak directly to you. The same principle applies to Shamanic Astrology. In the shamanic tradition, different cultures have different ideas about the meaning of the four directions. In the Lakota tradition, and other Native American traditions found in the Southwest, the interpretation of the meaning of the direction south differs greatly from the Celtic traditions, or the Wiccan traditions. Is somebody right, and somebody wrong? No. Different cultures have come to different conclusions due to different experiences, depending on what region or area they come from. If an astrologer works with one system of astrology for a long period of time, and that system works consistently and accurately, it is a good system. There are many systems of astrology that work. This is not an attempt to invalidate other forms of astrology. However, in the following classes I will be critical of some of the aspects of the astrological traditions. For example, it is my belief that a good portion of traditional western astrology today is patriarchal, and we should question its authority. This attitude also applies to what I am saying. It is important to keep questioning. In all honesty, what I am sharing with you is the feedback I have gotten from the hundreds and hundreds of people I have given readings. Many astrologers learn a system of astrology and then attempt to fit people and the circumstances of their lives into the astrological principles they have learned. What I am suggesting is to notice how people really are. Notice how the archetypes are evolving and apply them to now, then create astrology around that. Doesn't that make sense, to tune into how things actually are?

It is important to realize that ultimately we cannot really help anyone. I like to use astrology to inform people of all the possibilities available to them. When working with a person with a limited frame of reference, resulting either from their family, or their culture, the most helpful thing an astrologer can do is give them the entire mandala, the entire set of possibilities, and then not be judgmental about it. It is important to avoid statements that refer to good and bad. I begin every reading by letting the person know all the paths are valid and any approach to astrology that makes a judgment of good or bad is limiting. Many people come to a reading and one of the first things they ask is, "Is that good?" or "Is that bad?" We can't help it - we were born into a dualistic approach. But there is no good or bad with this. What we are really looking at is intent. We are assisting people in taking responsibility for their original intent.

What kind of intent am I getting at? If we have twelve men in a room and they all have Mars in Scorpio, they will *not* all be the same, but they will all have the same intent. It is for this reason that Shamanic Astrology can never be proven by mechanistic, linear science. Intent cannot be quantified or proven with statistics. Twelve men working on a certain project (Mars in Scorpio or any one of the other archetypes) are all part of an ongoing, artistic, creative process. They all have their own unique circumstances they bring to the project so their approach is affected by other factors in their lives. That's why Shamanic Astrology does not pigeon hole in anyway. If a person is willing to take responsibility for their intent, we can assist them by giving them the spectrum of possibilities and important clues about what their intent is.

When giving a reading or counseling a person, the first step is to give them a sense of all the possibilities. If a person is brought up in a culture that only sees red, white and blue, but as an individual they are turquoise green, or violet purple, then they are limited by the society that only sees red, white and blue. For them, the most liberating information is to know there are other valid possibilities, and it is okay to be different. I subscribe to the belief that the primary drive for existence is not survival, or the drive for power, or sex, but it is the drive or quest for meaning. It doesn't matter whether the meaning is external, and it doesn't require that there be some cosmic truth in it. As far as I am concerned, if there is some cosmic truth then that is dessert. The basic human drive is the quest for meaning, and there is no better system I am aware of for discerning meaning than Shamanic Astrology. Especially when you consider it is comprehensive and not locked into a patriarchal view. It is inspiring to share the larger picture with someone who really gets it. When a person is able to tune in to their inner quest, to their purpose, it clears the space for others to do the same thing. One of the greatest highs a person can have is to assist another person in seeing the light of their own life path.

I use the word *archetype* a lot. This term is used in a lot of different ways. *One definition is the original pattern of a model or any basic design*. In Platonic philosophy and in Jungian psychology, the term archetype is defined as *an idea or way of thinking that is associated with an original pattern*. In physics or the physical universe, archetypes are defined as *basic forms or basic patterns that are reflected everywhere*. At an early age I began to notice I could detect certain patterns associated with people I observed from afar. These were people I had never met and, yet I suspected I knew what kind of personality they had, how they got along their parents and other family members, even what they might be like as a lover (not necessarily as my lover, it was just part of what I picked up about the people I observed). I got strong impressions about their basic style as a person. I felt I was tuning into the archetypal pattern of their lives. That is what Shamanic Astrology is essentially about. It is a method of using the horoscope to tune into the archetypal patterns of a person's life.

We will look at the archetypes of the signs (not Sun signs, but the signs themselves as they apply to Shamanic Astrology). Once you know what the twelve archetypes are, you have the most important key for cracking the astrological code, and the whole script stands revealed. It could very well be that astrology itself is an archetype, and that is why it works.

I want to share two quotations that are core ideas in Shamanic Astrology. These quotes may not be easy to understand at first, but as the classes progress they will become clearer.

Charles Ponce' wrote a book called *The Game of Wizards.* There is a wonderful essay in the book called the "Nightmare of Astrology". He states:

> "I would like to propose that there is and has always been an organizer of unconscious perceptive functions in the psyche, that either seeks or contrives to find in *natural* phenomena a correspondence through which it may symbolically display itself. It may be inspired by external stimuli that display a pattern of organization similar to itself."

This is the old magical worldview. Shamanic Astrology is not cause and effect. It is something inherent in the psyche to look for the pattern, to look for external stimuli that are similar to what the internal pattern is. Astrology, particularly astrology that came from the rational world of the Greeks, created an archetype that now beautifully works in the system called Tropical Astrology. It doesn't really have anything to do with the star groups, as much as it has to do with the fact that it is a complex archetype itself. It works, because we have a need for such a comprehensive organizing pattern to operate and work from. Those who are open minded, and not locked into the rigidity of their system, will see how astrology that represents and validates all the possible paths is the most comprehensive approach. I am not saying there isn't anything else as comprehensive, and there may even be systems that are more comprehensive, but I do not know what they are. The only thing I know of that comes close is the I Ching. However, the I Ching doesn't have anything that corresponds to the individuality of a birth time, because it works with different principles.

Later on, we will have the chance to examine the four elements from the Jungian perspective of the thinking type, the intuitive type, the sensation type, and the emotional type. That is just one piece of the puzzle. It doesn't include the twelve valid paths for enlightenment, the past life themes, or what kinds of action a person can take to heal a wound. Systems that don't take all of this into consideration are more into type casting, or trying to fit a person into a specific role.

Every now and then I meet someone who claims they are not interested in finding meaning for their life. Some of the astrological archetypes are less interested in finding meaning. Astrological Taurus is one example. For Taurus, meaning comes from another realm, different than something they find with their mind. Strong Aries in men also tends to lack interest in the complexities of the psyche. However, even though some people may not be interested in the complexities of the psychological system to find meaning, they still have to have some sort of meaning, or some sense of direction and purpose.

A personal experience I had with this happened about fifteen years ago with guy I knew involved in the same meditation organization as I was, and in fact, he was my teacher at that time. He came down really hard on me once. He said my problem was I was too busy trying to find meaning, and that prevented me from being in the present moment. Since then, I have been aware of the fact that I may have a tendency for overdoing it. However, the quest for meaning doesn't have to be exclusive of attaining a state of beingness. It doesn't mean a person who reaches a state of beingness doesn't have any meaning in their life, but rather the quest for meaning ultimately leads a person to a state (or an awareness) where they don't even have to ask the questions.

The mandala is the model that works best. The Sanskrit meaning of the word mandala is circle. A mandala in oriental art and religion is usually represented by a circle or other designs that are symbolic of the universe. Mandalas are a representation of reality that tell the whole story. That's why the zodiac can be accurately viewed as a mandala. There is a beginning point, a mid point, and an end point that includes all the colors, all the Goddess and God issues; nothing is left out. Shamanic Astrology works the same way. There is no judgment about any one portion of the mandala being better or worse than any other. It is the wheel of life. The more comprehensive the better, and yet, parallel to that is the idea that we don't want to make it more complex than necessary.

The second quote I wanted to share is from my friend Jade Wah'oo, who is a Shaman by lineage.

> "All true shamanic ceremonies are the mythic re-enactment of cosmological phenomena. The underlying principle of mythic expression is the dramatic reenactment of cosmological phenomena." --Jade Wah'oo

Most of us have at our core a cosmology or mythos. Studying this material helps people to see how they can participate with the creation of their own personal myth, and then dream the dream onward.

An original myth of the Sumerian tradition, which later became Pluto and Persephone, and some of the other death and rebirth myths, is of Inanna and Ereshkigal. Something that is almost never taught in traditional western astrology is that Venus has a 584 day cycle. (See info on Mars/Venus Cycles at the back of the book.) It is a regular cycle. It rises as a morning star for about 260 days, then it goes retrograde and rises as an evening star for another 260 days. Then it "dies" or goes underground to be reborn in the morning sky about eight days later. The disappearance for eight days right before it reappears again in the morning sky was the original cosmological idea behind the death and rebirth scenarios. Venus dies and is reborn. In the original Inanna and Ereshkigal legend there is a character in the myth representing Mercury (Ninshubar). The myth involves Mercury coming to meet Venus. There is an actual point in the cycle where Mercury leaps up from beneath the horizon, or the underworld, as it were, and creates a Mercury/Venus conjunction. This phenomenon was expanded into an entire myth about human behavior. In virtually every tradition, the morning star represents something powerful, and impressive. In the Mayan culture, battles were planned to coincide with Venus appearing in the morning sky.

The last part of the theoretical foundation of this material can be summed up in the word synchronicity. The meaning I use for *synchronicity* is *events that happen together in time*. It is an acausal principle, not one of cause and effect. This ties in with everything else we have been looking at so far. It is part of the old magical worldview of As Above, So Below. If you know what cycles are happening within yourself, you know there are corresponding cycles happening outside of yourself. We are not just at the effect of this, but we are at the center point. Our awareness of it, our co-creation in that matrix, is what is really important. The class on aspects and initiations will bring the following principle across: *The universe is supportive of the human being who consciously participates with their cycles, who has awareness of events happening together in time and participates with the dance.* This is about taking responsibility for what our function in the universe is. This is about becoming conscious participants in the great mystery.

THE SCRIPT

The script of the horoscope is the dynamic that allows us to know what our intended process is and helps us to understand how we can best participate in and take responsibility for our chosen function in the current life.

I like to describe The Script as a symphony of three movements. (Please refer to pages sixteen and seventeen of this book for the outline of *The Script*.) I have listed four items, the one called Strategy is as important as the other three, but the Strategy is not as much a part of the dialectic as the other three. The first movement, or Thesis, is the original statement. I call this the lineage. This is what we come in with. This approach to astrology does not subscribe to the blank slate theory. When a person is born they have an original essence. This comes from the tribal ancestral history, and what is written in the genetic code. It is also associated with the past life themes. I am not particularly concerned about the absolute literalness of how these themes, past lives, genetic code, and tribal ancestral history, work together. That is a whole other speculation we could get into and have fun with, but is outside the scope of this class.

There are ways of looking at this that say only certain people reincarnate. Some people might have their experiences mainly based upon this life. Others experience events and circumstances in their lives that cannot be determined by what happened to them with their parents or their early environment, but clearly these situations are the result of an inheritance factor prior to this life. This factor might be coming from a genetic inheritance or from the past lives themselves. It depends on how a person wants to look at it. I believe at other times in history we wouldn't have to talk about past lives, because during more traditional times we did not have a global culture. It was a lot more common for children to follow in the footsteps of their parents. The whole thing was far more culturally bound. Lifetime after lifetime was spent with the same people. Today in any given family of four, maybe only two of them are part of the same core family, the other two often come from different lineages. They might even come from a totally different culture. That is why we are looking at all the factors blended together to come up with lineage.

Included in the lineage are the past experiences that contribute to our habits, addictions, attitudes, expectations, and the preset conditions. We are not a blank slate. The lineage is represented by the Moon position and the house position of South Node of the Moon. A comprehensive list of the lineage factors includes the sign position of the South Node, and any planets that happen to be close (conjunct) to the South Node. The planets conjuncting the South Node give clues about additional addictions that a person may be dealing with. The lineage is really the only part of the horoscope that has to do with traits such as characteristics of personality and qualities a person comes in with. Everything else on the horoscope has to do with current life intent.

Shamanic Astrology is sign based, but not on what is commonly referred to as Sun signs. I feel that only about two-fifths of all people are actually described by their Sun sign. A person is more like their Sun sign if they are born female and their Sun and their Venus are in the same sign, or if they are born male and their Sun and their Mars are in the same sign, or if they have major projections from the culture about their Sun sign. To a certain extent, Sun sign astrology seems to be part of a collective brainwashing program, because most of the Sun sign information out there includes all the judgments held against certain sign energies. It is interesting to note that it wasn't until about one hundred years ago people began categorizing each other by their Sun sign. This occurred because the only planetary sign people can know about themselves without an ephemeris is the Sun sign. Virtually the entire population, unless a person is born on the borderline between two signs, can know their Sun sign without the use of an ephemeris. Before Sun sign astrology became popularized, people gave their Moon sign when they were asked their sign. In Greek and Roman times, when the emperor used astrological symbols for his reign, the symbols chosen always came from his Moon position.

A person's basic personality is more closely linked to the Moon position than the Sun sign. The best qualities and traits are also associated with the Moon position. However, these traits and qualities are often what we tend to over identify with. I have found there is a directional arrow. The center of the being is with the Moon position when a person is born, and then the directional arrow is intended to move towards other parts of the horoscope.

The second part of the script is what I call the tools and equipment. These include five planets. These planets do not symbolize life purpose, but rather the tools and equipment available to a person to achieve life purpose. These five symbols are the Sun, Venus, Mars, Mercury, and Jupiter. Contrary to popular belief, the Sun sign is the least specific of the five, representing the general all-purpose principle that underlies the other symbols on the chart. It is best described as the fuel a person burns. If we look at the chart comprehensively then every area, such as relationship, creativity, right livelihood, everything on the chart burns the fuel of the Sun. For example, a person with Capricorn Moon and Aries Sun comes into the life with a Capricorn vehicle that must now fill up with Aries fuel. This symbolizes a dramatic change of gears. Conversely, an Aries Moon was running on high-grade aviation fuel, but if they have a Capricorn Sun their Aries vehicle is now filling up with the much denser fuel of Capricorn. It is important to understand the Sun sign is not archetype *specific* for the current life. For the specific archetype we look at Venus or Mars.

When looking at the script, the Venus position on a woman's chart represents the aspect of the feminine principle she is working on in the current life, or her current life intent for the feminine principle. The intent is determined by the archetype of the sign of the Venus position. One out of three or four women have Sun and Venus conjunct, and that means there is no ambiguity with the archetype. The Venus position is intended to lead, but it burns the fuel of the Sun. So when Venus is in a different sign than the Sun, the Venus archetype is more important. Looking at this from another angle there is an intended inner dialogue between the Moon (the old Goddess) and the Venus (the new emerging Goddess). The Goddess or the imagery from the archetype of the Moon represents the past, and that Goddess ideally dialogues with the emerging aspect of the Goddess or the imagery from the archetype of Venus.

On a man's chart the Mars position represents the aspect of the masculine principle he is working on, or his current life intent for the masculine principle. Only about one out of twelve men have their Sun and Mars position in the same sign. When this does occur there is no ambiguity about which archetype the man is working on. The same principle I described for women is true for men. If Mars and the Sun are in different signs, the Mars position leads, but it burns the fuel of the Sun. There is also an intended inner dialogue between the Moon and the Mars. Ideally, the old God or imagery from the archetype of the Moon dialogues with the emerging God or the imagery from the archetype of the Mars.

From this view the male and female principle are each represented as a twelve-spoked wheel. This means there are twenty-four archetypes in all, each archetype having a feminine and masculine expression. Each spoke of the wheel is presided over by a different God or Goddess, a different story, a different myth, a different set of principles. All are equally valid.

On a woman's chart the Mars position represents the magical masculine. Jung called it the "animus." This is a woman's inner and outer experience of the masculine. On a man's chart the Venus position represents the magical feminine, or what Jung called the anima. This is a man's inner and outer connection with the feminine. In our culture, where relationship is determined in many cases by physical attraction and romantic love, Mars on a woman's chart and Venus on a man's chart is the symbol for what they are most attracted to. In class three we will go into this information from the perspective of the sacred marriage, which means owning one's own internal masculine or internal feminine.

Question: *If someone has Sun, Moon and Venus all in the same sign is that balanced or easy?*

We are not in a position yet to make a clear answer. It depends on the archetype and the overall script whether it is easy or balanced. Certainly the archetype of the sign for all three planets is of the utmost importance for that person.

Question: *What is the sacred marriage?*

For women it is when they walk through life with their Mars on their arm at all times regardless of whom they are with, or whether they are with anyone at all. For men the same principle holds true, but it is the Venus position. This is similar to the Jungian material that says men and women need some connection, one way or another, with their anima or animus in order to have access to their creativity, and a mystical sense or an eros connection. Whether the external partner looks the way you want them to look is not as important as having the inner connection. However, Venus and Mars represent what a person is attracted to externally, and that is important information for a person to have. One of the more inexplicable things is why we are attracted to the types of people we are attracted to. When they get to be with the kind of person they are attracted to, many people discover it is either difficult or next to impossible to have a relationship with that person. Not everyone has this experience, but it is an amazingly common experience. Roughly two-thirds of all people have an attraction to the types of people who are different from what their true relationship intent is. When that happens it is an important issue to sort out and understand.

The Mercury position on the script is the tool corresponding to how we think, perceive, cognize, and communicate. In short, it describes the kind of mind we have in the current life. All five planets representing the tools and equipment of the current life intend to develop a dialogue with the Moon. In the area of communication, the dialogue is intended to exist between Mercury and the Moon. The Moon represents the old mind, the old ways of perceiving, thinking, cognizing and communicating. Mercury represents the tool for the current life. The Moon is the counterpoint to Mercury. If the Moon is similar to Mercury, and the South Node is conjunct, that indicates a strong identification with the past. The intent of the current life is to develop the qualities defined by Mercury with the qualities of the Moon as a foundation. Thus, the directional arrow is moving towards Mercury.

Let's take Capricorn Moon and Mercury in Pisces as a quick example. A person with a Capricorn Moon has a version of mind based on being the elder, a person who knows the principles, the rules, the law, and how to keep it together. They are in a position to have their lives structured in such a way they can show others they have it together, because they are the elder and can bring that across. Mercury in Pisces suggests that the new version of mind is to develop the ability to go into rapport, to merge with another person, to drop the sense of authority, and to innocently be with the other person in rapport. The ideal is to merge Capricorn and Pisces together in such a way that there is still an element of the Capricorn mind there. The challenge for the Capricorn mind is to let go and be in the present moment. The downside of the Pisces mind is they have no idea where the boundaries are. They are totally empathic. The Pisces mind identifies with whomever they are with in that moment. In this case, the challenge is to have a synthesis of Pisces and Capricorn in the area of the mind.

Looking at the sign position of Jupiter tells us what type of experiences will get a person to their life goals the fastest. The experiences associated with the sign or archetype Jupiter occupies are the kinds of experiences that assist us on our path to enlightenment. I call this the planet of the Vision Quest.

Question: Are you saying Jupiter is like a diving board for diving into life purpose?
Yes. For those people, who are not having life experiences associated with their Jupiter, they might do very well in a lot of ways, but they will have difficulty reaching their goals associated with life purpose. One quick example, let's say a person has a very serious type horoscope with Capricorn Moon, and Capricorn Rising. It's all about getting results and being the elder. However, they have Jupiter in Gemini. This is a very important clue. It means, when in doubt channel the divine comedian, when in doubt get in touch with the coyote, when in doubt, ask yourself; "What would Robin Williams do now?" In this example, Jupiter is quite different from what the rest of the chart indicates; yet it is an important factor not to be ignored. Jupiter in western astrology is the closest correlation to Chinese astrology. In Chinese astrology, some things are based upon the characteristics of an entire year. Jupiter is the year star; it stays in one sign for about one year.

STRATEGY

The tools and equipment are the antithesis or counterpoint to the lineage. Before getting to the synthesis, I want to talk about strategy. Strategy deals with the initiation cycles and aspects of the four outer planets of Saturn, Uranus, Neptune, and Pluto. The hard aspects are conjunctions, oppositions and squares to those four planets. Some people have chosen lifetimes where they are totally "at the effect of," or - melodrama rules! In other words their natal chart is loaded with squares, oppositions, and or conjunctions from the outer planets. The strategy represents the kinds of initiations and experiences that aid a person in getting to their goals in life. The aspects are precise, carefully articulated instructions on how to reach the goals. In many respects, this is the most useful part of the material, especially for those who are not interested in learning the other details of astrology.

The synthesis, or life intent, is represented by the angles of the natal chart - the most individuating features found on the chart. The Sun changes signs once a month; Mars changes signs every six weeks. Jupiter changes signs every twelve to thirteen months, and the Moon changes signs approximately every two and one-half days. However, the angles of the chart, the Rising sign, and Midheaven, etc. change signs approximately every two hours and change degrees about every four minutes. You have to know your exact birth time to know what the angles of the chart are. This factor individualizes the natal chart. Without knowing the angles of the chart we are limited to only knowing basic information, like what tribe a person comes from, or what archetype of the feminine or masculine a person is. I like to think the four angles of the chart correspond to four specific projects. I call them the life purpose projects and they all represent statements of intent.

The Rising sign is the portion of the zodiac coming up over the eastern horizon when a person is born. The Rising sign or Ascendant represents the Personal Identity Project. This concept is different than what is taught in traditional astrology. I am not saying the Rising sign is how you look, or your mask, or how you reveal yourself to the world or any of the rest of what's usually taught. Here the Rising sign is what you have actually signed up to work on. It is the mystery school you have entered, what you want to learn about, the type of training you have chosen for the current life. The Moon position, on the other hand, is the tribe you come from, or the training you already have several Ph.D.s in representing your mastery in this archetypal realm. Those with Aries or Libra Moon have already mastered that area of training. Those with Aries or Libra Rising are signed up to learn about that training or mystery school.

The corresponding angle, the Descendant, is the Partnership Project. The partnership project shows what mystery school a person has signed up for to learn about partnership and relationship. If we put the Ascendant and Descendant together, it creates an axis called the Relationship Axis. Class three looks at the Relationship Axis or the six paths of relationship from the perspective of relationship intent. Of the four angles, the two most important angles are the Rising sign and the Midheaven. The Rising sign is first in importance and the Midheaven is second. The Midheaven is the Right Livelihood Project, or contribution. Shamanically this is like saying the horoscope is your personal medicine wheel, and the angles of the chart represent the four directions. The common denominator for all the themes of enlightenment, or enlightenment paths, is represented by the Rising sign. Because most people have different ideas of enlightenment, it is better to say this idea is akin to "finding your place on the wheel." The bottom of the chart, or opposite point from the Midheaven, is the Home and Roots Project. This also creates an axis called the Foundational Axis, or Energy Axis.

These projects represented by the angles of the chart are all statements of intent. Coming back to the idea of how the horoscope is like a symphony, we create the symphony by putting all the elements together. The lineage is the first movement, the tools of the current life represent the second movement, and where it is all leading to, the dynamic of life purpose is the third movement.

I am looking for a word or short phrase that encapsulates these principles of astrology, similar to the natural science principles of the laws of thermodynamics, for example, that describe an equilibrium of forces. Shamanic Astrology has regressive and progressive aspects to the horoscope. If the regressive aspects are emphasized, then even if a person is perfect and absolutely right, there is no additional reward, nothing more happens to make them feel good. However, the lineage or mastery is also not intended to be disowned, but rather is the foundation a person stands on. The mastery and skill of the past achievements are intended to be available to assist in the successful undertaking of the current life purpose projects. The progressive portions of the horoscope show where, if the person does well in that area, there is a feeling of return. Part of the art of figuring and sorting all of this out, is to note which parts are regressive and which parts are progressive.

This is a homework assignment. Look at everything in your life. Make a list of all the things in your life you know you do really well. Then sort out which are the ones producing some return and which ones are not. It may be that this is an intelligence test. How many of us get into these traps of relationships and work where we keep doing the same thing over and over again, with no reward what so ever?

Question: *What about aspects on the chart that seem to be in contradiction, like there is no reward here, but it is conjunct the thing that is supposed to be getting you to the new territory?*
You are very right. What I am hoping is that by the fifth class we will have the tools needed to be able to sort out these paradoxes. Many times it is not so clear, and yet, many times it is. Next class, when we look at the lineage, we will find it is the key to different patterns. Most of the time we are so well intentioned. Often, the character flaws we have are the result of a simple misunderstanding. Nobody ever told us that there are certain areas that aren't intended to work. When all the pieces of a puzzle are clearly seen, the solution emerges. That's why it is important to see the pieces clearly. So we start with the part of the script that has to do with areas that are roadblocks, addictive patterns, places where we believe we should continue behaving in a certain way. We can even prove to the universe, with a team of lawyers stating our case to the cosmic judge, how incredibly well we have done. The fact remains there is *No Return*; box canyon, dead end. It is not a curse; it is simply an intelligence test to re-route energy into a different area.

Then we will look at using the parts of the horoscope associated with our intent, our life purpose issues, where there is a sense of magic, a sense of openness and expanse when we are on track with what we originally designed. Magic happens in our life when three things are in exact alignment. One, we have our tools together. Two, it is the right timing. Three, our desires are in alignment with our original intent. If any of these three things are off, at best we have to be patient, and at worst all kinds of weird things can happen. Most of us can relate to the experience of knowing we desire the right thing and we have our tools together, but the timing is wrong. No matter what we do, nothing seems to work for us. There may be other times when the timing is exactly right, but we don't have our tools together, or what we desire is not in alignment with our life purpose or part of our script. However, when all three elements are in exact alignment, things magically fall into place.

HOW TO DO COUNSELING USING THE PRINCIPLES OF SHAMANIC ASTROLOGY
Class Two
THE PYSCHODYNAMICS OF THE MOON

In this class we will look at the most important factors that set the foundation of the script. If we liken the horoscope to a symphony this is the first movement that sets everything up. The lineage, or Moon position, is the place to begin when looking at a person's chart. This is the Thesis of the script or the original statement of the horoscope. It is amazing how much information can be gained just by knowing the Moon position and the aspects to the Moon.

Traditional astrology describes the Moon as dealing with things like the emotions, the instincts, and the unconscious, and these things are certainly part of what we come in with as our lineage. The lineage is a combination of three things: past life themes, family history, and what is written in the genetic code. I also describe the Moon position as the tribe a person comes from, or what training a person has taken and mastered. Some of this material regarding the Moon as the lineage is found in one other school of astrology, called Esoteric Astrology. Shamanic Astrology does not really come from Esoteric Astrology, but in some of the books by Alice Bailey, and more recently Alan Oaken, some of what they have to say about the Moon is similar to what I am saying. However, even though there may be some similarities in how Esoteric Astrology looks at the Moon, Shamanic Astrology is a completely different way of looking at astrology. No other system I know of looks at astrology in this same way.

As I explained in the first class there are no good/bad judgments about any sign position in Shamanic Astrology. This is one of the ways we are reformulating astrology with this material. It is important to understand that all the Moon positions are valid. The judgments made about certain Moon positions in traditional astrology, like the notoriety reserved for Scorpio, Virgo, or Capricorn Moons, all considered heavy positions and not particularly popular, are judgments made by a culture based upon who has been in charge recently. We are attempting to get a view here that sees all the possibilities as equally valid. It is an egalitarian view, an Aquarian approach that says there are many paths to truth; one is not better than any other. The Moon and the South Node of the Moon comprise the only portion of the horoscope that actually describe innate personality traits. All of the other factors on the chart indicate statements of intent. The term intent describes what a person intends to learn about, experience, understand, and grow towards.

This class will thoroughly cover how the lineage issues work and weave in stories associated with some of the archetypes. In Shamanic Astrology the lineage is where we begin looking at the horoscope. The magic of this approach is, once you know what the twelve archetypes are, and how to work with the script, the archetypes can be plugged into any portion of the script. You don't have to know the individual meanings for Mars in Scorpio, Venus in Scorpio, Moon in Scorpio, or Sun in Scorpio. Rather, if you know the script and you know the archetypes, you have the key to understanding these symbols. They don't require individual precise definitions.

The first thing to notice is the sign position of the Moon, and then look at the strategy, or the angles from the outer planets to the Moon. These aspects give you some of the greatest clues about what is really going on, either with yourself or your client; but first look at the archetype of the Moon. It is especially important to determine the difference between the meaning traditional astrology has crystallized, and the actual meaning the archetypes are expressing today. Then, notice how this applies to the Moon position. There is a cultural overlay on the meaning of the sign energies that is extremely strong. Some signs are more affected than others. For example, if we say the Moon position represents a tribe, we can see that certain tribes are more favored and popular than others at any given time in history. It also makes a difference if a person is born male or female relative to the individual tribes (or signs). Hence, generally speaking, in patriarchal culture it is a whole lot easier to be born female with an earth or water Moon sign, than it is to be born female with a fire or air Moon sign. The reverse is true for men. It is much easier to be born male and have a fire or air Moon, than it is to be born male with a water or earth Moon, because of cultural judgments, currently in place, about certain tribes.

For example, if a person has Moon in Scorpio, it is like saying they have been a Scorpio for a very long time. It is where their mastery is. It is where their Ph.D.s are. Scorpio has been out of favor as an astrological energy since the take over of patriarchy. Therefore, it is difficult to continue to have the identity remain with the accomplishments and achievements of Scorpio training. If a person happens to have a Moon position that is judged by the culture to be a good one, or an acceptable one for their gender, or for the need of the times, then it is remarkably easy, especially in the early years, to continue on with the identity associated with their Moon.

Question: What is the evidence that shows the Moon represents the past?
Number one, the tradition of astrology has the Moon representing the instincts, the unconscious and things like that. For me, the evidence comes from noticing what is really going on with people chart after chart, and tuning into the mystery the charts reveal. I am sharing with you what I began to notice in the early days of doing astrology. I noticed over and over that this is the way the Moon works. It is the key to so many mysteries, and understood from this perspective clues begin to emerge. The main evidence that supports this approach is whether it works or not. What I am sharing in this class is not dogma. There are many other ways of looking at the Moon, but I suggest you try looking at it in this way and see for yourself how much is revealed.

A different angle on this is to consider the one thing that dying and being born both have in common. Both experiences require the complete loss of ego. When a person is born they don't usually remember what their past achievements were, and they don't remember what the agreements of the current life are. They come in innocent; there is an ego loss. Nevertheless we are not a blank slate. There are certain unconscious traits, certain instincts, certain habits that are there. I am suggesting it is the Moon position that captures that. The rest of the chart symbolizes what a person comes into the life to do. For example, the tools and equipment of the current life represent the new characteristics a person is working on, or what the *intent* is.

The symbolism of the Moon in Shamanic Astrology is not associated with a male or female identification. The Moon is not the female principle and the Sun is not the male principle. The Sun and the Moon are frequently principles of duality, but there are many cultures in the history of humanity where the Sun was seen as feminine and the Moon was seen as masculine. Therefore, both Gods and Goddesses, male and female mysteries, can be found in the symbolism of the Moon. I am not ascribing the Moon with any sort of gender identification. However, I will do that with Mars and Venus to a certain extent.

The other features of the investigation of the Moon include the habits and patterns of addiction, how to heal wounds, get one's power back, and deal with attachments. All of these issues are associated with the complexes of the Moon. The first thing is to get a clear idea about what the tribal ancestral history actually is. If you are working with a friend or a client, or are in any situation seeking insight into someone, know where he or she started. Know what their *habits, attitudes, addictions, and expectations* are. That expression captures an understanding of the Moon better than any other. Generally, a person's finest qualities are found in the Moon, and yet, it is where a person tends to most over-identify with, or get stuck. This brings us to the "law of the Moon." This law states, *Even If You Were Perfect With Your Moon, It Is Insufficient To Your Liberation.* In the first class, the homework I gave, was to sort out all the things you know you do well in your life, and notice which ones get you results, give you pleasure, validation, produce excitement, eros, and magic, and which ones do not. Separate out where it is you get a return, validation, and increase in happiness, from where no matter how well you do, none of the above seems to be the result. If one is attached to the Moon, if one's identification of self is with the characteristics of the Moon, then it is a diminishing return; at best, there will be ultimately boredom and redundancy. An excellent example is the thousands of people on the planet who are really successful, but aren't happy, because deep down they are bored. Boredom perhaps is the best case scenario for breaking attachment to the Moon. The worst case scenarios are all the different stories we have of addiction, and currently there are several forms. The dynamics of this will be clearer as the class progresses. Remember, when looking at the horoscope always look at the Moon first. Once you have a thorough understanding of what is happening with the Moon then you can look at what the intent is, but remember to start with Moon. Now let's look at some examples of the archetypes from the perspective of the tribal lineage, beginning with Aquarius Moon.

AQUARIUS MOON: Remember the Moon position indicates where the mastery is, or we could say a person with an Aquarius Moon has been Aquarius for a long time. One way to look at the Aquarian tribe is through the model of intergalactic politics. This describes the Aquarius Moon as a person who is not really from here (here being planet earth or third dimensional reality). They have come from elsewhere, like the Pleiades or Vega or some other off-world place and they are here on a mission. It is a challenge for an Aquarius Moon to be here because they have not been on a planet with such density before, and they are now coming into form. So where the Aquarius Moon had been previously comfortable, in a detached, cosmic overview type of existence, these qualities no longer offer the same advantages. They do have to be here, because they are making the journey or descent into third dimensional reality.

If one is not interested in the approach of intergalactic politics, we could say the Aquarius Moon folks are the ones who have been "om"ing out on mountaintops for a long time. They have taken the Buddhist view of getting off the wheel, of refining the consciousness and awareness to higher and higher levels, and that *was* their legitimate path. Remember, every one of the Moon positions *was* a valid path, but if the Moon is in Aquarius, that is where a person already has mastery. Chances are the current life is about changing gears into something different.

The third possibility is the Aquarius Moon was the ivory tower philosopher. They knew wonderful philosophical truths, but they didn't have to get their hands dirty. For example, they might have written books about relationships with the correct principles and ideas brilliantly expressed, but they were never really in any relationships themselves. The main quality, or teaching, or what is primarily learned in the Aquarius tribe, is detachment; sending out one's eagle, cosmic overview. It is within the tribe of Aquarius that we find the true definition of spirituality, as opposed to religion. I am not saying only Aquarius has spirituality, but the definition of spirituality is found in the Aquarius tribe: *Always expanding context, wherever you are in your life, always seeing the widest context. To be spiritual, in this case, is to continually expand the context.*

These are the trainings associated with the Aquarius tribe. On a practical level how does this information work? When a person is scared, over their head, or freaked out, they go into survival. They re-establish their equilibrium, by going back to their original roots. In any relationship, or any powerful encounter with anyone that causes a person to be afraid, overwhelmed, or over their head, the most loving thing you can do for them is give them strokes for their Moon. That helps them get re-established in their original center. We come into the life with the center of our being emanating from the Moon. Unless a person has the Rising sign and the Moon in the same sign (only one in twelve people do), chances are it is not the intent of the current life for the identity to remain with the Moon. Most people are changing gears into something different. Still, it is very loving to give a person a chance to breathe, to re-center.

How do you give Aquarius Moon strokes or the chance to re-center? In a close relationship where the Aquarius Moon has gone deeper than they have ever gone before, they will need a chance to get away, fly away. Let them have their space. Let them go meditate. Let them go into their intellect. Let them go into disassociation. This is what will allow them to get their original state of equilibrium. However, if that same Aquarius

Moon is demanding everyone they encounter treat them that way, and they remain detached, or in their intellect all the time, then it is an addiction and regressive. That person is simply holding onto what feels comfortable without the willingness to go into new territory.

There is a formula that works. In a state of balance and healthiness a person lives their Moon position about one-third of the time, because it is still the foundation, it is still what we are really good at. In a state of great healthiness, the Moon position is only done when it's fun. It should not be done when the person has an expectation of an additional reward, or when they feel pressured to be a certain way. Many us fall into the trap of feeling that we are selling out our identity if we don't continue to do the activities associated with our Moon. This principle will become clearer when we look at the *giver* Moon positions, like Pisces and Cancer.

Remember, the Moon positions are judged in different ways, depending upon the culture we are in. For example, if a woman has Aquarius Moon and Pluto or Saturn squaring her Moon, or some other difficult outer planet complex to her Moon, right off the top we can say Aquarius is not one of the tribes supported by patriarchy if you are born female. Hence, I have a large number of horoscopes of women with Aquarius Moon aspected by heavy Saturn or Pluto who are born into fundamentalist Christian families, and therefore experience immediate invalidation through their family structure. Another scenario might be a woman with an Aquarius Moon who is born into a situation where her brilliance or spirituality is denied or not reinforced; she might even be told she is stupid, or not that intelligent. This is just the opposite of what her lineage actually is. When the Moon position is not supported by the culture, or when there is wounding and a person is not allowed to feel good about their lineage, then there is a stage of development necessary in that person's life called *getting their power back.* This means re-establishing the starting point, and healing the wounds associated with the outrage or violation in connection with their Moon. I call this the hoax that happened in the beginning, where the person is led to believe that their best qualities are no good. At a certain point a person must be restored, or get to a place where they feel good about their lineage. That means the Aquarius Moon with heavy Saturn or Pluto to their Moon has the opportunity to get strokes for their detachment, brilliance, egalitarianism, avant-garde qualities, and spirituality. Then, they are better equipped to go into whatever the new territory is, as long as they don't over identify with the qualities of their Moon.

Now let's look at a man with an Aquarius Moon and *no* strong Pluto or Saturn aspects to his Moon or elsewhere on his chart. It is fairly safe to assume he was born into a family and a culture that has validated his detached intellect, and his linear, left brain, high speed, brilliant approaches to reality. He is an expert at that, and he continues to get validation for that. What happens when a woman meets this man, especially if the woman has some degree of development in the feeling function, and has the desire for interpersonal intensity? If she is a woman who desires for her man to share with her something about how he feels; what will happen? Nothing. He will express detached expositions about the theory of feeling, but there won't be a response in the senses, or in the interpersonal dimension. These are two examples of opposite things that can happen in the same lineage.

Women with fire Moons and men with water Moons have the tribal positions that are most contradictory to what the current culture deems to be true about that gender. I frequently see clients with this exact situation. It usually happens that these people reach forty, fifty, even sixty years old before they realize they have been living their whole life without their foundation. A common scenario that describes how this principle works is the example of a woman with a Sagittarius Moon. She may have spent thirty years of her life raising a family, or in some other position where she has mainly been a giver. She may have felt she had to do what the culture, the man, or the family said she was supposed to do. Therefore, she never had a chance to validate her lineage and now she is feeling angry. This is another example of someone who has to get their power back, and heal the wounds associated with the violation of their lineage.

Looking at the Moon as the lineage associated with a certain tribe, is in no way a claim that this is the comprehensive story of one's entire path. Rather, it represents the very specific karmic issues that set up the current life. This works best in a mythic sense, rather than looking at it literally. When someone has an Aquarius Moon and we make statements such as: this person has not been operating from the feeling function, has not been a householder, has operated from the higher chakras, and has come from refined or detached realms, we are not saying that person has never had any of the other kinds of experiences, but it works *as if they have never had any other kinds of experiences*. This is similar to what can happen when putting two charts together to determine the karmic links. Certain links cause the literalists to say; "Oh, you and that person have been lovers in a past life." I say it's not necessary to be literal. If certain aspects show up between two charts, whether it's true or not doesn't matter, it acts like it's true. In the same way the Moon positions act like they are the entire lineage. It is not possible to look at the horoscope and get the entire incarnational history of somebody anyway.

The lineage works in a beautiful way for therapy, because one is able to detect the complexes setting up the life experiences. The lineage acts as if that is all the person knows. The elements of the lineage are fixed in the character and are what a person most responds to, or where they are operating from unconsciously. For example, an Aquarius or Gemini Moon are both non-householder positions. These lineages indicate a person who doesn't know much about deep intimacy or bonding, but it doesn't necessarily mean the person has never married or never bonded at any time during their incarnational history. What those Moon positions suggest is that now they respond to life as if they don't know anything about deep intimacy or bonding. Right now our focus is on the issue of lineage, but the rest of the script may indicate the person is supposed to learn intimacy and bonding, or the script may indicate that intimacy and bonding are irrelevant in connection with their current life intent. These are issues we will look in the following classes.

Question: *I feel like I have identified too much with my Moon my whole life, and now I am turning that around and going in the other direction. Is that taking back my power?*

No, but what you are asking is exactly the direction we need to take this now. What happens when the Moon position is supported strongly by the culture, or has all easy aspects to it? I found that this scenario happens in the majority of the cases. Approximately three-fifths of all people find it is totally natural and easy for them to do their Moon. These people continue doing the activities associated with their lineage for as long as they can get away with it, or until they get bored with it. No matter what the strategy to the Moon is, unless the current life intent is the same as the lineage, which is rare, the intent is to shift gears from the lineage to something else. That's why we have a formula that says we only do our Moon one third of the time, rather than being attached to it. This is true across the board for every Moon position, regardless of whether a person has a hard strategy or an easy strategy associated with it.

The difference between people is what kind of strategy they have employed. There is the strategy of addiction, and the strategy of violation and invalidation. The addiction strategy is challenging because a person can live their Moon for twenty, thirty, or forty years and have a seemingly sufficient amount of validation for it. So what does it take to break them into the new territory? What motivates such a person to try something new? Boredom! It goes back to the issue of why millions of successful people aren't really happy. If a person has a wonderfully supported Moon position, and the culture likes it, the tendency is to keep doing it until they get bored with it. Stories of addiction and codependency fall into this category. Stories of people who give and give and give are also in this category. Then we have people with Moon positions that are immediately violated or invalidated by the culture. Both overall strategies are really the same, and represent an intelligence test to stop over-identifying with the Moon.

If you have a Moon position that has been powerfully judged against by the culture and you have heavy Saturn, Uranus, Neptune or Pluto aspecting the Moon, it is a double dose. Not only are there difficult personal aspects to your lineage, but also the culture automatically invalidates the lineage. There is a choice when a person is in circumstances like that. They can have a worldview that says they are victims and it's an unfair universe. They might even retain the best lawyers to go before the judge to present their case. The lawyers present a rock solid case proving their client has been a victim of unfair and atrocious treatment. Still nothing changes. Being right doesn't help. A better alternative is to look at the situation as a strategy to change gears. If a person doesn't get validation for their Moon, they are forced to develop a different identity.

I have often wondered why it works this way and if there couldn't be a more intelligent, less painful way to get people to try a different curriculum, or to check out a different mystery in life? Do we have to have such heavy violation and invalidation? So far I have found that this is the way it seems to work for a lot of folks. I am certainly not claiming this is the only way it has to be done, but I have found it is a common scenario. A lot of people go through a phase where they feel like a victim and they experience an oppressor, whether it is between races, male/female issues, or abuse issues, and so on.

The step beyond this experience is where one is able to see the larger picture. I am not trying to whitewash these experiences, or let any perpetrators off the hook, but it is often part of the strategy to go through a violation or invalidation experience, which then acts as a catalyst for a change of gears into something different.

The Moon represents our best qualities, so it is intended to *remain* as our foundation once we move on and no longer have our identity tied up with it. The point is to move to a place where there is no *attachment* to the Moon. Ideally, the Moon becomes a tool we can use whenever we need it. There are two kinds of attachment a person can experience in connection with their Moon: positive attachment and negative attachment. *Positive attachment* occurs when the Moon position appears to work well and the person gets validation for those qualities. This might be the Cancer or Capricorn Moon type the world calls on to take responsibility over and over. Not only do they do it, they do a great job every time, and everyone tells them what a wonderful job they did. This is positive attachment. If the Moon position is supported by the culture or feels relatively good, it is easy to keep doing it and over identify with it. *Negative attachment* is when the Moon has hard or difficult aspects, such as squares or conjunctions from Saturn, Uranus, Neptune and/or Pluto. In the case of the Capricorn Moon with hard aspects the person might go through twenty years really angry and resentful because they don't get any respect, and no one really takes them seriously. Ironically, for lifetimes they were respected and revered as the elder. This is an example of a case where a person doesn't get any validation for their Moon whatsoever. What is the way out on this one? To realize life is not about always getting validation. It's "getting the joke" that you already have a Ph.D. in that area, and now it is time for someone else to be identified in that role. It is understanding that neither type of attachment works.

SCORPIO MOON is a good one for further illustrating these principles. Scorpio has not been in favor for about five thousand years. We have to go back to the great matriarchies, back to the age of Taurus, to find a time when Scorpio was in favor. However, Scorpio is still a valid approach to reality inspite of the cultural judgment against it. If a person has a Scorpio Moon, it means for lifetimes they were working on Scorpio, they were in Scorpio school and they are a Scorpio adept.

What is the nature of Scorpio training? The first part of Scorpio training, and this applies to all the water Moons, is learning to feel the feelings. One way or another, the student in Scorpio school must be in touch with the feeling function. The second part of Scorpio training, which is different from the other water Moons, is learning to command the experience, to be a master of how the life force energy works. The Scorpio path, throughout the ages, has been associated with the path of sorcery. It is tantric energy, meaning that *life force energy itself is the path to God.* It is Scorpio's job to command that experience. It is combining will and desire into a wonderful working team. The autonomous self is simultaneously in touch with desire, because on the healthy Scorpio path there can be no denial of desire. This contradicts the traditional western interpretation of Scorpio as being secretive, or repressed, or denied. This is not the true essence of Scorpio, but rather what Scorpio has had to be to survive. A person with

Scorpio Moon usually feels on a deep level that if they really came forth with the power, depth and the intensity of what they are feeling, and what they know, and what they desire, it would be dangerous for them. I have seldom met anyone with a Scorpio Moon, particularly women, who did not resonate in some way with the motif of having been burned at the stake.

A person with Scorpio Moon comes into the life with a background of having totally felt everything and having commanded it. What I mean by commanding it is, say at birth a person has a ten speed sports car and rather than being in a family or a culture that only lets them run in third gear, they have had the opportunity to investigate the higher gears. When they begin to investigate the other gears, especially the first few times they are trying it out, the experience is wild and out of control and they are in over their head. However, eventually they learn to command all ten gears and they know how and when to use each gear.

Scorpio learns mastery and command of the feelings. What happens when the Scorpio master is born into a culture that invalidates the feeling function and invalidates Scorpio? What do they do? One option is the repressed version, where they feel compelled to keep who they are, and what they know, secret. The other option is the expressed version, represented by the Scorpio Moons who are very much in touch with their will, and still into running the energy. These types are what our culture refers to as control freaks. Scorpio training has a required curriculum that includes classes in Control 101, 102, 103 and so on. If the Scorpio student does not learn command and control of the feeling function and life force energy, they fail Scorpio school. That's why the Scorpio Moon remembers their best traits are command and control, and running the energy. It was what the world needed them to do in the past. Their mantra was *I Will That My Will Be Thy Will*. Here there are three wills, and two of them belong to the Scorpio tribal member.

It is as if God wants Scorpio to do that. When Scorpio Moon comes into the life, they remember their best qualities are to be willful and run the energy. They instinctively know the principles of sorcery. So what does it take to break the attachment to the expressed version of positive attachment to Scorpio Moon? I have found a person gets over positive attachment to Scorpio Moon by creating circumstances in their life totally beyond their control so they learn how to let go and surrender. This means no matter how good they are at focusing their will, moving the energy, and using sorcery, the circumstances they find themselves in are just too much. Eventually, depending on how stubborn they are, this breaks their attachment to the will.

Every Moon position has carefully articulated strategy to break attachment and all strategies are tough, relative to their specific tribe. Scorpio's strategy isn't any more difficult than any other strategy, but it is their own strategy unique to their predicament of attachment. For those of us who don't have this one to deal with, it sounds like a rough one. Now if a person is negatively attached to their Scorpio Moon, they have never really felt their power. Due to their life circumstances they have never really allowed themselves to feel their feelings. This causes the energy to become blocked on the inside, and often results in illnesses like cancer or heart disease. These are situations where the Scorpio Moon must become aware to get their power back. I have found the majority of people with Scorpio Moon are in negative attachment rather than in positive attachment.

Comment: Get back that control.
Well, it's not get back the control, it's get back the feelings; where one can have permission to be in a position to respond and not be attached to the results of their will.

Question: What about the sexual addiction of Scorpio Moon?
If it is an expressed version of Scorpio, their operating reality is life force energy, and their intent is to be surrounded in life force energy as the path to God. If that particular Scorpio pattern includes bonding and relationship issues, it almost always shows up in some of the most obsessive forms of connection. Many people who get into Scorpio addictive sexual patterns have partners that are quite willing to participate, so it is not always about controlling the other person. In this case the problem is simply over identification with a state of reality a person already knows everything about. For example, if the Scorpio Moon has Mars in Aquarius, and Aquarius Rising, they will experience magic in a dimension vastly different than what Scorpio represents. If the Scorpio Moon remains stuck in the Scorpio dimension they will eventually get terribly bored and want to explore new possibilities. The tendency for everyone is to prefer to be with our Moon regardless of what our Moon position is, because that is what we know. It is comfortable and familiar, even if it has become boring. Some of the Moon positions, especially Scorpio, Capricorn, and Leo, are more stubborn, making it tough to shift into something different. Even if you could absolutely, conclusively prove to them there are no further rewards for continuing to live their Moon and that there are amazing rewards in something else, they might still choose to remain attached to their Moon. This is a way of astrologically describing a masochistic pattern. A person keeps doing the same thing, even though it hurts, because they are so stubborn they think maybe *this time* they will convince the universe to give them the reward they believe they rightfully deserve. They know they did a great job at this before, and they were rewarded. They know they are still doing a great job, and they are convinced they should still be getting rewarded. Logically, to them, it should still feel great, and they wonder why it's not working.

In the astrological schools that use karma and past lives as part of their teaching, it has become common (especially with some of the less popular Moon positions that include things like control and power), to make the judgment that a person misused their power previously, so they are experiencing difficulties now because of the past misuse. It is absolutely *NOT* useful to look at it this way. That approach, even though it is couched in karma and past lives, is simply a recycled version of guilt and judgment. It is far more useful for the Scorpio Moon to understand that if they are now blocked in the use of their will (negative attachment) it is not a punishment, but rather they simply went as far as they could in that training. If a person has five Ph.D.s in Scorpio training, and they were really good at it, they are much more likely to be attached and it will take an extreme strategy to convince them to let go of it. Otherwise, using the model that says a person is being judged, or punished, or they misused their power, tends to keep them at the effect of the exact same energy. I never make any judgment that a person screwed up or misused their power, rather they simply went as far as they could with that training and now it is time to shift to something new. To me, it's typical that this culture would disempower Scorpio by saying they misused power.

The joke associated with the Moon position is, when you no longer over-identify with your lineage through either positive or negative attachment, positive or negative identification, then you have access to your Moon in a healthy way. You get to use it whenever it is useful or whenever it is fun. The lineage is the foundation that serves the current life purpose and when understood in this way, you automatically get to use your Moon about one third of the time.

Comment: It seems to me people feel insecure using their Moon and they don't always get strokes at that point.
This deals with the issue I mentioned before about when a person gets over their head, freaked out or scared, and they want to go back to where it's safe. I can speak from experience on this regarding Capricorn Moon. For me, if I am scared or powerless, the best way to get back into center is by having something responsible or important to do, and then having someone tell me I did a great job. Put me in a position of being elder in some way, and I am right back to center, because that is my original lineage. However, if I that's all I am doing, then I am operating out of addiction. If all a person does is operate from their Moon position there is no real eros or joy in it. How I deal with my tendency to over-identify with Capricorn Moon is tell myself, "I am only going to do this if it is fun!" I have even changed my creative fantasy behind what I do. Instead of looking at my work as representing something responsible to do, or a way for me to contribute something valuable and worthwhile, I now look at it as if I am an entertainer, and the most important person for me to entertain is myself. If I am not entertaining myself, I am wasting my time, because otherwise the activity is redundant and regressive.

Now let's look at the giver Moons. The *giver Moons* consist of *Pisces, Virgo, Cancer, and Capricorn.* These four lineages do not really have an identity save what they do for others, although they all have different reasons for giving. *Capricorn* knows the law; they are the elders. What is the downside of that lineage? It is the teacher that needs the students more than the students need the teacher. *Cancer* represents responsible nurturing, they are the ones who keep the families together. The healthy version of Cancer is the woman who loves her children without thinking, "If I love my children then they will love me back." It is a healthy arrangement. There is nothing neurotic about it. Cancer's downside is not having a personal identity. The identity is only operating through the tribe, through the lineage, through the children or progeny. This is not limited to just physically having children. It also has to do with having a seed (a project, a cause, a mission) and being committed to the seed until it grows to what for it is maturity. *Pisces* lineage is a more transpersonal version of giving, and being in a position to be of help. The spiritual path for Pisces is like a "Generic" Boddhisattva. I am not saying all Pisces Moons are Boddhisattvas, but it gives the essence or flavor of the lineage. In the Buddhist teaching, Boddhisattvas are the ones who have already worked out their own personal stuff, but rather than leaving, rather than going to the celestial realms, or going to the absolute, they stick around as normal, ordinary people to be of help. It is the healthy side of service, where it is a joy to be of service and make available to the world what it is they do best. *Virgo* is the impersonal version of being a giver. Virgo represents absolute, resolute, dedicated focus on the sacred work. For example, archetypally, Virgo was in position to do the ceremonies for the solstices and other sacred timings, because if those ceremonies weren't done properly the Sun wouldn't return, the crops wouldn't grow, the rains wouldn't come on time.

It is very common these days to have a lot of support groups dealing with codependency issues and what is called addicted giving. In fact, the whole thing has become so widespread, it has almost gotten to the point where people are led to believe that being a giver, *period*, is neurotic and something is wrong with giving. In reference to the lineage, if a person has a Moon in one of the four giver signs, they *were* legitimately on the planet to be a giver. There is a healthy way of being a giver. How do you tell if it is a healthy version of giving? If a person is legitimately here to be a giver, they receive a return or reward, and there is an increase in joy and pleasure in the giving. They don't have to think, "If I give, something comes back." Rather, it is a natural process. When the current training is taking place in a giver tribe, it is worthwhile to be a giver.

A person with a giver Moon comes into the life fully expecting, and legitimately assuming, if they continue to give they will get a return, and life will be enjoyable. Logically, it is legitimate to think there will be a return if one previously had a return. What is remembered is how being a healthy version of a giver generated happiness and success in life. Unfortunately, now it is the Moon; so now it is an intelligence test not to be over-identified with the past mastery. A person with a giver Moon, who is out there giving and giving, may begin to notice as they go through their life there is a diminishing return, or they aren't getting back what they legitimately feel they should be getting back. In our culture it tends to be the woman who serves the guy, or serves the company, or serves the project; giving their best, hoping someday he'll change, or it will change, or something good will happen. Nothing does; nothing changes. Logically, on a linear level, one conclusion drawn is, "I must not be doing it well enough." So they start giving even more, and they notice there is still no response. The next conclusion they reach is, "it's an unfair universe, something is wrong," and they begin to develop the shadow side of the giving complex. This can go all the way to its most neurotic form where they end up trying to force the person they are with to respond in a certain way.

Question: *Are you referring to the shadow associated with the descendants?*
Can be, that is part of it. I very much appreciate the Jungian idea of the shadow. In Shamanic Astrology it is part of the Pluto strategy. When we get to the portion of the

class about strategy, the shadow will be found in the symbolism of Pluto. However, the Moon complex is another area where we can see the unveiling of a shadow element. For example, the shadow side of Cancer is expressed in Cancer Moon conjunct Pluto; or the Pluto in Cancer generation, where they believe they have the right to force the offspring to be a certain way, because they have loved them so well, or provided for them so well. Until a person gets the joke, the last desperate act is to force the company, force the project, force the friend, lover, husband, children to act as they should act, because you can show how much you have done for them. However, these scripts usually set up situations where the giver Moon is forced to give up their attachment and over-identification with their Moon. So, no matter how much they give, life does not respond positively to their giving efforts; there is no additional reward that results.

Let's look at this on the flip side for a moment. If a person's Venus, Mars, or Rising sign is in one of these four giver signs, how can they tell if they are on the right track? If they are legitimately in a circumstance to be a giver, there is a return that naturally comes as a result of their giving. Let's say a woman is Cancer Rising and she keeps attracting men who need her help and she willingly takes care of them, doing everything she can to grow them up, feed them, and support them, but she notices she is never getting anything back. At a certain point, when she develops enough self-love, she discovers she has been casting pearls before swine, and she has the right to ask or even demand the universe send her a return for what she has given. When she is able to do this, then she knows she is on the right track with Cancer Rising. If it is the progressive aspect of the horoscope, not the lineage, but something a person is newly working on, then there should be a return; there should be support for it. Okay, so what about all the experiences where a person, legitimately on the path of giving, didn't get anything back? Consider it practice, but at a certain point a person has practiced enough, and if they still aren't getting anything back, it is time for them to start looking for a return.

People with giver Moons are good at being responsible, being of service, giving, and loving, but it is not intended for the identity to remain there. It is intended for the person to finally give up the attachment to those qualities and shift to something different. Then when they have shifted the center of the being to something different, they get to have their Moon and access it anytime they want. It becomes a source of joy, and the healthy foundation they stand on to reach their goals for the current life.

At this stage, for those who are unfamiliar with looking at astrology this way, this may seem exceedingly complex and overwhelming. But, I assure you by the time all of the classes are completed; we will have contributed great simplicity to understanding the core issues in a person's life using Shamanic Astrology. What we have discussed in this class lays the foundation for everything else we are going to deal with. It is important to understand how to use the Moon position, because it lays the groundwork for looking at the rest of the chart.

The South Node of the Moon gives additional information about the lineage, because it describes what the person's job was in their tribe. Every two and a half days a different tribe comes through, but what house the South Node of the Moon is in describes what the expertise was in that tribe. This further contributes to discovering where a person's fixations, addictions, and attachments are. For example, Scorpio Moon with South Node in the eighth house indicates a person who had the Scorpio job in the Scorpio tribe. It is like a double, triple Scorpio statement. However, if the South Node is in the seventh house, that is the Libra job in the Scorpio tribe. This represents the type of Scorpio mastery that expressed itself in pair bonding, in marriages, in partnerships that were one to one, or non-hierarchical. A person with Scorpio Moon and South Node in the seventh house had many experiences of being with what they believed was the soul mate, and were they ever attached and addicted to each other! They didn't have a separate identity, because their identity operated through the intensity of the tantric union.

On the flip side, if the South Node is in the first house, that indicates the Aries job in the Scorpio tribe. This might be a person who was tantric with many individuals, never really developing a long term, bonded type relationship with any of them. They were mainly on their own. A typical example is the tantra teacher who literalizes the teaching with a lot of different students. This might also occur with the South Node in the fifth house, or ninth house, because the emphasis is on exploration and experiencing independence.

When looking at the Nodes, use the meaning of the house position to clarify the job. The first house is Aries, the second house is Taurus, the seventh house is Libra, the Eighth house is Scorpio, the ninth house is Sagittarius, and so on. In Shamanic Astrology the house position of the Node is more important than the sign position of the Node, because the Nodes remain in a sign for over a year, but they change houses every couple of hours. Therefore, the house position of the Node is a more individualistic aspect than the sign position. I suggest you try out this method of looking at the Moon and the Lunar Nodes on your chart and on the charts of others. See if it works to look at it this way.

HOW TO DO COUNSELING USING THE PRINCIPLES OF SHAMANIC ASTROLOGY
Class Three
MARS, VENUS, AND THE RELATIONSHIP AXIS

The first goal of this series of classes is to provide everyone, whether an astrologer or not, with powerful tools that will impact their effectiveness in giving assistance to another person, or dealing with their clientele, or assisting them to better understand their own lives. The second purpose is to include the shamanic ingredients in using astrology. The third is to introduce you to the script I use when I am doing a reading. My hope is that people will try out these principles to see if they work.

So far, we have looked at the Moon position as lineage, and we have begun introducing the archetypes of each sign. One of the most important things to understand is that Shamanic Astrology is *archetype driven*. If you understand the specific archetypes and the whole array of images and symbols associated with each sign, it is easy to combine the archetypes with the script in a way that doesn't require a lot of technical knowledge. This enables you to quickly understand what is going on, either, with yourself or with another person.

This class will look at Venus and Mars from several different directions and how they function in the script. But first, it is important to know about three basic ways the twelve sign energies interact with each other, because this information is essential for understanding the dynamics of the script. Some of the sign energies interact harmoniously and with resonance. They like each other, and are in some degree of harmony with each other. For example, if Aries energy happens to connect with Sagittarius energy there is a resonance that occurs. This is an example of a trine between sign energies. Some sign energies don't interact at all well with each other; their interaction is more like a war, or creative engagement. The interaction between these two types of energies produce either a cathartic, catabolic, difficult, unpleasant reaction, or a motivational reaction where something has to give, a "divine discontent." A typical example of this type of relationship between signs is Aries with Cancer or Aries with Capricorn. This is an example of a square.

When sign energies have no connection between them it is referred to as an inconjunct. The term inconjunct includes the astrological aspects formed by a quincunx, defined as two signs within one hundred and fifty degrees of each other, or a semi-sextile, defined as two signs within thirty degrees of each other. In the second century Ptolemy wrote the astrological treatises that became the cornerstone of western tropical astrology. What he did was organize into a body of knowledge what was known about astrology at that time. Ptolemy considered so-called quincunxes and semi-sextiles, or inconjuncts, to *NOT* be aspects. At that time the definition of astrological aspects required there be a relationship or connection between the energies. Inconjuncts are examples of astrological energies that have no relationship between them.

I consider this third way for signs to interact with each other to be a disconnect, because there is no communication between the two energies. If we look at Aries and Virgo, we find there is nothing in Aries that includes the language of Virgo, and vice versa. A person with an inconjunct, who is not consciously attempting to figure out how these energies work, might manifest a situation where they are seen by one large group of people as one type of person, and by another large group of people as a completely different type of person. For example, the person may appear to be quiet, shy, and even inhibited in their personal life; but an aggressive, directed, leader oriented, dynamic type in their business life. Who is this person really? It is like the right hand not knowing what the left hand is doing. Disconnect. However, on a progressive path, when those two energies have that kind of relationship (or non-relationship), then there is a way out called alchemy. This involves creating a consciousness large enough to encompass both non-communicating, disconnected energies. A unique synthesis is the result of that process. The synthesis produced by an inconjunct is different from the synthesis that results from a square, or conjunction. The Aries/Virgo inconjunct produces a synthesis that looks completely different than the synthesis that comes out of Aries/Cancer. With the Aries/Cancer combination (because they square each other) the synthesis comes out of the war or struggle between the two; it is not an alchemical path. To determine which of the two factors is intended to win requires clues from other portions of the chart, primarily the Ascendant, and possibly the Jupiter position. However, this is not an alchemical path.

VENUS AND MARS

First we will look at the Venus position for women, and the Mars position for men. Then we will reverse it and look at it the other way around. In Shamanic Astrology the Mars position on a man's chart is the main symbol for the archetype of the emerging masculine identity, or what a man intends to work with in the current life and incorporate into his being. Jung's definition of masculinity was "to know your sword and to know how to use it." However, this is not a war-related imagery. The word "tool" could be used instead of sword. Every one of the twelve Mars positions represents a different sword quality, or a different version of masculinity. It is well known by now that many of the aspects of the feminine principle have been discounted, disowned, not taught, or not accepted in patriarchy. It is less well known that the same thing is true for the masculine principle. In Shamanic Astrology, the male principle is represented by a twelve-spoked wheel (the twelve astrological energies), and every spoke of the wheel is presided over by a different God, a different story, a different set of myths. The same is true for the female principle; only each spoke of the wheel is presided over by a different Goddess, a different story, a different set of myths. This means there are actually twenty-four different archetypes in all.

The Mars and Venus positions on a person's chart represent statements of intent. The Mars position on a man's chart represents the new intended version, or identity of the masculine. The Moon position represents the already existing identity. The Mars position represents the current life intent for finding fulfillment in the masculine. Ideally, a relationship is created between the old God and the new God. If a man has Moon in

Aries and Mars in Cancer, the old God (represented by the Moon) is quite different from the new God (represented by the Mars). This creates a dynamic interaction between these two images. They do not like each other, and their interaction is cathartic. Remember, in Shamanic Astrology there is no judgment about any one of the paths being better or worse than another. All paths are valid and all scripts are intended to work. The relationship between the Moon and the Mars position might not feel very good when there is a dynamic interaction between the energies, but the person will be motivated to figure out how to synthesize the two. Again, it is like divine discontent. The person is driven; they may be ambitious. They will feel a need to get somewhere with that combination, to find a level of comfort. In contrast, a man with Moon in Aries and Mars in Sagittarius is on a resonance path or has a coasting situation that is not as difficult or challenging. However, because Aries and Sagittarius are so similar they may not be motivated to check anything else out. Men who have an inconjunct between their Moon and their Mars are facing a greater complexity and challenge associated with figuring out that kind of interaction. A good example of this is Moon in Aries and Mars in Virgo.

One way to work with this material is to do an inner dialogue between the old God and the new God. Imagine what the Aries God might say to the Cancer God? Aries is the rugged individualist, black and white, dualistic in their thinking, everything is external, spontaneous, competitive, not a householder. Mars in Cancer is the emerging God, who is the good husband, the good father, a good provider, someone who is here to learn how to do responsible nurturing. The challenge is to figure out what kind of dialogue Cancer might have with Aries. In our culture, men do not usually get reinforced for Mars in Cancer, so there is often a sense of anger about that. *I believe the anger, rage and grief of men today occurs when they do not get to do their Mars*. Men have an inborn, often unconscious, desire to get to do their Mars. Certain Mars expressions are readily promoted by our culture, and certain ones are not. This is much the same story *Women's Mysteries* have been increasingly aware of in the last twenty-five or thirty years. For women, the entire spectrum of femininity was not being honored or even allowed by our culture, until the feminist movement began to change that. Women and men on the front lines of the avant-garde women's mysteries have made a lot of progress towards validating the full spectrum of femininity, at least in archetypal and psychotherapeutic work. The good news is now the same thing is beginning to happen for the male principle. However, it is still in process, as all of the Gods are not yet fully known, but are now emerging.

The first thing I do, when I have a new male client, is to look at the dynamic interaction between the Moon and Mars to see what is going on. This can be quickly seen in the ephemeris by looking up the person's birthday. Approximately nine out of ten times it is possible to tell what the Moon position is, and ninety-nine out of one hundred times it is possible to tell what the Mars position is using the ephemeris, even *without* knowing the exact birth time. Once you know what the Moon and the Mars positions are it is simply a matter of plugging the archetype into each position to get a sense of what is going on with that man.

Here is a practical example of how this can be used in personal counseling work, or relationship counseling scenarios, or in your own relationships. What a woman most needs to know about a man is to honor his Moon one-third of the time, and his Mars two-thirds of the time. This formula is not intended to be literal, but the principles do work, because this allows the relationship to be in balance and growing. For example, if a lover, a son, or a male friend with Aries Moon goes into survival because they are scared, freaked out, or in over their head, then the most loving thing we can do for them at that time is give support for their Moon. How this translates out for men with Moon in Aries is they need time to go out with the boys, or be involved with some sort of sporting event, something that has to do with aggressive play that has no particular higher meaning. It doesn't have to be about anything. It just needs to be fun play, and sometimes even competitive. If you know a man with Aries Moon who never gets to play aggressively, it is safe to assume he is very angry. Conversely, if a man with Aries Moon is *only* doing Aries type activities, where six out of seven nights he is at the bowling alley, or the pool hall, or out on the golf course, then he is addicted to the Aries Moon, and is not working on the progressive aspect of his horoscope. The idea is to have balance, with the emphasis being on the Mars position or the current life intent. The most loving thing anyone can do for the person who is really out of balance is to honor their Moon, but remember, the progressive aspect is to honor the Mars (or Venus, if it is a woman) two-thirds of the time. This is very personal information. For example, for many men with Mars in Libra, the last thing they would ever admit is they are personally vulnerable in connection with their relationships. Yet, the thing they most desire is to be known as a good partner. They care about the relationship more than anything else, whether they easily admit it or not. If the man with Mars in Libra has Sag, Aries, or Gemini Moon, he was not interested in relationship in the past, and he might find it difficult to admit that relationship is his area of greatest vulnerability. When women and men know this material they can respond to the their partner in a loving and progressive way.

Let's look at Mars in Sagittarius as another example of how this works. What is it that Mars in Sag most needs to work on, or what is the sword quality of Mars in Sag? This is where a man needs to be affirmed for his own spiritual path, his consciousness, his own quest for meaning, and for his ability to do that on his own. If the man also has Cancer or Capricorn Moon, or one of the other householder Moon positions connected to commitment and bonding, and his current life intent is to be on a bonding path, and to be taken seriously in relationship, then the most healthy response the woman in his life can have towards him is to make certain he has plenty of time to go off by himself, pursue his own spiritual path, and to honor him for his consciousness and his mind. With this combination, giving support only for his ability to bond or be responsible might prevent him from being an independent self (separate from relationship). Mars in Sagittarius is a valid part of who he is and part of what he genuinely needs to express, in addition to his need to bond and be committed to a family or a project.

An opposite example is Mars in Cancer with Moon in Aquarius. In this case, the old God is a consciousness-oriented yogi type. The emphasis was on raising his consciousness to get off the wheel, with a desire to be separate or detached, and to keep from getting too involved in the emotional and the physical. Yet, in the current life, Mars in Cancer indicates the very thing that most needs to be worked on is responsible nurturing, done in such a way that he gains validation for his ability to do that. This man might be the most expert visionary in the whole ashram, but if he doesn't get a chance to take care of a family, or be a householder, or be committed to a seed until it grows to what for it is maturity, his Mars is not being validated or honored. Then, ultimately, if he is not getting to do what his Mars intent wants to do, anger and confusion will result.

The exact same situation we have looked at for men and their Mars and Moon positions occurs for women and their Venus and Moon positions. For women a similar inner dialogue occurs between the old Goddess and the new Goddess.

Question: *I am not sure what you mean by the old Goddess and the new Goddess.*
If we look at the Moon position, gender irrespective, each lineage will have different Gods and Goddesses, different myths, different stories that are associated with that lineage. For example, the Goddesses associated with Scorpio Moon include Kali, the Goddess of death and destruction. She is the one who notices when it is time for something to die, and she performs that function. Kali is the goddess associated with autumn. Plants die and seeds go into the ground. Other Goddesses associated with Scorpio are Madame Pele, the Hawaiian Volcano Goddess, Hecate, the original Greek figure that later became the imagery of the witch, and the Cretan Snake Goddess, to name a few. These all represent original primeval Scorpio Goddesses. If a woman has Scorpio Moon these Goddesses represent the lineage, or they are the old Goddesses.

Question: *What are the new Goddesses?*
The new Goddesses are represented by a woman's Venus position. The Venus position represents the emerging, or new, aspect of the feminine principle being worked on in the current life.

Question: *What about people who have their Mars or Venus conjunct their Moon?*
For the purposes of our analysis so far, the only thing we can say is that the old version of the God or Goddess dialogues with what the God or Goddess intends to do now. It is still the same archetype, but the way it expresses itself is different relative to the age we are in now, plus there are other factors. However, we are only working with the tools or second portion of the script now, we are not yet to the third movement, which reveals what this is all leading up to. The same principles I am sharing with you now, about the dynamic interaction with the Moon and the Mars position or the Venus position, is the same kind of thing that happens with reference to the angles of the chart representing the life purpose issues. However, that is another part of our story. Still, there is a lot a person can get just from looking at *this* information. If we look at the woman's Venus or the man's Mars it genuinely does represent what is being worked on in this life and, one way or another, it does have to be dealt with. Knowing the full spectrum of the archetypes gives us an advantage. Otherwise what are we faced with? According to traditional astrology, a woman with Venus in Scorpio has an unfortunate

Venus position. Judgments are made for and against certain sign positions or archetypes based upon who has been in charge recently (in this case patriarchy). These judgments are a product of the cultural prejudices. I would love to see a system, or a world, or a culture, that allows for the full expression of all the different Gods and Goddesses. It is up to us as individuals to create such a world, by becoming aware of the full expression of both the masculine and feminine principle and honoring the Gods and Goddesses in all of their forms, without prejudice.

The same principle of resonating, conflicting, or disconnecting energies apply to the Moon and Venus for women. One of my favorite examples is a woman with a Cancer Moon and Venus in Sagittarius. With this combination, the lineage (Cancer Moon) is represented by the nurturing Mother whose identity is based upon being a giver, what she contributes to the family, progeny, clan, structure, and so on. It is a householder position. The shift is to Venus in Sagittarius, which is like a philosophical version of Diana (Artemis). She is the virgin amazon, very intelligent and keenly interested in looking for the meaning of life. What would these archetypes or sign energies have to say to each other? There are no known myths where they have an interaction. Does this mean the two archetypes are a bad combination to have? Traditionally this type of astrological combination for a woman represents a conflicted feminine principle, because the virgin amazon has no interest whatsoever in what Cancer is about. If you have this combination it is not a neurosis. It means you have to dream the dream onward, and allow yourself to be in a position to create a new myth, and new stories that synthesize the two energies. In some cases we can find wonderful stories from the past to illustrate the dialogue between the old Goddess and the new Goddess, or the old God and the new God. At other times we have to create new images. In reality, all the archetypes are being dreamed onward at the turning of the Ages. We are all, one way or another, involved in the process of coming up with new images for all the archetypes.

The Venus position on a woman's chart helps to answer Freud's legendary question; "What does woman want?" The answer lies in knowing what sign Venus is in at the time she was born. Therefore, if we look at the standard imagery of a heterosexual relationship, the Venus position answers what a man needs to know about a woman. The same formula we used for the men applies for the women; honor her Moon one-third of the time and honor her Venus two-thirds of the time.

I have noticed these principles cut across gender lines in relationships. For example, two men in a gay relationship will both wish to be honored for their Moon and their Mars. Two women in a lesbian relationship will both want to be honored for their Moon and their Venus.

Question: *What happens when there is an aspect such as a square between the Moon and the Venus? It seems like, if you are honoring the Moon, you might be actually offending the Venus.*
It can be like that. The Rising sign material is the clue in some of the most difficult combinations that allows us to work out the conflicts. However, I don't want to get into

that yet, so relative to what we are introducing now, the formula one-third, two-thirds still works. Another way to answer this question is to look at it as a directional arrow. For example, for a woman with Aries Moon and Venus in Cancer, the directional arrow is moving from Aries to Cancer, but the foundation or the Aries heritage is not intended to be disowned. Another way to say this is when a woman is born, the center of her identity is with the Moon, but as she goes through life, she is shifting the center of her being, the center of her identity, from the Moon through Venus, to the Rising sign. The same principle is true for men only the shift is from the Moon through Mars to the Rising sign. For some people the shift is difficult or challenging, for others it is easier, depending upon the relationship between the old identity and the new identity. If a person has reached the place of workable synthesis, and they are totally comfortable with both ends of it, even if it started out as a square or an inconjunct the formula of doing their Moon one-third of the time still applies. The original identity is still there, and the person still has access to it, but the major identity now resides with the Venus, not the Moon.

Question: *Maybe I misunderstood you. At first I thought you said the idea is to integrate the Moon and the Venus, then I thought I heard you say we are shifting from the Moon to the Venus.*
Both things are true. There is a directional arrow. We start out only knowing about the Moon. If Venus or Mars and the Moon are similar, the shift may take place relatively quickly. If Venus or Mars is vastly different from the Moon it may take that person a long time to make the shift, but the intent is to shift to Venus or Mars. Once the directional arrow or the center of the being has shifted to Venus or Mars, the Moon is still there, but it is no longer the primary center of the being.

Question: *So we are shifting it through integration?*
Yes. It is not that you disown the Moon and leave it behind. What happens is the main center of the identity is now with Venus or Mars, and the Moon is still part of it. With some of the more difficult combinations, it may take some good creative thinking to figure out how to bring this shift about without disowning or violating the lineage.

Question: *In terms of the directional arrow coming from the Moon and going to the Mars or Venus, how is the nature of that directionality {sic} different from the directionality {sic} of the Rising sign?*
The answer to that goes back to the script itself, or the three movements of the symphony. The Thesis, or first movement is the lineage; the Antithesis or the second movement includes the tools and equipment we use to get to the third movement or Synthesis, which is the destination. Included in the tools and equipment are the Venus or Mars as the guise, the robes, the character, the identity we take on in order to reach the goal, which is the Rising sign (along with the other angles).

The Sun sign is another element found in the tools and equipment that adds more complexity to our understanding. The Sun sign is also a statement of intent, but it is not "archetype specific," unless it is in the same sign as the woman's Venus or the Man's

Mars. If the archetype of Venus or Mars is the same as the Sun, then that person is burning the fuel of the same archetype. However, if the Sun is in a different sign than Venus or Mars it is important to remember that the imagery or archetype of the God (Mars) or Goddess (Venus) is the emerging archetype, and they burn the fuel of the Sun. A synthesis is intended to take place with the Sun/Venus or Sun/Mars combination as well, when they are found in different signs. For example, a woman with Venus in Pisces and Sun in Aries is different than the woman who has Venus in Pisces and Sun in Pisces, because the fuel of Pisces is radically different from the fuel of Aries. However, regardless of what the Sun sign is the imagery of Venus is dominant. That's why the formula for relationships is to honor Venus or Mars two-thirds of the time and the Moon one-third of the time, without much reference to the Sun.

So many difficulties in relationships can be cleared up just by knowing this information, and by having the willingness to do some creative negotiations. Let's say a woman is in love with a guy who has Mars in Aquarius, and there are all kinds of difficulties in the relationship. He is frequently detached, and not willing to share his inner life. He is too intellectual, and all he wants to do is meditate. If the woman is mainly Scorpio/Pisces, his way of being is a polar opposite from her way of being. If she projects onto him her desire for him to be more like her, the relationship is in trouble. However, if she recognizes his Mars in Aquarius is not a neurosis, but is a valid part of his psyche, and she learns how to give him love for that; then if there really is intended union between the two of them, it will work more smoothly, because she has given him a gift. He may, then, in admittedly ideal circumstances, wish to also honor the part of her he has not been aware of, or understood. Otherwise what happens? If the person we are with doesn't have the characteristics we think are the right ones, we might end up thinking something is wrong with them. The fact is, depending upon Venus or Mars; their expressed qualities may be an absolutely valid part of who they really are.

Question: *What about Moon in Aries, Venus in Virgo?*
Ah yes, the good old Aries/Virgo combination. This is a wonderful example of how an inconjunct sets up very confusing signals. Let's say someone is fully into their Aries side, spontaneous, fun loving, playful, straightforward, and one never knows what they are going to do next, and that is the thing that is most delightful about them. This is why Libra and Aries can often make a very dynamic combination. Libra is very tactful, and believes everything is supposed to be done in appropriate ways, so they tend to have a strange fascination with wild Aries. They may be mortified by Aries behavior and disbelieve a person could actually act in such a way and get away with it, but they seem to find something exciting about it. It seems to produce a sort of eros for Libra. Meanwhile, when the Virgo side of the Aries/Virgo combination kicks in, the person shuts down, becomes much more clinical, extremely analytical; all of sudden they have very precise standards, and everything is interior. When men face the Aries/Virgo challenge in a woman, it is difficult for them to figure out what is going on. Just when they are ready to accept the fact she is wild, free spirited, independent and fun loving, she turns the other way and becomes the separate, aloof, critical, Virgo Priestess. It can be extremely intriguing or immensely frustrating.

Now, what about the woman who has these two Goddesses battling it out, or trying to understand each other? In this case the directional arrow moves from Aries to Virgo, so two-thirds of the time honor Virgo, or honor the Priestess for her sacred work and her sacred space. Honor the precision of her ability to see the patterning of life, and let her set the standards for her work. Do not try to cause her to be different than the way she is. However, don't forget, one-third of the time honor her Aries side; promote the child, and the competitive, playful, spontaneous side of her. Both of these images are very nontraditional and challenging for a woman to work with in the current culture.

THE MAN'S VENUS AND WOMAN'S MARS

The next portion of the material is to look at a man's Venus and a woman's Mars. I want to keep this part distinct from what we have looked at already. The material we have covered so far stands on its own from the perspective of the Gods or Goddesses and the evolving aspect of the male or the female principle. The woman's Mars and the man's Venus are the complementary other side. Our culture emphasizes romantic love and physical attraction and therefore trains or programs us to look for someone out there who has the characteristics or qualities we find attractive. The cultural belief projected onto us says when we find the person that matches our inner picture, we will find our own "happily ever after." The qualities we are attracted to in a mate are similar to those defined by Jung as the anima or animus. On a woman's chart the Mars is the *magical masculine* or animus, and on a man's chart the Venus is the *magical feminine* or anima. On a practical level this is what we are attracted to externally. Each of us has a wiring to be with a certain kind of energy. There are thousands of men and women in this culture who have found someone with just the right characteristics to inspire feelings of intense physical attraction and romantic love, and then they discover the relationship doesn't work easily, and in many cases it doesn't work at all.

The anima (the magical feminine), or animus (the magical masculine), is not the same as relationship intent. However, there are two important levels of the anima or animus to understand. The first level is what we are attracted to; the second level is our own inner aspect of the male or female. On a woman's chart Mars is her own inner masculine. On a man's chart Venus is his own inner feminine. Owning these qualities for ourselves is referred to as the sacred marriage. The sacred marriage in this context is when a man or woman walks through life with the inner partner on their arm at all times, regardless of whom they are with, or whether they are with anyone at all. The sacred marriage occurs when women own their own Mars and men own their own Venus and are no longer trying to project it onto a partner. The same archetypal material we have been working with applies here as well. For example, a man with Venus in Virgo has a great desire to be with the Virgo archetype, to impress and even to bond with the Virgo archetype. This may not have anything to do with what his true relationship intent is. (We will look at that issue later.) Understanding the man's Mars or woman's Venus gives us the main clue as to why many people keep chasing the same kind of person over and over again; yet their desire for a certain type of relationship is never fulfilled. This happens because the kind of partner they are attracted to does not necessarily have the same intent for relationship. However, it doesn't work to simply tell someone to stop being attracted to that type of partner. From a psychotherapeutic perspective the absolute hardest thing to change is what we are attracted to, particularly the chemistry part of it.

RELATIONSHIP INTENT

Approximately two-thirds of all people find that what they are attracted to, and what their intent is for relationship, are two very different things. About one-third of all people find those two things are in sync. Two separate parts of the chart deal with relationship; the Venus and Mars material, which shows what we are attracted to, and the relationship intent, symbolized by the relationship between the Rising sign and the seventh house point. This is a feature of the third part of the script. Relationship intent describes what a person is here to learn about and achieve in the area of relationship. It might be to learn how to bond, or to do family, or to be a free spirit, or to be a tantrika. There are six different possibilities altogether.

The main point is, even if you have a Venus or a Mars that doesn't work for your relationship intent, it is still a part of your psyche, and there are ways to integrate and incorporate that into your life. For example, I have Venus in Virgo. My entire life I have been absolutely fascinated by the Virgo archetype. In fact, I have almost made it a personal crusade to re-vision and help the Virgo archetype get over the violation and mistranslation that has happened to it in patriarchal astrology. My whole life I have attempted to have different reflections of my Virgo anima be impressed with me and love me, based upon how much I loved and understood them. Unfortunately, relationship intent on my chart is about bonding, Libra Sun, Libra Rising. What I finally understood, years ago, was I could not do my relationship intent with my anima. My only remedy was inner sacred marriage, which incidentally is an ongoing thing. Just when I think I have it, along comes the next lesson. I began incorporating the Venus in Virgo woman into my life by inviting her to show up to do a lot of my readings and talks. I love her so much I have been able to incorporate her as an invaluable resource. This has enabled me to walk through life with the High Priestess woman on my arm at all times. I am no longer trying to marry her externally, or trying to bond with her in a traditional marriage situation. If I had Virgo Rising or Pisces Rising, my relationship objective would support my being with the Virgo woman in a successful external relationship. However, I have Libra rising, and most of my mistakes in relationship had to do with projecting the Libra relationship intent on my Virgo anima. I will explain this phenomenon more thoroughly when we get to the Relationship Axis Women with problematic Mars positions, (such as Mars in Scorpio, Virgo, Pisces, or Cancer) often find, due to the culture's judgment about these qualities not being strong, healthy, examples of masculinity, that they are forced to take responsibility for their own Mars position. This is especially true if the problematic Mars position also has heavy outer planet strategy conjuncting, squaring or opposing it. Remember, in this system the hard aspects from the outer planets to the inner planets represent the strategy. In every case I have seen, especially when women have Saturn and/or Pluto to their Mars, or men have Saturn and/or Pluto to their Venus, it is virtually impossible for them to have a relationship with the type of person they are most attracted to that works easily. When this occurs does it mean they lack in merit, or they are being punished, or they simply got a bad hand this time? Not at all. Rather, the strategy is a specifically rendered, articulate instruction about how to reach the goal. Outer planet aspects to the Venus or Mars indicate the necessity for that person to accomplish the sacred marriage. This means they take responsibility for the qualities of their own Mars or Venus, rather than projecting it on to a partner.

To understand this better let's look at a woman with Mars in Scorpio. There are three possible stages of development with this type of Mars position. The first stage involves a series of relationships with the type of partner they find most attractive. We've seen Scorpio's predicament in the current culture. Here, experiences with Mars in Scorpio partners are frequently destructive and difficult. Things often happen in the structure of the relationship that are dangerous. The relationship does not represent ease, or flow, or harmony. This woman might go into a masochistic pattern of repeating the same mistake over and over, hoping the next time, with the next partner, it will be different. However, the problem is her attraction to this kind of energy and until she becomes aware of the pattern, she will continue to repeat the same mistake. This is in no way a reflection on how good she is at relationships, or whether she is lacking in merit, or is experiencing the return of bad karma she acquired in the past. It is simply a situation that forces her to accomplish the sacred marriage.

The second phase happens when it occurs to her that once again her relationship is not working, and she realizes it is the type of man she is choosing for her relationships that is the problem. It is likely she will decide to never get close to that type of man again. Ultimately, what she is doing is denying or repressing her external connection with Scorpio energy. Phase one and phase two are at the effect of the external imagery. Sooner or later the third phase has to show up. The third phase happens when she is able to take total responsibility for her own Mars. Mars in Scorpio for a woman is about taking command of her own life force energy, or getting in touch with her own tantric energy, totally feeling the feelings, and being able to go deep into the interior of her feelings and her deeper passions. This is very different than suppression or repression; rather it is calling out the passion and the feelings, and mastering them. Once a woman has taken responsibility for her Mars, she can walk into life and encounter the masculine energy she is attracted to without being overwhelmed by it. She can tell the difference between the healthy and unhealthy version of that energy. Even if she encounters a healthy version of her animus she won't feel a need to act on it, because she is sufficient unto that energy within herself. She may choose to engage with the energy externally, but at that point her choice is not out of need.

A different set of circumstances occurs when a woman has Mars in Pisces or Cancer. This woman will have a desire to be with a man who is well developed in the feminine, close to his feeling function, who is giving, protective, nurturing, and a totally safe space. If she has heavy Saturn or Pluto aspecting her Mars, she will tend to keep running into negative versions of this type. As in the last example, the first phase of her experience has her continually finding herself in relationships that don't work, but not necessarily for the same reasons. She may find herself with someone who is not the type of man she ultimately wants, so she projects onto him her inner picture, trying to force him to become her inner picture. If the man is an Aries, Sag or Gemini type, she might wonder why he isn't more attentive to her feelings, or why he isn't more responsible, or why he doesn't share his inner life with her. In this case, the woman is projecting her Mars onto the man in her life, which ultimately won't work. As in phase two of our first example, she will decide to not get involved in intimate relationships. She denies this is something she wants in her life. She denies her desire to be in a relationship that is nurturing to her. Instead, she chooses not to deal with the issue, to avoid relationships, and just be with herself.

The third stage, as in our last example, occurs when she learns to own the qualities of her Mars for herself. A common mistake is to assume that a woman with Mars in Cancer or Pisces is the same as a woman with Venus in Cancer or Pisces. It is important to know the difference. A woman with one of these Mars positions desires to be nurtured by her partner in her relationship. A woman with Venus in Pisces or Cancer is learning how to nurture others. If a woman has Mars in Pisces or Cancer and she is not getting the nurturing or the giving she desires from her relationship, in her confusion she may decide she is the one who has to be nurturing and giving to her partner. She decides to be Cancer or Pisces in someone else's life. This is absolutely backwards! If a woman has Mars in Pisces or Cancer, her intent is to take responsibility for that function within herself, or to be *self nurturing.* Ideally she creates her life in such a way that it is loaded with people and/or experiences that give to her, where she can experience being nurtured. If that doesn't happen with the love object externally, then she must learn how to do the sacred marriage; she must learn how to nurture and give to herself. It is important to remember if a woman has Venus in Cancer or Pisces, she is legitimately here to be the giver and nurture others. However, if the woman's Mars is in Cancer or Pisces, to get the sacred marriage, she must learn to nurture and give to herself.

Question: *Is the woman's Mars attracted to the man's Mars?*
Sometimes. It depends. In this system, only the Moon position is literal; the other things on the chart are statements of intent. So, a woman with Mars in Cancer may encounter a number of men with Mars in Cancer who have not sufficiently developed any characteristics of being a responsible giver. This is particularly true if any of these men have a Sag or Aries Moon and Mars in Cancer. In this case, it is unlikely a woman with Mars in Cancer perceives him as an animus figure, unless he has moved into the Cancer realm and is actively working on his intent.

Question: *Would the Rising sign be more evident then?*
No. As far as taking one aspect of the chart to determine that, you look at the Moon. However, looking at this from a different angle, let's suppose the woman with Mars in Cancer has done the sacred marriage, and she *then* becomes involved with a Mars in Cancer man. In the long run this is a great connection, because if she is not tremendously needy of him, she can actually be of assistance in helping him develop his own Mars in Cancer. She can give him support for his developing ability to be a giver.

This comes back to the example of twelve women who all have Venus in Cancer or twelve men who all have Mars in Cancer; they are not all the same, but they all have the same intent. Depending upon a lot of different factors, they may have already grown into their Mars or Venus, or they may still be working on it. However, if a woman genuinely desires to be with a man who is a giver and that is part of her script, being involved with an Aries Moon and Mars in Cancer is a far more promising track than being involved with a man who has Moon and Mars in Aries. At least the Mars in Cancer is legitimately here to work on the giving aspect.

Question: *I have a lot of gay friends I do charts for, and I never know what to do with that opposite sex sign.*
This material works the same way for gay couples. When I was living in the Puna area of Hawaii, a large part of the population was lesbian couples, and I was an astrologer they trusted, so I did a lot of readings for those circumstances. I have also done a lot of readings for gay men, but I have done more for gay women. In both cases I found the same situation. When two women are together in a relationship, one of the women invariably has her Mars in the archetype the other woman already is or is working on. This same principle holds true for two men in a relationship, but it is the Venus archetype the partner is already, or is working on.

Question: *So the attraction factor is the same even though the gender is different?*
Ninety-five percent of all women in lesbian relationships that I have worked with were in unsatisfying or abusive relationships with men first and later got into relationships with women. I found that about seventy to seventy-five percent of the time they were dealing with wounded animus imagery. Again let's take the Mars in Cancer or Pisces example. This says her desire is to be with a partner who is very beautifully connected to the feeling function, very sensitive, safe, and giving. If every experience this woman has is with men who are totally the opposite of her animus, she may conclude it is not safe to be with a man. Therefore, in order to satisfy her intimacy needs she finds a person, gender irrespective, who is a safe animus imagery. This works with any archetypal combination. I have not yet found any archetypal information that always translates out as heterosexual, homosexual, or bisexual.

Question: *Is it difficult to have the sacred marriage if the Venus and Mars are in the same sign?*
Not really. It all depends upon the relative difficulty or ease of that archetype. There are a number of interesting situations we can look at. On a man's chart if the Sun, Venus, and Mars are all conjunct, or even quite commonly, if a man has Sun and Venus conjunct, this generally indicates a man who is anima possessed. He is bonded in so tightly with the feminine imagery he often finds it difficult to individuate into his male side. This type of man usually goes totally against the masculine stereotypes of our culture, and demonstrates his sensitivity, knows how to honor the feminine, knows women and how they feel really well, and has women friends rather than men friends. The problem is he is too much into that, and women find it difficult to respect him, because he is possessed by the feminine and he doesn't have his masculinity. This same

thing can happen with women who have a Sun/Mars combination, except it is called being animus possessed and the woman is too identified with the masculine principle.

Question: *Doesn't it depend upon what sign it is in?*
Absolutely. This phenomenon is more likely to be seen if a man's Sun and Venus are in a more traditional feminine imagery, like most water or earth signs. The most important thing to remember is the idea of the sacred marriage. Sooner or later we all have to get the sacred marriage. There are people out there who seem to have ease and harmony between what attracts them and what their relationship intent is, as well as having their aspects and archetypal combinations in harmony with each other. These are the people who, at a fairly young age, or through an easy series of circumstances, find a wonderful person to be in relationship with. Frequently, that means they don't have sufficient motivation to work on the sacred marriage. However, I also know plenty of people who haven't been in traumatic relationships and have still successfully worked on the sacred marriage! Not everyone in a good relationship has had to work at it. For some it was just a given. The main thing to understand here is that there is not a logical connection between a person's merit, knowledge, or wisdom about relationship, and how well they are doing with it. Other factors are at play.

Comment: *I feel a whole lot better, in fact my whole row feels better!*
I find the greatest contribution of this approach is that it does give a lot of breathing space. Rather than being tightly bound into a limited cultural perspective of the way things are supposed to be, or to be under the apparent incredible oppression of Saturn or Pluto complexes that make us believe we are somehow flawed, Shamanic Astrology is an affirmation of many valid ways of being human.

One of my favorite ways of illustrating these principles is to use the ephemeris to look up famous people, such as musicians, actors and actresses, because these people have readily identifiable traits. Here are a couple of examples. Using the birthdate for the musician-singer Neil Young, the ephemeris tells us he has an Aquarius Moon. Archetypally we could say he is not really from here. The eccentricity, progressive avant-garde, different than normal, idiosyncratic, totally into being his own unique self, that describes the Aquarius archetype, describes Neil Young and his music. In addition, he has Mars in Leo. I find it quite remarkable how many of the male rock musicians are Mars in Leo, like Bono the lead singer of U2 as another example. Mars in Leo says the current life intent of the masculine is to be center stage, to have a love of performing, to walk in self-confidence and self-love.

The ephemeris also tells us that Neil Young has Venus in Scorpio. The Scorpio archetype seems to show up in the type of women Neil Young gets involved with and the type of relationships he has. He gets intensely into one woman for long periods of time, and tends to be quite secretive about his relationships. He doesn't share that aspect of his life with people. In addition, Neil Young has Sun in Scorpio, so the male archetype of Mars in Leo is burning Scorpio fuel. This is a dramatic example of combining diverse archetypes, (Aquarius, Scorpio and Leo) and how they can manifest in a person's life.

Another example of very distinct characteristics is jazz musician Charlie Parker. There was a remarkable and amazing movie about his life, called *Bird*. This is a guy who was totally into the most avant-garde aspect of playing the saxophone. He died at a very young age, due in part to his terrible addictions to heroin and other drugs. From the ephemeris we learn that he had Moon in Pisces, Mars in Scorpio, and Venus in Virgo. The movie depicts him as very committed to his wife and children for a long period of time. If the movie is accurate, his wife was very cold and extremely critical of him. These qualities fit his Venus in Virgo. It seems he couldn't get out of being with that kind of woman. The Virgo archetype also showed up in his music. As a creative individual he had an ability to get into the feminine universal pattern of life. He was born in 1920 with a Moon position in a water sign. This tells us right off that he wasn't validated for his best qualities, especially his deep connection to his feelings and his passion. This is why Pisces Moon and strong Pisces are frequently associated with drinking a lot, or the depressive side of their feelings, where they allow themselves to sink into the shadow side of feelings. It was his deep connection with the feminine principles of Scorpio, Pisces, and Virgo, that inspired his music, and gave him at least one healthy way to express himself. These examples help to show how the archetypal material can give us an understanding of people.

It is important to realize no astrological formula exists that accurately says who should or shouldn't be together. The reasons behind why two people come together and get involved in deep intimacy with each other are part of the Great Mystery. No system of any kind can accurately determine who should or shouldn't be together. However, once two people have decided to be together, I know of no greater set of clues for sorting out how the relationship can best work for each partner than what we have been looking at in Shamanic Astrology.

I have seen some relationships work really well even when there was no connection between the anima or animus of either partner. Often, when a person first hears this material they think the best type of person to be with is a healthy version of their anima or animus, or a healthy version of someone who has the qualities they find the most attractive. This is not necessarily so. I can give you just as many examples of couples that are each other's total inner picture and the relationship is addictive, or confused, or pointless. The thing that keeps them together is that the other person looks exactly like their inner picture, but their interaction with each other is completely different from their relationship intent. Now, what if you are in a relationship associated with your relationship intent, but your partner is not at all like your inner picture? If you really love each other, and have every intention to work through it, knowing each other's inner picture and knowing it is a valid part of both your psyches, gives you clues on some wonderful creative ways you can work with each other. For example, if a woman's main feminine characteristics for the current life are her consciousness, intellect, individuality, and creative progress, and she winds up with a partner who has Venus in Scorpio, a compromise will have to be reached for the relationship to be successful. What is his inner picture? His inner picture is something like a tantrika; a woman who is the embodiment of exotic expressed sexuality, someone running the energy in a provocative way. This is not a neurosis for the man. However, if the woman in his life has no connection with that image relative to her own feminine mysteries, but she understands his desires in this area are a valid part of his psyche, she can consciously choose to validate this area of his life. Once she understands what he is attracted to or what he desires, she can agree to give him four hours Wednesday night and three hours on Saturday morning to explore the tantric realms. She might even agree to put on special lingerie, and learn some of the more exotic kama sutra positions as part of the exploration process.

Now, if a woman has Mars in Pisces or Cancer and the guy she is with is, in many ways, self-centered, and not a very giving person, this is contrary to her inner picture. Her inner picture of the masculine is for him to share his inner life, and be giving. I don't mean sexual stuff here. I mean sharing feelings and being close just for the sake of being close. In this case, if he is truly interested in the relationship working out, once he understands her need for sharing and closeness is a valid part of her psyche, he would agree to give her a few hours Thursday night and Sunday morning to be close and share feelings, even though he doesn't fully understand how to do this yet. The idea is to mutually negotiate so that each partner's needs can be fulfilled. Otherwise, one way or another, a person has to have a connection with that part of their psyche. Let's use the example of the man with Venus in Scorpio. If the woman in his life has judgment against tantric expression and sexuality, what will happen is one day she will discover his secret stash of pornography, or that every Thursday night he is out at a topless bar. Obviously this is an extreme example of a certain type, but it is one of the twelve. It could be just the reverse. It could be a guy who has Venus in Aquarius, whose inner picture is a woman who wants to meditate with him, dream together, and who will make love in the higher chakras. It turns out the woman he is with is a Taurus/Scorpio type, where everything is real basic and real physical. The same kind of disconnect can happen. His inner picture is a valid part of his psyche. For the relationship to work and be exciting, each partner must be willing to learn about their partner's inner picture.

Another common problem occurs when a man or woman gets into a relationship with someone who is not anything like their Mars or Venus position, so they project onto their partner what their inner picture is, even if their partner is not that type. If a man has Venus in Scorpio and his partner is not that type, and he is continually trying to get her to be that type, there can be a real violation for both partners. This incites anger between the partners real fast, even though ultimately it is just a misunderstanding. When two people learn to understand and accept each other, the violation caused by misunderstanding is cleared up.

THE RELATIONSHIP AXIS

The Relationship Axis is based upon the Rising sign and the seventh house point. The Relationship Axis represents the third phase of a threefold process. So far we have looked at the synthesis of the Moon and the Venus/Sun combination, and the Moon and the Mars/Sun combination. These combinations may be easily synthesized or they may have difficult challenges connected to the synthesis process. Where is this leading? How does relationship intent fit in? The relationship intent answers the question of why a person would even want to be in a relationship. If someone is going to bond, or marry, or be in a conscious partnership with someone, why do it? In Shamanic Astrology there are six reasons or six relationship paths. Our current culture recognizes only two paths, the family path, and the soul mate path. The soul mate path has typically represented the idea that a person is only fifty percent by themselves, and if they can find the other fifty percent, they will be complete. On the family path it doesn't matter that much whom you are with, as long as they are a good provider, can provide a safe space for the children, are concerned about the seven generations to follow, and are interested in being a pillar of the community. These are two valid paths. However, I am suggesting there are four more paths.

There are twelve signs, or six pairs of signs that form an axis. They are Aries/Libra, Taurus/Scorpio, Gemini/Sagittarius, Cancer/Capricorn, Leo/Aquarius, and Virgo/Pisces. These six paths describe what kind of relationship works best for a person. For example, a woman with Sag Moon, Venus in Aries, and Sun in Aries is a wild, spontaneous, free spirited non-bonding, non-householder type. However, if she has Cancer or Capricorn Rising, a major change of gears in intended to take place. Here is a woman with no clues on how to do the family path, but in the current life she is somehow working on how to develop family and community. Chances are she will not do the traditional version of family, but it is still her path to bring into form some aspect of home and roots, and/or to find something to believe in, where she is making a concrete contribution to the collective.

The Aries/Libra axis is the emerging version of what I like to call nonhierarchal conscious equal partnership. It is a bonding relationship path. It doesn't matter what you do together, as long as you do a lot together. It is process-oriented relationship in learning how to bond. If a person doesn't have any background in their past life themes in bonding, then this is moving into new territory. My life is an example of that one. I have South Node in the first and a Capricorn Moon, which says I was absolutely independent, and self-sufficient in the past. Now I have North Node in the seventh with Libra Sun and Libra Rising. It is potent bonding statement almost to the point of overkill. It is clear that my intent is to learn how to bond one way or another! My ability to be on my own, at this point, is irrelevant.

Capricorn/Cancer is the new version of the family path. It does not necessarily look like the traditional family. Today it often looks like the desire to find spiritual community; to develop a completely new version of how to make it safe for the children, have security in the best sense of the word, and have continuity from one generation to the next. This is definitely a householder path.

The Taurus/Scorpio path is the life force energy path. Each of these paths can be illustrated by using this question: How do you know if you are on the right track in a relationship? The answer for the Taurus/Scorpio path is found in whether they are getting their batteries charged or not. They must experience an increase in life force energy. Something must happen that plugs them into their feelings, and into their eros. Ideally, they find their relationship causes them to experience greater strength and energy at the end of the day, than what they had at the beginning of the day. When the relationship is healthy it is increasing their life force energy.

The fourth path is Virgo/Pisces. This is the path of the helpmate. In this case two people are together, not because the relationship is the most important thing, but because "the work" is the most important thing. How does a person on this path know if they are in the right relationship? They know they are on track if their partner is supportive of their sacred work. If a person on this path is obsessed with either finding a relationship, or with a relationship they are already in, to the detriment of "the work," then they are on the wrong track. Those with Virgo/Pisces are designed to be helpmates for each other in their dedication to the sacred work.

The fifth path is Sag/Gemini. This is called the path of the quest mate, represented by two people who are together in a healthy way as long as they are both riding in the same direction, or are on a similar quest. Maybe they are working with the same spiritual teacher. Ideally, they consciously honor each other's space and give each other room to take individual command of their own path. This relationship path is radically different from our traditional understanding of bonding.

The last path is Leo/Aquarius and is the most radical path of all. On this path two people choose to be together because their partner is easily able to promote, advocate, and empower them in ever greater experiences of their own uniqueness, sovereignty, independence and power. Two people on this path might be across the table from each other and one of them says; "You know, I am really fine on my own, and I don't need you." The other person says; "I know that, and I am fine on my own and I don't need you." Then a spark goes across and they say, "Yes, but wouldn't it be amazing to dance at this level!" The relationship comes about as a choice, not out of neediness. They are two masters who completely recognize the autonomy and sovereignty of each other. The interesting thing about this path is, if for other reasons such as Moon, or Venus position, a person finds they get into being dependent in a relationship, the Leo/Aquarius path requires they are busted of that dependency; it is disallowed. Circumstances force them out of the relationship because they are dependent. The second possibility happens when Leo/Aquarius is with someone who is dependent on them; then they are required to break their partner of that dependence. So a shifting back and forth occurs until the point is reached where Leo/Aquarius is completely independent and they can find someone who is able to choose to dance with them at that level. For many on the Sag/Gemini or Leo/Aquarius path, relationships are not that big of a deal. However, for those on the Leo/Aquarius path who have an intent to bond for other reasons, such as Venus in Libra or a lot of planets in the seventh house, they will have to learn to bond within the context of the Leo\Aquarius path.

This is not a cookbook. No one specific formula works all of the time. Not every combination expresses itself in the same way. If we threw all the different combinations into a hat, the scenario unfolds something like this: One-third of human beings are pair bonders or would like to be. One-third of human beings are into serial monogamy, meaning they can be fully intimate with only one person at a time, and in these speeded up times those relationships may take place one right after the other. The third possibility is one-third of human beings are capable of being fully intimate with more than one person at a time. Cancer/Capricorn or Libra/Aries are more likely to bond or have a monogamous relationship than Taurus/Scorpio. There is a version of Taurus/Scorpio that is completely monogamous, although their reasons for being monogamous are different than the reasons Libra/Aries or Cancer/Capricorn are monogamous. For Taurus/Scorpio when monogamy is a choice, the technique is to put all of one's intent into the relationship with no energy leaking out to others. That means the partner one is committed to is experienced as all men or all women, depending on which aspect the partner is representing.

Using the astrological material there are three valid reasons for monogamy. One reason is described by the Libra/Aries path, where the relationship is the spiritual technique. The second reason is the Cancer/Capricorn path, where the bottom line is to maintain the integrity of the family, especially if under patriarchal rules. In patriarchy the emphasis has been on the nuclear family, and the kinship system has been destroyed, so a woman desires and deserves the full attention of the man in her life. The third possibility is the Scorpio/Taurus path that is designed to respond to energy. If someone on the Scorpio/Taurus path responds to an energy that is the most powerful energy they could ever image, they might not notice any other for thirty years. I call this defacto monogamy, because it involves being fully locked into the energy of another person. Taurus/Scorpio may have reasons for being in a committed relationship, like Venus, Mars or Jupiter in Libra, but still Taurus/Scorpio is in its integrity when it responds. The important thing for Taurus/Scorpio to know is that it doesn't always mean they must literalize their response.

Each of these paths is uniquely expressed through a blending or synthesizing of the other factors on the chart and each person's own life experiences. What I have described is the basic intent of each of the six relationship paths. For a full understanding of the relationship picture on a person's chart it is necessary to look at the Moon, representing what the emphasis *was* on for relationships in the past, Venus and Mars, representing the feminine and masculine intent for the current life, and the strategy, represented by the aspects from the outer planets to Venus and Mars. The final ingredient in the relationship puzzle is the relationship intent described by the Relationship Axis. All of these factors together assist our understanding of what the challenges are and what the intent is for relationship in the current life.

HOW TO DO COUNSELING USING THE PRINCIPLES OF
SHAMANIC ASTROLOGY
Class Four
THE TOOLS AND EQUIPMENT OF THE SUN, MERCURY, AND JUPITER

Question: *When the lineage happens to be the same as one of the current life tools, or the Rising sign, how does one work with that situation?*

There are several ways to answer that, however, I don't want to get into the Rising sign material or the other angles of the chart yet; we will do that later in this class. If the tools and the lineage are in the same sign, the person is essentially working with the same archetype in essence, but not in content. The directional arrow is moving in a way that encourages the person to let go of attachments and expectations involved in the old imagery of that archetype. The challenge is to create a new version of the old archetype. For example, five thousand years ago the content of Cancer was matrilineal and was expressed through a matriarchy. A person born in the 1800's or early 1900's experienced a patriarchal content for Cancer that involved the close-knit nuclear family, with the man as the lord of his household. In the 1890's the family situation looked drastically different than it does today. The essence of Cancer remains the same from age to age and includes things like concern for the children, the family, and the seven generations to follow. The essence of any archetype remains the same, but the content changes to reflect the times. Now, at The Turning Of The Ages, it is Cancer's job to participate in creating or inventing its new content to reflect the present times. The new content will still have at its core the same essence of concern for the children and the family and the seven generations to follow, but the shift and change in content is moving towards new and hopefully more vital and healthy forms of expression.

Question: *Isn't it also possible that a person can stay addicted to the old patterns?*

Yes, very much so. This principle applies to any of the combinations with the Moon. For example, a woman with Venus in Sagittarius and Moon in Cancer might stay stuck in Cancer and never move into Sagittarius, because the culture tends to validate her Cancer Moon more than her emerging Sagittarius identity. The challenge for Moon in Cancer and Venus in Cancer is to avoid falling into the trap of being stuck in the old version of Cancer and to actively participate in the emerging version of Cancer.

Question: *So the idea is that now a person is using Cancer to get to a new goal, instead of using Cancer to be in the Cancer of the past.*

Yes. To summarize this point, there is a regressive way of looking at the horoscope and a progressive way of looking at the horoscope. The regressive approach is when all the planets, including what you believe the Rising sign is about, support the Moon through negative or positive attachment. The progressive approach is when all the planets, including the lineage, are supporting the new projects of the current life represented by the angles of the chart.

Before we go into the strategy, or how the aspects of the outer planets affect the inner planets, let's fill in the other characters in the script and some other basics, like where Othe houses, elements, and retrogrades fit in. The characters of the script we have examined so far are the Moon and the South Node of the Moon representing the lineage, and the Sun, Venus and Mars representing part of the intended tools and equipment for the current life. What's missing are Mercury and Jupiter.

MERCURY

Mercury is the current life tool for how a person thinks, perceives, cognizes, and communicates. It represents what kind of mind or computer a person is learning how to use. Just as we looked at the dialogue between the Moon and Mars or Venus, it is useful to have a similar dialogue between the Moon and Mercury, or the old way of thinking and the new way of thinking. The sign position of the Moon shows how a person cognized, perceived and communicated in the past. The sign position of Mercury indicates the current life intent for the thinking process or how a person *intends* to cognize, perceive, and communicate. Therefore, the Moon and Mercury set up a dynamic interaction between the old way of thinking and the new way of thinking. Again, there is a directional arrow from the Moon to Mercury. Remember Shamanic Astrology is almost completely archetype driven. The archetypes, and how they interact with one another, show where a person is coming from, where they intend to go, and what type of challenges might be involved along the way.

Let's illustrate this using Moon in Aries and Mercury in Capricorn. Even if these two sign energies are not in exact square to each other, the relationship between Aries and Capricorn is a "creative engagement" because the essence of both energies doesn't interact well together. That's why even a twenty-five degree aspect between Aries and Capricorn still sets up an archetypal conflict. This brings up an important point. The reason this system is archetype driven rather than aspect driven is because I believe the integrity of the archetypes is a stronger, more powerful reality than the aspects. For example, Cancer and Virgo or Cancer and Taurus may form a sextile by aspect, and is considered a harmonious aspect in traditional astrology, but archetypally they are vastly different. That's why in Shamanic Astrology a sextile is not necessarily an easy aspect; a lot depends on the influences of the culture and the signs and planets involved. Archetypally, Cancer and Taurus look more like opposites, and can be challenging energies to combine or synthesize. Cancer is a giver energy, the nurturing mother, and householder; Taurus is a receiving energy, the courtesan, and focuses on intimacy as an art form. Neither of these archetypes has much in common. I sometimes find the squares between archetypes easier to deal with than certain combinations of sextiles. The bottom line is that the archetypes themselves drive this system, not the aspects.

Mercury shows what the new intended expression of the mind is for the current life. The old mind (Moon) and the new mind (Mercury) interact with each other. To understand how this interaction takes place it is important to know about the four elements associated with each sign: fire, air, water, and earth. These elements are similar to the Jungian system of the four psychological types. Fire is intuitive, air is thinking, earth is sensation, and water is feeling. Because of the way language is used in our culture, intuitive is often misunderstood for feeling. In the Jungian approach, fire or intuitive is an active, archetypally masculine quality. It is like the tip of the arrow, the tip of the spear, boldly going into the unknown. It is the creative version of mind, not the detached version of mind, but rather a dynamic aspect. The intuitive function, or fire element, includes Sagittarius, Aries, and Leo. Air is the thinking function, and is also masculine. It has to do mainly with detachment and objectivity, being able to step back away from things. Fire is right brained and air is left brained. Fire is not controlled by any particular analytical logic; it is continually creative. Remember, one is not better or worse than the other. When we look at astrology as an entire spectrum there is nothing better or worse about right brain or left brain. Rather, it represents a comprehensive mandala and all the possibilities are valid. Mercury is usually associated with the principle of thinking. The element of the sign and the sign position of Mercury represent the way a person's thinking processes are intended to take place. If Mercury is in one of the three air signs, Aquarius, Gemini or Libra, the thinking is left brained, detached and objective. It is thinking times thinking, or thinking squared. In other words, what we normally think about thinking happens when Mercury is in one of these three signs. It doesn't mean thinking is wrong, or faulty, or flawed; if Mercury is in one of the other elements, it simply represents a different style of thinking.

Earth signs represent the sensation function, and have to do with the senses in the physical or practical dimensions. Earth is feminine. When Mercury is in one of the three earth signs, Capricorn, Virgo or Taurus, the thinking is operating from the *left brain of the Goddess*, or the left brain of the feminine; the analytical, rational aspect of the feminine. The water signs, Scorpio, Pisces, and Cancer, represent the feeling function and are right brain feminine or the *right brain of the Goddess*. The water element is not analytical. It is not rational. It does not plan things out; it exists in the present moment. In fact, both fire and water live in the present moment. The biggest difficulty a person may experience if their horoscope is heavily concentrated in fire and water signs (not just Mercury but most of the other planets as well), is not having any objectivity. This type of horoscope is constantly in response, constantly living in the present moment. People with this type of chart are usually jealous of the people who are able to step back and have objectivity. Conversely, a horoscope heavily concentrated in earth and air signs represents the left brain analytical type. These people have everything planned out so they know what is going to happen before it happens. It is very civilized. Often, they believe the people who are having all the fun on the planet are the fire and water types, who are completely into the present moment all the time.

When the Moon and Mercury are combined they may form a fire/earth combination or a water/air combination. The fire/earth combination is sometimes called the locomotive. They have vision and imagination and a powerful intuitive function that takes them into the unknown (fire) and yet they also have the ability to get results (earth). Look at how many thousands of people there are who have great ideas, and never get anything accomplished. There are just as many people who are really good at getting the job done, but never have a creative thought their whole life! The fire/earth combination is a dynamic synthesis of these two qualities. In ancient alchemy, the air/water and fire/earth combinations were the most alchemical elements, similar to the quincunx or inconjunct relationship we have already discussed. These two types of combinations require a person to develop a larger container of consciousness so both elements can more easily co-exist. Otherwise they don't have any communication, because there is no logical connection between them.

Unlike the fire/earth or air/water combinations, the fire/air combination is similar in nature. Both are masculine and both are non-organic. They get along well with each other and they do not require an alchemical process to interact or communicate with each other. However, if the Moon is in a fire sign and Mercury is in an air sign, due to their similarity, it may be more difficult to shift the thinking process from the Moon to the Mercury. So each combination represents its own unique challenges and gifts.

The elements of the signs are associated with either the male or female principle; fire and air are masculine, earth and water are feminine. This does not refer to gender, but rather the archetypal principle of masculine and feminine. Many men are working on the feminine principle and many women are working on the masculine principle. Within this framework, masculinity as an archetypal quality refers to a movement away from the organic (earth and water) dimensions towards spirit and consciousness using will and intellect, and ultimately moving off the wheel of life. The archetypal feminine refers to the opposite tendency, moving from spirit and consciousness (fire and air) into the organic realm (earth and water), with the intent of bringing spirit into matter. These qualities are irrespective of gender. Shamanic Astrology is not gender driven. However, a man with a horoscope represented by all fire and air signs (all masculine signs) has nothing within his make-up to connect him with earth and water (the feminine signs), because he is born male. Two possibilities exist for such a man. One is he has to connect with earth and water through the polarity version of relationship by getting with an earth and water woman. The musician Robin Williamson a member of the Incredible String Band in the late 60's, is a good example of this. He is known as a marvelous Celtic, Scottish, storyteller, musician. I found his entire horoscope consisted of fire and air. Not one thing on his chart was connected to earth or water. He was pure logos, a total light being. Going to his concerts, I observed the woman in his life embodied archetypal Virgo/Scorpio. She was a heavy, dark, brooding kind of woman who ran his business for him. At his concerts people often whispered, "What is he doing with that woman?" She appeared to be the total opposite of him, and yet his chart suggested his connection with her is how he stayed on the planet. She grounded him and connected him into the organic somehow. Admittedly this is an extreme case, but this is one way it does work. The other possibility for men with all fire and air signs manifests as their being the ones who study yoga and follow the laws of Manu. The laws of Manu say, if you want to get enlightened, avoid women at all costs, stay away from them, don't get entangled with that aspect of life. It represents a radically dualistic path. This is the type of man who is only going towards expansion of consciousness, only going towards the masculine side of life. Again, this is not a typical situation, but it illustrates the point.

Conversely, if a woman has only earth and water signs she has no connection to the masculine principles of consciousness or logos. She has two choices. She might also have a polarity oriented relationship, with a man who strongly embodies the fire and air principles, or she might associate with other women who are completely Dianic. These women are totally involved in an approach to spirituality that denies there even is a male principle. It is a radically polarized view, like a version of the witches' coven that altogether denies the logos principle. This is rare, but it does happen. I have also noticed men with all earth and water automatically get fire and air by virtue of their gender. Similarly, women with all fire and air seem to automatically get earth and water just by being born female.

Question: *What do you mean by "automatically get?"*
Earth and water are feminine. By being born a woman, even if she has all fire and air on her chart, she is able to ground the consciousness, because the elements of earth and water are in her physical body. This is not necessarily completely automatic and it usually requires an action, like having a child, or having a garden, or some other type of activity that activates the organic water and earth within her. The opposite is true for the men, only they need an activity that activates the inherent fire and air qualities.

Question: *You are not talking about the elements here in regard to just the Moon and Mercury, but in relationship to the whole chart?*
Yes, the whole chart. We started with the more important ingredients and now we are expanding and bringing in other parts of the script. Especially when looking at Mercury, it is important to know the element as well as the sign, to help clarify the clues about the current life intent for thinking. For example, when Mercury is in a water sign, that person's thinking, logic, or type of computer exists in a medium of feeling. If the emotional life of a person with a water sign Mercury is healthy, they can be brilliant, but if they are not together emotionally they find they don't even know what two plus two is anymore. It is feeling function driven. The unique thing about water is it doesn't seem to be able to come into its power without a human connection. People with Mercury in a water sign can't get enlightened without being around other people. They must develop the ability to go into rapport, to merge, to connect in some way. People with *Mercury in Cancer or Pisces* are particularly good at the rapport or merge approach. *Mercury in Scorpio* includes another ingredient called the *eros of logos*. This is the opposite of the type of people who find thoughts alone interesting. Some people find total joy in taking thinking to its logical conclusion whether it has an emotional content or not. Not Scorpio. Because, for Scorpio, it is the passion of the mind that is the most interesting. If it is not something that turns them on, it won't engage their mind, because Scorpio comes from the emotional depths. I have Mercury in Scorpio and have tended to get angry when people accuse me of being an intellectual. I explain rather passionately that my intellect may appear to be functioning properly, but I am not interested in ideas for idea's sake, I am emotionally committed to what I am expressing!

If Mercury is in an earth sign, practicality and the physical feelings are what are most important. Each earth sign has its own unique perspective. *Mercury in Virgo* is an amazing approach for perceiving the web, the sacred patterning of life, the web of "spider woman." It's like watching a crystal grow under a microscope, perceiving the way things move in accordance with the lawful patterning of life. *Mercury in Taurus,* despite having a reputation for being dull, or slow, or dense, is actually very thorough. I sometimes call it *cow mind.* Cows may chew their food for several hours and then the food goes through four different stomachs. This lengthy process thoroughly digests the food. Similarly, Mercury in Taurus may go through a lengthy process to learn something, but once they have learned it they have thoroughly learned it. *Mercury In Capricorn Is Aware Of The Entire Structural Reality In Form, And In Law, From The Godhead To The Densest Entrapment Of Spirit In Matter. It Is Like Sacred Geometry.* It also represents responsible thinking with a keen attunement to what the rules are, or how things really operate in third dimensional reality.

Mercury in a fire sign (Sagittarius, Leo, or Aries) intends to go into new territory and call out what they see and learn. It is an adventure. It has a creativeness to it. Remember the Mercury position is the statement of intent, so not everybody uses their Mercury as intended. However, their intent is to shift to using Mercury as the new style of thinking, without discarding the old style of thinking completely. Rather, the challenge is to process and synthesize the two, with the emphasis or directional arrow moving towards the archetype of Mercury.

Question: *You talk about the Sun as a person's fuel, is that like a person's style, or the way they go forward toward their Rising sign?*
It depends upon the Venus or Mars position. If a man has Sun in Pisces and Mars in Aries, the style is more likely to be Aries, not Pisces. The Mars or Venus position gives us a clear sense of the archetype, and then that archetype burns the fuel of the Sun. Their style is partially described by the fuel, but it is not always the dominant style. If a person has a Capricorn Moon, with Sun and Mars conjunct in Aries, they have a Capricorn vehicle that is now filling up with Aries fuel. Aries fuel is a high-grade aviation fuel. The Capricorn vehicle previously burned an incredibly efficient, long lasting, fuel. Aries and Capricorn fuel are radically different from each other, and require the same kind of creative thinking that blends the Sun together with Venus or Mars.

This principle of blending or synthesizing the archetypes is also true for the Sun and Mercury position. However, a large percentage of people have the Sun and Mercury in the same sign. It is more likely for Mercury and the Sun to be in the same sign, than Venus and the Sun, or Mars and the Sun to be in same sign. That's why people who do *not* have Mercury and the Sun in the same sign, are considered mental individualists. This is an aspect other astrologers have pointed out, and is not unique to this system. Additionally, other astrological approaches say when Mercury and the Sun are in the same sign, Mercury is subsumed into the Sun and Mercury becomes what the Sun's energy is. I look at it the other way. The principle of Mercury is always the principle of Mercury, but when it is burning the fuel of the Sun, they are subsumed together. The maximum elongation of Mercury is twenty-eight degrees away from the Sun. That's why there are a limited number of combinations for Mercury and the Sun. A person with Sun in Aries could not have Mercury in Virgo. Mercury is either in the same sign as the Sun or in the sign preceding or following the Sun sign. So if the Sun is in Aries, Mercury will show up in Pisces, Aries, or Taurus.

Question: *I have a conjunction in fire and water, with Moon in Pisces and Mercury in Aries, How does that interact?*

The old mind, Pisces Moon, represents the aspect of thinking that merges. Essentially there is no objectivity or separateness to that type of mind. When Pisces goes into rapport with another person they believe what the other person believes. They are strong in what the other person is strong in. They are passionate about what the other person is passionate about, until they meet someone who has opposite beliefs, and then they go into rapport with that person. Generally speaking, Pisces doesn't have much individuality associated with their thinking. This is not a judgment against Pisces, because this version of thinking is tremendously useful and helpful in counseling, and in forms of close intimacy. The challenge is to move towards Mercury in Aries, which says, "I think what I want to think, and I do what I want to do." Aries has no sensitivity to the other person. The delight and joy of Aries is its naive innocence; it only sees itself. So this is an example of a huge change of gears. Someone with this combination never loses the Pisces end of their thinking, but there is a directional arrow from the old way of thinking to the new. A person still gets to do the old version of thinking (Moon) some of the time, but the greater identity is intended to be with the new version of thinking (Mercury).

MERCURY RETROGRADE

When looking at Mercury Retrograde, it is important to eliminate the dualism found in our culture that has us believe Mercury Retrograde or any retrograde planet is the negative formulation of that planet. What would happen to a society where consensus reality was right brained, and the majority lived in a fluid, continually creative space, without reference to pattern, order or logic, and most everyone lived in an eternal now, when Mercury went retrograde? In that society people would suddenly be doing things logically and rationally. They would have great difficulty in functioning in the usual way, because everything taking place would be opposite of what they assumed was normal. History has some similar examples. Coffee and coca leaves hit Europe just before the time that is known historically as the *age of enlightenment*. Little cafes everywhere had coffee and the avant-garde eagerly partook of the new drug. One of the greatest under-reported stories in history is how many of these people, upon their first experience with coffee had bad trips. At the time coffee was introduced, the prevalent consciousness in Europe was very superstitious. Most people feared the church. However, many of the common people were still heavily into nature religions and the cycles of the seasons, but the original power of these religions had degenerated into plain old superstition. The introduction of coffee acted as a catalyst that lined up their minds in a logical, linear way. The sudden shift from the predominantly right brained thinking to the left brain thinking was difficult for most people to handle. Conversely, in the 1960's consensus reality was predominantly left brained or logical and linear. At that time a whole other set of drugs came in to overturn or shift the polarity to a more right brained way of thinking. The shift in polarity depends upon what consensus reality is at the time, but it doesn't mean left brain or right brain thinking is better or worse than the other. Both are valid and serve a purpose.

Mercury Retrograde shifts the polarity of how the mind spins. It is a time when consensus reality no longer works. During Mercury Retrograde the reverse polarity becomes the dominant reality. A person with Mercury Retrograde on their natal chart in a right brain sign (a water or fire sign), has the most revolutionary, avant-garde position there is for Mercury, as well as the most alienated position. A person who handles it well really has something amazing to contribute to the culture. For the person who is not well adjusted to this aspect, profound alienation results because they feel so drastically different from everyone else.

I have found it interesting to note when Mercury Retrograde changes direction in the progressed cycles. (This information is more advanced but worthwhile if you understand it.) For example, when I was born Mercury was retrograde, and when I was nineteen it went direct by progression. That time marked some of the most fundamental changes in my life. My whole personality changed; even my direction in school changed. I switched majors in college from chemistry and physics to eastern philosophy. I became far more confident in myself and shifted from being an introvert to being an extrovert. When I look back, it is clear Mercury reversing direction was linked to these dramatic changes. I have also seen this principle occur when the progression causes Mercury to shift from direct to retrograde. If a person has Mercury Direct on their natal chart, but due to other factors they express as an introvert, the change in the direction of Mercury reverses the polarity. Mercury going direct or retrograde isn't always connected to shifting from being an extrovert to an introvert or vice versa, but Mercury going direct or retrograde either by transit or progression is shifting direction and reversing the polarity.

When transiting Mercury goes retrograde I do make allowances for the shift. Mercury Retrograde is a powerful time for doing creative work, or a powerful time for doing inner spiritual meditative or inner quest processes. If properly understood and participated with, Mercury Retrograde is a great time. But beware! If you expect things to work externally in a logical, linear way as they usually do, much frustration and difficulty could ensue.

Comment: I have known people who have Mercury Retrograde on their natal chart and when Mercury goes retrograde in the transits it seems to be the time when they get everything together.
Yes, I have had the same experience. A person who really has it together during Mercury Retrograde can count on most people messing up and thereby make amazing inroads at that time!

Comment: *I have noticed the same principle seems to work for people with Venus Retrograde.*

Yes. This principle is true for Venus and Mars Retrograde too. I have found Venus Retrograde associates with sacred marriage. Venus Retrograde on the natal chart or Venus Retrograde by transit urges us to see no one else is out there, and ultimately we must dance with our own inner partner. A person with Venus Direct is more likely to be plugged into the consensus reality views of how relationships work. In April, 1993 Venus went retrograde in Aries. A brilliant example of the effect at that time was the number one best seller *Women Who Run With the Wolves.* The awareness of the wild woman archetype was prevalent. In addition, people who attempted to work out their relationships, on the level of the relationship, were in deep trouble. This phenomenon included people who were trying to project or communicate to their partner how happy they were with the relationship, and how great they felt about how it was working. A common experience I noticed, was no matter how articulate they were in expressing these feelings, it wasn't good enough. That's because Venus Retrograde isn't about the external reality; it is about working with it internally.

Comment: *I was married to a guy for a few years that had Mars Retrograde, and when I asked him to do anything, he would say okay, but then he wouldn't do it. He could never just respond to a request. He refused to respond until it was coming from his own inner place. It was as if he didn't want to hear it, if it seemed like an order.*

That makes sense. The most superficial element of Mars, as understood by more traditional astrology, is similar to the soldier following orders, and everything is external. What you are describing is a more inward direction for Mars, more internal than external. It goes along with the theme of a retrograde being more of a revolutionary direction and alienated direction, and not wanting to go along with what the average beliefs are associated with that particular energy.

The outer planets, Jupiter on outward, are all retrograde every year from four to six months of the year, so there is very little that is individualistic about their retrograde cycles. Mercury goes retrograde about three times a year, for approximately three weeks each time. Venus retrograde occurs only once in about 18 months. Mars retrograde is the rarest retrograde cycle taking place only once every 26 months. It is important to have an understanding of retrogrades because they can be seen visually in the night sky. The early skywatchers thought they were quite impressive, although, most of them may not have had an understanding of what was behind the phenomenon as far as the physics or astronomy of it was concerned. Still, it was an amazing thing for them to observe a planet, in its regular orbit and in its regular cycles, suddenly stop and go the other way. Retrogrades are important in Shamanic Astrology, because they can be observed and experienced in the night sky.

JUPITER AND LIFE INTENT

Jupiter represents another feature of the tools and equipment of the current life by describing the types of initiations or experiences a person must have to fulfill their life purpose. Jupiter has been known as the *year star*, because Jupiter takes about twelve months to move through a sign. This creates clusters or groupings of people occurring every twelve years, who all have Jupiter in the same sign. Therefore, Jupiter is similar to Chinese astrology because in Chinese astrology every twelve years people are born under the sign of the rat, or monkey, or dog and so on, and these signs give certain characteristics to the year and to the person born in that year. Within the framework of Shamanic Astrology the difference between Jupiter and Chinese Astrology is that Jupiter describes the kinds of life experiences that get a person to their goals the most quickly.

Jupiter is closely linked with the actual mystery schools (represented by the four angles) we have signed up for. The angles of the chart change approximately every two hours. The degrees of the angles change about every four minutes. More than any other factor, the angles of the chart are what truly individuate the horoscope. Without knowing the exact birth time we can determine what tribe a person came from, what archetype they are, and what fuel they burn, but the exact birth time is necessary for determining the four angles of the chart. Throughout the history of astrology, the most important angle has been the one coming up over the eastern horizon called the Ascendant or Rising Sign. Shamanic Astrology refers to this as the east point on the medicine wheel. The Rising Sign or Ascendant represents the personal identity project. The best, fastest, and most powerful way to get to the personal identity project is to use the methodology described by the archetype of the sign Jupiter is in.

Also fitting into this system is the North Node of the Moon. Remember the Nodes of the Moon are the time track. The South Node of the Moon is the origination point and the North Node of the Moon is the destination point. The house position of the South Node indicates what the major was in the university a person got their Ph.D. from, or it says what job they had in the tribe they came from. The house position of the North Node is the destination. It describes what job the person has signed up for in their current life mystery school. If a person has Libra Rising, they have signed up for Libra school or they are now joining the Libra tribe. If they have North Node in the fourth house they have signed up for the Cancer job in the Libra tribe.

The Midheaven describes the mystery school of Right Livelihood, career, and contribution. The North Node and Jupiter are applied to this area of the chart in the same way as they are applied to the Rising Sign. The fastest way to accomplish the Right Livelihood Project is with the help of Jupiter. The house position of the North Node further indicates the type of contribution a person intends to make on the planet. If a person has Capricorn Rising and North Node in the tenth house (the Capricorn job in the Capricorn tribe) it is a clear that Capricorn is the intended goal of the current life. Now if this person has Jupiter in Gemini that describes how the person gets to the goal of Capricorn the most quickly. Jupiter in Gemini says if this person is too driven, taking everything too seriously, and they know they have an important duty to perform, or they are scared of the pressure of having to get results, that's when they benefit from tuning into their playful, lighthearted coyote side. They need to get some humor and fun into their life. They need to see the joke in what they are taking so seriously. When things get too heavy, they can ask, "How would Robin Williams deal with it?" The idea is to channel the divine comedian, or do something crazy, off the wall, unexpected.

Question: *The South Node represents the job you had in your Moon tribe?*
Yes. For example, if a person has a Capricorn Moon and South Node in the tenth house, they had the Capricorn job in the Capricorn tribe. If however, they have the South Node in the seventh house, the Capricorn Moon was also into partnership bonding. So the emphasis in the past was on defining who they were by who they were in a relationship with, totally being a giver, holding it together, and being a great provider in a relationship.

Question: *How does this relate to rulerships?*
I don't do much with rulerships. Some astrologers have that as the basis of their system and it works well for them. Shamanic Astrology, however, is archetype driven. From what I have determined, rulerships shift and change from one age to the next, yet the associations between planets and signs continue to have a certain resonance.

Shamanic Astrology considers the angles of the chart to be of the utmost importance. Virtually every house system available has the same angles. There is little controversy on that particular issue. I consider the intermediate house positions to have much less importance. A person can show me a chart run on five or six different house systems. Two or three of the charts may have Venus in the eighth, and the rest may have Venus in the ninth. I am not going to turn this into a technical class by explaining all the rationales throughout history of why they found different ways to divide up space or time into twelve different regions, because it is one of the most esoteric and obscure aspects of astrology. When a planet or node is near the border of two intermediate houses I deal with this issue by reading it for the next house regardless of the house system that is used. In the above example, I would read Venus as if it's in the ninth house. In most cases, the house meanings for the intermediate houses blend nicely, anyway.

I do use houses when I am doing interpretations; I haven't totally thrown them out, but they're not nearly as important as the angles or the archetypes. What I do is apply the archetype of the sign associated with the house. The first house is the Aries archetype. The second house is the Taurus archetype. The third house is the Gemini archetype and so on. This corresponds to the Zip Dobyn's school of astrology, as well as Ptolemy's way of looking at it, and that keeps the whole issue of houses simple. The great thing about Shamanic Astrology is that it is not necessary to construct the whole chart to get a great deal of important information about a person. A lot of information can be gained by knowing a person's birthdate and looking it up in the ephemeris.

It is not my intent to invalidate other approaches to astrology or house systems. There is brilliant work done with many of the things I have put on a lower scale of importance. This system has evolved through noticing the key symbols that define the most important issues in a person's life the most quickly. However, there is a precedence set for this approach to the houses by the most popular school of astrology in Europe that has thrown out houses altogether. This is the Harmonics version of astrology and it uses a forty-five degree dial.

KARMIC LINKS

Something I did not bring up in the relationship material was how to look at the so-called karmic links. This way of looking at the chart really works. The karmic links are not absolutely literal. If I say a link shows past life ties, it doesn't necessarily mean those two people literally had past lives together. Karmic links operate on a mythic level, so they work as if they are true. Whether they are literally true or not doesn't really matter. We all have an underlying myth or series of myths that describes our life. The South Node is an especially potent symbol for determining karmic connections. Past life links are indicated when two horoscopes have either the Moon or South Node within ten degrees of the other person's personal planets (Moon, Mercury, Venus, Mars, and/or Sun) or a major angle. The faster moving planets are the more potent links. Since the Moon moves the fastest, South Node to the Moon is the most potent link. However, Venus, Mercury, Mars, and the Sun are all personally potent. South Node to Jupiter, Saturn, Uranus, Neptune and/or Pluto are not as personally significant, because these planets move much slower, and there is a greater cross section of people that link up due to the length of time these planets stay in the same degree, yet they do form a connection.

Question: I have done family charts, and the thing I have seen the most of is the South Node of the older relative being conjunct the ascendant of the grandchild.
Yes, that is a good example.

Question: How about a square from a personal planet to the South Node?
For the most part, because the cycle of the Nodes is a wave function, and it is not the same as the orbit of a planet, I considered squares, sextiles, and trines to not have the same power as conjunctions and oppositions. I have seen some good work done with squares, although not nearly as powerful as the conjunctions and the oppositions. The South Node conjunct another person's personal planets indicates the past life karmic links, and you can tell interesting stories about that.

Comment: My ex-husband had South Node conjunct my Venus and Jupiter.
I call South Node/Venus past life intimacy. These are two people who have been with each other before. There is a certain level of connection that need not be proven. There is already acceptance there. However, this does not necessarily make for a great relationship. What it means is there has already been something in place. I have found in many cases that some of the most addictive relationships can come from that connection.

Another powerful past life connection is when a person's Moon (lineage) is connected to one or more of another person's personal planets. A future karmic link is determined by the conjunction of the personal planets to another person's North Node. There is something dharmic about that type of link, something to be learned that has to do with the final destination point of the North Node. If the Moon or the South Node connects with one of the angles, South Node conjunct the ascendant for example, this is one of the most overwhelming links having to do with the future and the past. It is a past life connection that also has a future destiny or intent. It represents two people who have been together before and are together again because it is progressive for them and they are moving on to a new expression of what they were already working on. So this is a very important connection.

Then there are the links that are pure potential, like North Node conjunct another person's Rising Sign. It is possible nothing ever happens with that link. On the other hand if these two people have charts that, according to the traditional rules of astrology are out of whack, the one thing going for them is they are both working dharmically in the same direction. Therefore, the North Node/Rising Sign connection has a fantastic pure potential. If a couple has this aspect along with other aspects that are in sync, such as the same Rising sign or harmonious connections between their Mars and Venus, it shows they are definitely heading in the same dharmic direction.

The next step is to blend the archetypal meaning of the planet with the lineage issues. For example, I have noticed Moon or South Node to another person's Mars works like past life comrades, blood brothers, people who died in the barricades for each other. South Node conjunct another person's Sun works like that too. This connection indicates the same basic community or family group, a group that has been together and has the same interests.

Those who wish to be critical of the so-called karmic links might argue that a statistical survey using the parameters we have been discussing would turn up hundreds of thousands of people connected to any one person's chart. Even if we narrowed the search to include only those people with karmic links living in Tucson, Arizona who have their South Node conjunct within five degrees of the Venus of the person conducting the search, chances are good several hundred people would turn up with that connection. Do all of these people have a past life connection with each other? I bet if the researcher met one of these people the two of them could share stories as if they had known each other in the past, but whether they literally did or not, is not the point.

Question: *Does the Node give to the planet, or vice versa?*
Using the example of Pluto to the South Node, the person with Pluto would have performed the action to the person with the South Node. The one with the planet is the one who is the doer when it is a planet/node connection.

Question: *If a planet, say Venus, is just barely into a new sign, does it take on some of the characteristics of the previous sign?*
No. This is an important question. This is one of the basic principles that underlie the shamanic approach to astrology. The shamanic approach of looking at the archetypes

does not recognize a cusp. I have recognized a cusp in the intermediate house areas, but not the signs or archetypes. So zero degrees, two minutes of Libra is not any more or less Libra than any other portion of the sign. The integrity of the archetype of the sign is not changed by how close it is to the other sign. When a person is born at the end or beginning of a sign, if that person displays the characteristics of the other sign, it's because they have either their Venus, Mars, Moon or some other important factor in the other sign. The sign's integrity is within the thirty-degree zone. There is not a unanimous opinion on this, but an extremely well known astrologer who has written eloquently on this issue, is Liz Greene. She absolutely teaches the same principle of the integrity of the signs being within the thirty degree range. However, there is a way to look at a sign in the first ten degrees as being different than the same sign in the teens, or twenties, etc. It is similar to the difference between straightforwardness and complexity. For example, if we look at a Moon position twenty-five Capricorn or a Moon position twenty-eight Scorpio, those degrees represent a comprehensive development of that particular lineage.

Comment: *I find that for people who have the last degree of a sign, it is like a last gasp, where they recapitulate everything. It seems like they want to do everything at once, as opposed to five degrees of a sign where it seems a lot slower, as if they are getting used to it.*

Yes, and if we look at the Moon as potential addiction to the old identity, the late degrees have a very intriguing paradox, because on the one hand the person truly is an adept, and secondly, they sure don't want to let go of it. Their challenge is to not be too over-identified with the old identity.

This brings us to the importance of the house position of Jupiter. It is not as important as the sign, but it is important relative to the issue of the fastest path or a useful way of getting to the Rising sign or the Midheaven. For example, if Jupiter is in Sagittarius in the tenth house, it says the way to quickly reach the life goals is by questing for the meaning of life or connecting with an expanded vision in the area of Right Livelihood. This principle also applies to the Moon and the other personal planets. First it is important to understand the lineage, or archetype of the Moon, then notice the house position of the Moon, because this indicates where a person must use their lineage in the current life. The Moon represents what you already know and have mastery in. The house position shows where the mastery of the Moon intends to be expressed into the current life. People with Aries, Sagittarius, or Gemini Moon are from tribes that didn't focus on bonding or relationship. If their Moon shows up in the fourth or seventh house, they have an interesting challenge to integrate their mastery in either a relationship or family situation. So the house position of the Moon represents a feature of current life intent.

Question: *What does the Moon in the second house represent?*

That house position is associated with the mysteries of Taurus. It has to do with the "I have" statement, one's possessions, the physical reality of the person, the sensation function, being a receiver.

Comment: *Robert Hand said the second house is things I attach myself to and the fourth house is the things that attach themselves to me.*

The difference is the second house is about personal issues. The fourth house is about family issues; about responsibly holding things together for the family.

RIGHT LIVELIHOOD

The Midheaven is associated with the Right Livelihood. The Rising sign and seventh house point create the Relationship Axis. Similarly, the Midheaven and the opposite point at the bottom of the chart, or the Home and Roots area, also create an axis called the Energy Axis or the Foundational Axis. This axis describes the current life intent for Right Livelihood, family and roots, how we create our security in life, and the development of the inner and outer aspects of the foundation of our personality. Just as the Moon represents the foundation of self from the past, the Foundational Axis relates to a future foundational intent.

The sign on the Midheaven is the creative fantasy that stands behind Right Livelihood. The Midheaven does not define the job a person is supposed to have, rather it reveals whether a person is on the right track with their profession or not, or what element underlies the successful expression of the Right Livelihood. Let's illustrate how this works by using the example of a musician. The Midheaven describes how the person intends to approach their chosen career. So a musician who has Libra on the Midheaven has as their intent to sing the type of songs the greatest number of people will like, because for them it is important to be well liked. If the musician has Capricorn on the Midheaven everything they do is a career move. If Aquarius is on the Midheaven their desire is to sit at the synthesizer (or whatever their chosen instrument of expression is) charting out beautiful, celestial music simulating the thoughts of God. If Scorpio or Taurus is on the Midheaven the music is designed to plug them into life force energy and to induce orgasms for themselves and others! For Scorpio or Taurus the energetics of the music is what is most important. If Aries is on the Midheaven they must be able to play, have fun, and get to do what they want to do. Gemini on the Midheaven must have a connection to their creative muse, and requires that the music be something a child would like. With Sagittarius on the Midheaven there is an absolute hatred of having to do the same routine over and over again. They must do something that expands them out to wider vistas.

All of the angles, the right livelihood project, the personal identity project, the relationship project, and the home and roots project, are mystery school degrees. For example, if a person has twenty-nine degrees Virgo Rising, virtually the entire first house is Libra. The first house is the "I am" statement and represented by the archetype of Aries. If the entire first house is mostly Libra, then that person's "I am" statement is expressed more through the Libra archetype. However, the mystery school of the personal identity is twenty-nine Virgo, not Libra. There is a tremendous Libra influence for the first house, but the twenty-ninth degree of Virgo is the actual current life Personal Identity Project mystery school. There is a huge difference between the Rising sign and the first house. The entire first house can reveal, as in the traditional meaning of the first house, aspects of appearance, self-expression, and initiative, but it is the degree of the ascendant's sign that most captures the personal identity project mystery school. If a person has twenty-seven degrees Gemini on the Midheaven and five planets in Cancer in the tenth house, the Cancer planets in the tenth house are extremely important with reference to tenth house Capricornian issues, but the mystery school of Right Livelihood is still the twenty-seventh degree of Gemini.

Question: Do you get into the qualities of the signs, Cardinal, Fixed, Mutable?
Thanks for asking that. Not too much. Not as much as the elements. The reason is cardinality, mutability, and fixity change from one age to the next. For example, in the age of Taurus, the constellation Taurus was aligned with Aries and had cardinal qualities associated with it. Now Taurus is a fixed sign and has a different meaning today than it did then. Every two thousand years or so there is a shift as far as the emphasis on whether a sign is fixed, mutable, or cardinal. Today the cardinal signs are moving into the fixed constellations. So the horoscope can still be divided into its component parts and it may show up as being heavily fixed, mutable, or cardinal, but what is most important is the archetype, not the fixity or the mutability of the chart. That's why I don't place a high level of importance on the qualities of the signs. I have found the archetypes are much more important and revealing.

In the next class we will explore the issue of strategy (determined by the aspects from the outer planets) and how it reveals some of the biggest differences between people. Some people have very melodramatic lives and often appear to be totally "at the effect of" circumstances, or events happening beyond their control. The dramatic events that transpire in their lives force them to grow and change. Other people have relatively uneventful lives, coasting lives, cruise control lives, maybe even boring lives. The issues of melodrama versus cruise control, or other approaches, are all based upon the kind of strategy a person has on their chart to get from point A to point B. One approach is not better than another. This is one case where I could *almost* make a judgment that it is better these days, at the turning of the ages, to have the melodramatic strategy, the catastrophic strategy, the strategy driven by divine discontent. During these speeded-up times a person who has a horoscope with all cruise control might get left behind, or miss out on the party. I could almost go that far. Maybe I would go that far only to get us over the prejudice that still exists in a lot of astrology that says, to have a lot of squares and oppositions is not good.

Saturn, Uranus, Neptune and Pluto are initiators and represent very specific, beautifully articulated instructions for how to fulfill the original life purpose. Ultimately, our goal is to get to the life purpose issues, or the spiritual objective, as quickly as possible. The strategy indicates the way to most quickly accomplish the original life intent and how to wake up as fast as possible. That is what we are learning to get clues for in a non-judgmental way, in a way that reveals the entire spectrum of possibilities, and always has as the bottom line the Aquarian Dispensation. The Aquarian Dispensation *says every human being should have the freedom to take personal responsibility for their own evolutionary path. Any form of class, caste, or dogma, is part of the old age.*

HOW TO DO COUNSELING USING THE PRINCIPLES OF SHAMANIC ASTROLOGY
Class Five
THE STRATEGY OF SATURN, URANUS, NEPTUNE, AND PLUTO

Question: Last class I asked about how the house position affects the Moon in the current life, and we used the example of my Moon in the second house and you said it means whenever I nurture people I should get pleasure out of it. That doesn't really tell me where to use the lineage, it says when I am using my lineage I should get pleasure from it. It doesn't tell me when to use my lineage.

The intent is for you to use your lineage in a second house way. The precise way of formulating this principle is to note the house the Moon is in and that indicates the sphere of life activities where the lineage is intended to express in the current life.

Question: So how does that work if the Moon is in the second house?

The second house represents personal pleasure. Therefore, if Cancer Moon, which has to do with what you do for others, shows up in the second house (or Taurus house), then it is on you to take the giving energy of your lineage and turn it into something that is now for your personal pleasure and satisfaction. To further illustrate this let's look at this from the angle of a nonbonding lineage such as Gemini or Sagittarius. If either of these Moon positions show up in the seventh house (or Libra house), the challenge is to take the energy of the lineage that did not operate in the area of relationship and learn how to use it in that area. All of the above scenarios represent a kind of alchemy. The challenge is for your Cancer Moon to learn how to operate in a second house way.

In the previous classes we have looked at the entire script, except for the strategy. The strategy is derived from the four outer planets, Saturn, Uranus, Neptune, and Pluto, and how they aspect the personal planets. These planets describe the kind of life agreements a person makes when they incarnate. They set up the pattern of events in a person's life. The outer planets represent the encounter with external experiences that prompt or promote action of some kind. People who do not have any hard aspects in their personal horoscope, have what is called a coasting life, unless they have a Moon position or personal archetype that is out of favor in this culture (like Scorpio or Virgo). For the purposes of determining the strategy, the hard aspects are the conjunctions (zero degrees), squares (ninety degrees), and oppositions (one hundred and eighty degrees), within a ten degree range or orb of each other.

Question: Is it only with the outer planets that the orb is that large?

To determine the strategy we look at the outer planets in their aspect patterns to the inner planets, so in Shamanic Astrology the orb is always up to ten degrees. I find the principle works up to ten degrees and sometimes beyond. Amazingly, I have seen Pluto/Moon aspects, Saturn/Moon aspects, and a few other outer planet aspects, of fourteen or fifteen degrees that still work, although that is more rare.

People without hard aspects (or a coasting chart) are similar to those born into an aristocratic family at the height of the British Empire. This was a time when everything went well for the ruling caste. They retired to their country estates as early as age thirty, and not much happened after that. The absence of the hard aspects was something that was longed for, because then a person had the privileges of the ruling class. People with coasting charts have an expectation that the world is in harmony. This attitude is partially responsible for the dualism found in the traditional astrology books, and the reason the trines (one hundred and twenty degrees) and sextiles (sixty degrees) are considered the easy aspects, while squares, oppositions, and conjunctions are considered the hard aspects. Interestingly, I have found, at The Turning of the Ages, coasting lives are not particularly useful because there is not enough motivation to move into new territory, or to make use of the talents and skills already in place. Even so, there is still no script that is better or worse than another, and all scripts are valid, and have a specific doable intent.

SATURN

No one gets out of having some encounter with Saturn strategy. Even people who don't have hard aspects to Saturn, still must encounter Saturn by virtue of the Saturn transits at some point in their life.

The ephemeris is useful for determining the type of strategy a person is dealing with or what outer planet transits might be affecting them. It is not necessary to be an astrologer to learn how to use the ephemeris. Simply by knowing the birthdate of a client, (the birthtime is not necessary for determining this information), one can easily observe if Saturn or Pluto is conjunct the Moon, or in hard aspect to Venus or Mars or the Sun. Using an ephemeris lets you know right away if a person has a Saturn Complex, or some other strategy involving any of the other outer planets. One of the first things I look for is the type of strategy a person has.

Saturn represents the rules of the game, the principles, the boundaries, the law. The content of the law changes when we shift from one age to the next. Five thousand years ago the laws that governed society were different than the majority of the laws we have now. We are born into whatever the consensus reality beliefs are. We can't get out of it. It is impressed upon us. If a person has a Saturn Complex, they *absolutely* can not get out of it, and probably find they are continually experiencing heavy encounters with the laws of the ruling culture. In the last five thousand years, the Saturn Complex has had a content that includes guilt, atonement, and original sin. These three issues have supported the notion that a person is not okay just the way they are, and they have to prove themselves to the *fathers*. The *fathers* could be a literal father, or God, or any external authority figure. This means they live their lives in a way they hope will earn them approval from the fathers and includes adopting the ethical judgments and morals of the ruling culture. That's why people with a Saturn Complex tend to compare themselves to the standards of the culture to determine how well they are doing with their life more than any other type of complex.

Part of the programming inherent in the Saturn Complex is the belief that there is a logical connection between a person's merit, how good they are, how well they perform, and what the return is. The fundamentalist view of karma that says; "As you sow, so shall you reap," is an example of Saturn programming. I am not claiming this is an untrue principle from some perspectives, but with a Saturn Complex, a person is constantly hit over the head with the fact that there is no logical connection between how well they are doing and the reward they receive for their efforts, even though they are led to believe there is. No matter how hard they try to act in accordance with the principles and morals of the ruling culture, or how motivated and driven they are to live their lives as perfectly as possible, there is no additional reward that appears as a result.

Question: *Are you saying with a Saturn Complex, doing your best in that area of your life won't produce the reward or benefits a person expects?*
Yes. Where the Saturn Complex shows up on the natal chart is where a person is shown over and over again that the approval or rewards they expect for how good they are in that area, never really manifest in a concrete way. Saturn in hard aspect to the Sun hits a person across the board, because it is hitting the fuel. The entire chart burns the fuel of the Sun so every area of life is affected. Saturn in hard aspect to the Moon shows up as heavy boundaries and limitations and judgment associated with the lineage. This means the very thing a person is best at, the thing they have three or four Ph.D.s in from their past, is now continuously being shown to not be good enough. The term I use to illustrate this is, "Not Okay!!" I once had an old William Blake painting called *The Judgment of Adam* that perfectly captured this imagery. It depicted the Father God as a severe character pointing his finger at Adam who had his head bowed in shame. It was as if God was saying to Adam, "Not Okay!"

The way out of a Saturn Complex is to see that there is no logical connection between your merit and your rewards. When you are really able to understand this, then you can relax. You will probably still be a person who is driven, achievement and accomplishment oriented, hard working, and a perfectionist, because those qualities are inherent in you. The difference is now you are doing it because it's fun, or because it seemed like a good thing to do that day. The drivenness and other qualities become just another personal trait, like having red hair and green eyes, or being left handed. In the same way, some people have a Saturn Complex and some don't.

Until a person figures out the hoax of the Saturn Complex, they usually experience one of two patterns. The first pattern is the feeling that the finger of the Father God, or the constant judgment of those who are in power (the authority figures), is real. These people end up beating the external authority figures (the parents, the teacher's, the CEO's of the company, etc.) at their own game, by outperforming them using their same principles. The other pattern expresses as the rebel who rebels against the principles of their family or culture. Some examples of how this has manifested are, the son who refuses to take over the family business and disgraces the family with outrageous behavior, the daughter who interracially marries or marries "beneath" her, or the political activist who fights the system. However, the rebel is still beholden to the same energy, the same external law in reference to what they are in reaction against, and they are ultimately giving their personal power away to external authority, because the same type of energy is still running the show.

Comment: *Even if they don't have a father around it seems like a complex of their own mind, where they mentally crack the whip, and tend to be an overachiever, feeling like they are never doing it well enough or getting enough rewards from their efforts.*

Absolutely. I remember about fourteen years ago when, for the first time, I was getting a handle on my own Saturn Complex. (I have a Capricorn Moon, and Saturn conjunct Venus, a strong Saturn Complex.) I started doing vision quests around 1980. I often went out alone to the wilderness area in Joshua Tree National Monument outside of Los Angeles. It was a wonderful place, where I was completely alone and able to get into the silence and space of the area. It seemed to be perfectly designed for vision quests. One time I went there specifically to get deeply in touch with the significance of my own Saturn Complex. It wasn't long before I began to feel panicked, because I thought my Dad was going to find me there. This feeling was constantly bugging me. For hours I practiced a dialogue of what I was going to say to him when he appeared. I imagined him saying: "What are you doing out here, boy? When are you going to be responsible in your life? What is this about? Isn't this just another big escapist thing you're doing?" Through the internal dialogue I was having with my father I finally understood, on a profound level, that there was not one chance in ten trillion of him showing up there, and the fear I was feeling was connected to the inner Saturn principle I carry around in my head. I realized that, even when I was out in a remote area where my father would never find me, I couldn't get rid of him. That's when I finally began to understand my inner Saturn Complex.

The Saturn principle people carry around inside requires them to check in for duty. They feel they must be able to give their name, show what relationship they are in, what bank account they have, and what their contribution is at all times. Until a person gets the joke of Saturn, this is a difficult predicament, because they will continue to beat their head against the wall, believing at some point they will receive validation and reward, and they never will. If there were an easy way to get through a Saturn complex, I would definitely be teaching people how to do it. As far as I know, there isn't. It is not that simple. The more precise the complex is (within only a couple of degrees of exactness for the conjunction, square, or opposition), especially with regards to the Moon, the more challenging and difficult it is to understand. A person can be so addicted to it that they literally have to go through it ten or twelve times, each time becoming more excruciating than the time before. That's why some make it and some don't. In my own case, with the Saturn/Venus material, I actually had a heart attack and almost left this earth over a relationship that didn't work. I knew I had done everything exactly right. I had done my best for the person I thought was my divinely appointed partner, and it still didn't work. In every case the way out of a Saturn complex is self-love, but what does it take to get there? Often a person insists on going through every possibility of attempting to prove that, if they have a certain degree of merit, they will receive a certain reward. They create for themselves increasingly more excruciating examples of hitting the wall, until they finally get the joke. The *joke* is another way of saying: *It Wasn't Intended To Work! Being Driven And Motivated And Doing Everything Perfectly Does Not Bring An Additional Reward.* It simply is *not* intended to work like that. When a person gets the joke, they can actually change the parameters of the game. They can choose a different set of Gods and Goddesses to have as their leading edge. They can replace Saturn with something else. There is only one day of the week named after Saturn (Saturday). When a person gets the joke, they realize that there are six other days of the week not governed by Saturn. The whole purpose of the Saturn Complex is to reroute the energy into new territory.

One of my favorite statements about Saturn was made by one of the best astrologers in America, Robert Hand. I heard him tell the following joke in a talk he gave. He was describing Yahweh, one of the original images that became the central Father/God figure in the Hebraic tradition. Robert Hand said, "Hey, I don't have anything against Yahweh, he is a perfectly fine god. The trouble with Yahweh is he thinks he <u>is</u> <u>God</u>--as if he is the *only* symbol for God."

Question: *What about South Node conjunct Saturn?*
Usually when the South Node is conjunct Saturn there is an extremely deep seated attachment of some kind. For example, South Node in the tenth house conjunct Saturn represents a person who, for lifetimes, has been the elder, the one who was required to keep it together, and now they literally cannot let go of that position. The paradox associated with a planet conjunct the South Node is, a person really does have to continue to use that mastery, but not be attached to it at the same time. The trick with Saturn is how to be responsible and irresponsible at the same time; how to have a duty and hold space, and at the same time not be attached to it. In other words, know that you will always be a serious person, but don't take yourself seriously. If you can figure out how to do that, you have it licked. South Node conjunct Pluto is especially difficult to let go of because it is an even more obsessive and deeply welded together old pattern.

Question: *Is the attachment phenomenon true whether it is an opposition, conjunction or square, or is something different expressed in the different aspects?*
For the sake of understanding the complex, it isn't necessary to have them distinguished, because they all represent the complex. However, an opposition is analogous to the power and intensity of a full Moon. The person is definitely more aware of what the situation is. My favorite way of explaining the square is Dane Rudhyar's phrase: "Crisis in Action." Something has to give, but generally the person doesn't know what it is. It is like being blind-sided. Unlike the opposition, the square does not have as much awareness of the situation. So the square usually involves circumstances that cannot be prepared for. Something happens to break apart the status quo. The Saturn square is usually experienced more unfair than a Saturn opposition, even though they are both unfair, because the opposition has a greater awareness about what is going on.

A predominant feature of a Saturn Complex is the issue of fairness and unfairness.

Heavy Saturn complexes are almost always experienced as unfair. This is partly due to the discovery that there is not a logical connection between your merit and what the return is, which feels unfair. It *is* unfair. One of the best ways to deal with Saturn is to understand that some things simply aren't fair. Sorry, "fare" is what you pay to get on the bus. Greek tragedy is a great example of Saturn strategy at work, where the hero or heroine didn't do anything wrong, they just encountered limit conditions beyond their control.

Comment: *They were set up by the Gods.*
Beautiful. They were set up by the Gods. Each of the strategies is like a setup.

Comment: *But you are God and you set it up yourself.*
That is just what I was going to say. I believe the basic human enterprise is the quest for meaning. A model that describes how this works uses the imagery of a person dying, and going before the Lords of Karma. True Saturn, not patriarchal Saturn, and the other planets (or Lords) are all there gathered in counsel. The first thing the person is told is what is on the balance sheet or the ledger, what they owe, and what is owed them. Then a creative negotiation takes place. The person brings to the table what their desires are, what they intend to have happen in the next life, and what their objectives are. The Lords of Karma let them know how much rope they can have. For the sake of an example let's say the person was footloose and fancy-free for lifetimes, (Aries Moon with Aries job in the Aries tribe) out on the trail having adventures, having fun, and doing it extremely well. The Lords of Karma assume this consummate Aries will want to do the same thing again, but maybe this time they would like to check out the Leo or Gemini job in the Aries tribe. However, they are shocked when the Aries adept says, "I am pretty damn bored with that. I have been doing that for a long time. I want to check out being a householder, and I am interested in investigating personal intimacy." The Lords of Karma scratch their heads and say, "Hum, are you really sure about this? You know this is very different from what you have been doing?" Then they consult their records and note that this master of the Aries tribe has accumulated enough merit to investigate this new territory; and they agree to let him or her take on the challenge. However, the Lords of Karma caution and warn them of the potential struggle associated with new, unfamiliar experiences and their Aries background will not give them many tools or clues on how to handle these experiences. The Aries master remains determined, assuring the Lords of Karma they want to take on this challenge and they are looking forward to the change. Then just before going down the chute to incarnate, the Lords of Karma say, "Remember once you are born you must carry out the agreements you have made. It will do you no good to raise your fists to the heavens and tell God you have changed your mind!" This example works in the reverse with a person who has been a householder for a long time and a wonderful loving parent (a master of the Cancer tribe). They also might decide to try something different and unusual, like signing up for the Aquarius tribe where they must learn detachment and cosmic overview. Again, this represents a completely different approach to life from what the Cancer adept has been doing. Both of the above cases represent a major change of gears, and the outer planets describe what strategy is in place to change those gears.

When looking at Saturn from the therapeutic perspective it is useful to know if the client has a Saturn Complex on their natal chart or is going through a Saturn transit, such as Saturn going across their Moon, or squaring their Sun. If the person is in a Saturn transit, or approaching one, you can give them useful information on how to participate with the cycle. These transits usually cause the person to experience a state of depression they can't escape from. In fact, I have found this type of cycle is *intended* to be experienced as depression. It is not a time when you can get out of the depression, uplevel your mood, or escape into the abstract or etheric. Unfortunately, our culture does not train people that there are certain times in a person's life where a depression can be useful. Carl Jung said once, "In an age that has become demythologized, it does not mean the Gods and Goddesses do not still exist. What it means is the only way they can really get our attention, is in our illnesses and our depressions." If you are in a Saturn cycle, pay attention to the interior; address the depression on its own level. There are many people in these cycles squirming around trying to find a solution to getting out of the space they are in. Our culture promotes this escapist attitude by coming up with antidepressant drugs that can sometimes create a violent physical reaction when given during one of these cycles. It is important to give ourselves permission to experience the depression on its own level, and to let it lead us to a greater understanding of ourselves.

Question: *The depression comes from realizing there isn't a reward?*
That's part of it. The other part of it is, in a Saturn cycle the various ways in which we feel good are taken away. During these cycles the brain chemistry doesn't function in the same way as in a more *normal* time; the endorphins and serotonin are not secreted. All the various things we like doing to uplevel our mood, don't work!

Comment: *I have been through a major Saturn transit recently and I really took time out to understand what Saturn means to me, and I feel it helped to put everything into perspective.*
Indeed, yes. Thank you for bringing that up, because I don't want to leave Saturn without bringing in what usually happens at the end of a Saturn cycle. The Saturn cycle, for nine out of ten charts, is about eight or nine months long, if you take into account the retrograde loop of the planet. Saturn moves across the planet, backtracks over it and then comes across it for a third time, which usually takes about eight or nine months. What I have noticed is that by the end of the cycle, in most cases, the most positive useful feature of the initiation happens. This is the point where a person gets clear about something. It is a definition point where something comes into form.

At the beginning of a Saturn cycle you will feel depressed, as if something has to give. You feel yourself becoming increasingly aware of what isn't working in your life, be it your job, your relationship, your lifestyle, where you are living, your outlook on life, your goals and so on. A mythic description of how this works is as follows: You are called before the reviewing board and their job is to test you by asking you what doesn't work in your life. You must answer truthfully and also be willing to get rid of, or change, what doesn't work. Saturn won't let you get away with anything; it really pushes you to look at your life and provides an ideal opportunity to truly see what doesn't work. Then at the end of the cycle, if you have done the work properly and made the necessary changes, you'll be able to clearly pinpoint what *does* work. That's when you declare your intent. That's when you state who you are, what your place on the wheel is, what you are good at, and that's when things will work harmoniously with your original intent. The end of a Saturn cycle is the completion of an alchemical process, where the base elements have been transformed into gold. Saturn crossing the Rising sign (or any angle or planet), could be imagined as a large lead cauldron labeled the Personal Identity Project (the other angles and planets are labeled accordingly). During the process of these nine months the person is caught in the cauldron. They are so bound into it they can't get out of it. Inside the cauldron are all the different elements of the personal identity bubbling and boiling until it is brought to critical mass. There is no escape, but the alchemical process is taking place and the base elements are being transformed into gold. At the end of the cycle the gold is produced. That's when the cauldron vanishes and the person emerges transformed into their mature form. Saturn cycles represent a maturation process where a new level of maturity or development is reached. Because Saturn has a thirty year cycle, Saturn transits are a thirty year development reaching its maturity point.

Question: *It seems like a person could be going through a Saturn transit most of the time?*
If a person has Saturn heavily impacting their natal chart, like Saturn in a grand cross, then transiting Saturn comes around every seven years and trips off the T-square. This results in that person having a lot of initiations involving the Saturn principle.

Question: *What is the orb on a transit?*
One degree.

Question: *You mentioned the difference between oppositions and squares, but not conjunctions.*
A conjunction is a blending together of two or more planets. So, if Saturn conjuncts a planet, it "Saturnizes" that planet. If the Sun is conjunct Saturn, no matter what sign the Sun is in, it's practically like being a Capricorn. If the Sun is conjunct Uranus, no matter what sign the Sun is in, it's practically like being an Aquarian. If the Sun is conjunct Neptune, it's practically like being a Pisces. The quality of the outer planet impacts or overwhelms the Sun or any of the other personal planets it might be conjuncting. Hence, if you have Saturn conjunct any of the personal planets, then built into your script is a dynamic encounter with limit conditions in that area. This means you will probably be a more sober, serious person, with a need to accomplish something, but hopefully you'll get the joke. Because once you get the joke, you will enjoy the process, rather than constantly trying to get rewards based upon your merit, or trying to please the external authority figures.

Question: *Is it inactive for part of the transit?*
No, it is not inactive. The initiation cycle is a window of time.

Question: *So if Saturn is coming back it is active the whole time?*
Indeed it is. Although, the more intense moments may occur when it is within one degree. The transit sets up the parameters of the initiation, creating an initiation window that lasts from the time Saturn (or any one of the outer planets) first enters a one degree orb to the planet or angle, until the last exact conjunction.

Question: *Then on its last pass, once it has passed the exact degree, the initiation is over?*
Yes, I do not have a one-hundred percent opinion on whether it is over on the last pass when it hits the exact degree, or when it gets one degree beyond it. I take creative license on this depending upon the person I am sitting with. If I see they haven't really dealt with it, then I am likely to extend the initiation window to one degree after. However, if the person has been working with it really well, then I use the date it exactly conjuncts that degree for the last time as the graduation point, or the point of completing the cycle.

Saturn as strategy is serious strategy. However, for those people who have figured out how to deal with Saturn in an intelligent way, a Saturn transit represents a time when hard work pays off. This means if we really understood how Saturn works we might only have to work one year in seven. Of course, there are some of us that would work every year anyway, because it's fun. People who have lots of Gemini or Aries, or some other archetypal sign that likes to play, will find this information interesting, because if they worked with the principle correctly then they would only have to be hard working and serious one year out of seven. The catch is it would have to be real seriousness.

URANUS

Uranus strategy falls into the category of being "at the effect of" and operates through uncontrollable, unplannable, unpredictable experiences that have as their intent to bring about change in the areas where a person is stuck. Uranus' job is to act as a monitoring device that checks out where a person has been in a holding pattern, or crystallized, or something has been a certain way for too long. Uranus does not judge good or bad; it just notices what has been in place too long and goes to work changing it. By what means? By whatever it takes! Saturn hits everybody in much the same way by setting up limit conditions, but Uranus is unpredictable. People who are into change, and not into anything that represents conservative type things, or holding onto crystallized patterns, enjoy Uranus. In other words, people who like change, like Uranus strategy.

Question: *You mean they like shocks and surprises?*
Yes, they roll with the punches. The best way to deal with Uranus strategy is to roll with the punches, and trust in the fact that when you do, it is taking you in the direction you need to go. Treat every experience with an open hand. No attachment to anything is possible. If two people are in a relationship and one person has a natal chart loaded

with Uranus strategy and the other person has a natal chart loaded with Capricorn or Saturn (which means they like commitment, stability, attachment, and consistency), the two innate personalities are contrary to each other. The only responsibly oriented people that can handle an encounter with a Uranus type are those who thrive on polarity.

Question: *Is this because one type is predictable, and the other type is totally unpredictable?*

Right. The basic nature of the Uranian type is unpredictable. When the stable, predictable, reliable, and consistent person is hit with a Uranus cycle, chances are they won't enjoy it much. During any Uranus cycle be prepared to change habits of twenty years. The generational Uranus opposition cycle that occurs around age thirty-eight or thirty-nine is one of the most important cycles we encounter. I have often thought it might be interesting to do a statistical study on how many people come for their first astrology reading in that cycle, or how many people go into to therapy at that time.

Question: *Would you comment on men who are stuck in their Saturn role and how a Uranus cycle affects them?*

My experience is based upon the readings I do. Seventy-five to eighty percent of my clientele are women. They often come for a reading during their Uranus opposing Uranus cycle and tell me about their relationships with the men in their lives. What I have heard from them leads me to conclude that women are more likely to shift in a Uranus cycle, and more likely to do something positive with the cycle. Men are more likely to fight against the cycle and resist change. However, just image the number of men impacted by this cycle that don't have anyone to talk to about it, or don't have the tools to deal with the kinds of changes it generates. It is intriguing, because as recently as thirty years ago the majority of the people who even talked about this were men. This is what generated all the stories in the culture about men who reached a certain age, hit their mid-life crisis, and then took up with younger women. For a long time those were the most common stories, but now it has shifted. These days, when women hit this cycle they are making rapid leaps forward in their own evolution and their own spiritual path. All of a sudden many of these women end up feeling younger than they felt when they were twenty. Often this is when they get into intense physical fitness, or go through a "young" stage where they are no longer interested in the man in their life. This is becoming a common scenario. Women seem to be growing at a faster rate than men, especially in these cycles. At least that is what I am hearing from the people I am working with these days, although, I am sure the male scenarios are still taking place.

Uranus is part of the strategy of evolution and change. My experience with looking at charts and what people are reporting as their experience has led me to conclude that Uranus cycles are not really as difficult as Saturn or Pluto cycles right now. What Uranus forces upon a person is a time when they have to flow with whatever happens. They have to let go, and allow the changes to take place, otherwise the events that occur get ever more dramatic until the person does let go. I find Uranus cycles are only catastrophic if a person holds on too tenaciously. The purpose of Uranus, as with any of the strategies, is to take a person towards their original life intent. For example, a person might have on their original script, as part of their original dream, to be philosophical, contemplative, and inward looking. If they have never had an opportunity in their life to address the inner, because of an intense Saturn Complex, or for any number of other perfectly valid reasons, when they reach a Uranus cycle they might end up being run over by a truck, and spending six months in traction. Now they find themselves forced to address the original life dreams, because the events have forced it. Another example is a person who has on their original script the intent to travel, to be an adventurer and explorer, to see the world, but numerous reasons have prevented it, such as no money, not enough time, or no one to travel with. When a Uranus cycle hits they win the lottery, or they meet someone with lots of money who wants to take them on a trip around the world. Uranus produces unexpected, unplanned-for events that are designed to take you in the direction you had originally intended to go.

Comment: *I feel the Uranus cycle I am in right now is doing that for me. With my Aquarius Moon, and Venus and Mars in Aquarius it is forcing me to look at the shadow in myself, feel every feeling, and realize how many times I have had a lot of rage and I didn't know it. I feel like the gift of it is diving into it and connecting with my passion. I am getting so much energy from the rage that I feel I could almost punch my way through a wall or move a mountain. It is empowering and that connects me to my core that is passionate and alive. I think it is that process that brings a person to the point where they get what their life purpose is. So now I have more energy to do the things I want to do, because I have addressed the rage and the changes that are taking place in those other cycles.*

So from that perspective, what a Uranus cycle can do, in breaking up the crystallization, is get things moving, create action, and produce change.

Question: *What does Taurus Rising and Uranus in Gemini in the first house indicate?* How close is Uranus to the ascendant?

Answer: *Pretty close, about five and a half degrees.*
It is not close enough to be a major Uranus complex. If Uranus was less than five degrees from the Ascendant, and the closer to the Ascendant the more intense the complex, then it would be considered a major Uranus Complex. However, when Uranus transits that area of the chart it may involve unexpected developments that force you to pay attention to the needs of Taurus Rising. If Uranus was angular with Taurus Rising or Uranus merged with that point, then we'd get an extremely unique, different-from-normal, eccentric, unusual, version of Taurus Rising; like a flamboyant, avant-garde sense of self.

A therapist, working with someone in a Uranus cycle such as Uranus going over their Sun, or in their Uranus opposition, can be certain what the person is going through is not a *normal* time in their life. They may feel they are *not* in control of their life. This is useful information when counseling a couple who have had a stable relationship for ten years and now one of them is acting in strange, bizarre, and unpredictable ways. The erratic behavior of the partner going through a Uranus cycle is not a reflection on the partner who is not going through that cycle, and the behavior is not going to last forever. Now, if a person starts a relationship with someone in a Uranus cycle, or one of the other mid-life crisis cycles, and the relationship survives the cycle, the person who was not in the Uranus cycle will observe the person who was change before their eyes. That's why it is difficult to formalize, in a structured way, any new relationship during an outer planet initiation cycle, because these cycles create a situation that is not in *normal* time.

Question: *How long does a Uranus cycle last?*
When combined with the retrograde loop it lasts about a year.

NEPTUNE

Neptune is the planet of the dream and the vision operating through events and circumstances that create confusion and induce an identity crisis. The purpose of Neptune strategy is to get a person to tune in on a transcendent level to the original dreams and visions, but this strategy cannot be successful unless a person is willing to let go of what they think they know, who they think they are, and where they think they are going. Therefore, the confusion or identity crisis is intended to bring about a change in the way a person sees themselves and their place in the world. Ultimately, it is intended to reveal a new level of their personal vision and new possibilities they may choose.

As with depression, our culture does not believe there is anything useful or okay about an identity crisis. Instead, the dominant Saturn principle operating these days says a person must know who they are at all times. What I am suggesting is, that during a Neptune cycle it's okay to *not* know anything. Many traditional cultures understood this. The Australian Aborigines have the walk-about. The Native Americans go on vision quests. In the most extreme version of the vision quest the person goes out and says, "I know nothing, send me a vision." Even the chiefs and shamans do vision quests. The point to understand with Neptune is the more empty a person can be the better. It corresponds to the principle of completely emptying the water from the glass, so there is room for fresh, new water in the glass. This is not an easy thing to do. So what we need are support groups for people dealing with these initiation cycles.

Question: *Is it helpful to hang out with a whole lot of other people who don't have a clue?*
What is helpful is to know at least you are not alone. The support of the group helps to give a person permission to participate with what is happening. (Otherwise, when a person is in a Neptune cycle there is still a lot of pressure on them from the culture to continue to perform at the same level.) Can you imagine what it would be like in corporate America if they kept the horoscopes of their employees on file, and when a person went through Neptune square Neptune they were given a six-month sabbatical with pay? What a wonderful opportunity that would create for a person to really tune in to the intent of the Neptune cycle, while providing the space that would allow them to fully refresh their vision.

The misunderstanding of the intent of a Neptune cycle is similar to the whole dilemma of what happened with women and their menstrual cycle. The pressure from today's culture says there should be no difference for women during that time; but in the past, women had command of those days. They did not do business as usual. Instead, it was a time to refresh and go back to their roots. This is a mystery beyond what I can put any content into, because I don't know what was actually done in those three to five days, but it was no doubt different in different cases.

Comment: The other women of the tribe took the children and the duties, so the woman could go off to the Moon lodge to be by herself or with other women in the same cycle.
Yes, the culture was supportive of that sacred time. The purpose of those few days was for the women to get in tune with the Earth. Some were meditating; others may have gone through a chaotic process of some kind such as raging and screaming, or whatever. The important thing was, the women were in control and it was their own business what they did during those days.

Comment: We hear the women were kicked out of the village during those days, and we think, "Oh how terrible," but it wasn't necessarily a terrible thing.
What I am talking about is a time when the menstrual cycle was a sacrament controlled by the women. There wasn't any fear associated with it and it wasn't a forced segregation. As patriarchy took over it became less and less controlled by the women, until it became the situation we have today, where the woman's menstrual cycle is no longer honored as a sacred time by the society as a whole. Rather it has been thought of as more of a *curse* to be conquered (with drugs when necessary) so women can continue to perform at the same level as every other day of the month. It is time now to re-empower these mysteries in new ways appropriate to our times. The best and most useful way to participate with a Neptune cycle is to give yourself permission to not know, to not have all the answers, to be okay with feeling confused. When people give themselves permission to be confused in the right cycle, they are cooperating with the strategy. I've often thought about marketing a T-shirt for people going through a Neptune cycle that says: *I Am Confused.* Underneath that it says: *But This Is The Time In My Life When I Get To Be Confused!* The back says: *Confusion Can Be A Very High State!*

Question: How long does a Neptune cycle last?
A year to a year-and-a-half depending on the retrograde loop. A Neptune cycle takes place whenever transiting Neptune forms a hard aspect to any of the personal planets, or when Neptune reaches its square to itself around age forty or forty-one. For most people this mid-life crisis cycle comes right on the heels of the Uranus opposition. The Uranus opposition brings about change, while Neptune provides an opportunity to bring in the new visions and new dreams to direct the energy Uranus has changed. Following Neptune is the Saturn opposition that helps to bring into form the changes and visions brought about by the Uranus and Neptune cycles. Ultimately, these cycles are intended to move a person in the direction of their life purpose. That's why knowledge of how to consciously participate with these cycles is important.

A Neptune Complex is symbolized by Neptune in hard aspect to any personal aspects, such as Neptune conjunct the Sun, opposing the Moon, or squaring Mars. Let's illustrate this by looking at a sixteen or seventeen-year-old who has a strong Neptune Complex. This youngster has been called in to the high school guidance counselor, because it is time for him or her to declare what they plan to do when they leave high school. The pressing question is whether they plan to go to college or trade school, or get a job right away? If their counselor has access to the student's natal chart and they know the student has a strong Neptune Complex, the counselor could assure the student that, contrary to the pressure from their family, peers, and school to state their purpose, they really don't have to know the exact answer to that question right now. The counselor might further explain to the student that being a visionary is a strong part of who they are, and life will continuously expand in front of them, and their direction or purpose may not be clearly defined for quite some time. In fact, for them there really is no advantage in narrowing it down so much. Then the counselor volunteers to assist the student in writing an answer designed to satisfy those who want one.

This is a loving and tolerant way of approaching a Neptune Complex that is not realistically supported in our Saturn-based culture. However, let's imagine this type of scenario did take place. Ultimately, what would happen to the young students with strong Neptune? Eventually, due to the nature of how Saturn cycles operate, there would come a time when life presented them with the necessity of making a concrete choice. That's when they would *get* what it is they were to do and then they'd commit to doing it.

Most people with a Neptune Complex on their natal chart can relate to the following experience: They are lying in bed at night unable to sleep, because all the talents, all the abilities, all the skills, and all the things they can choose to do are running through their minds faster and faster, but they can't figure it out. It just does not compute. The best strategy for dealing with this dilemma is to *NOT* try to figure it out. Let it go even more. Don't try to compel the beauty and the value of how Neptune works, because Neptune keeps expanding the vision into new territory, if we are willing to cooperate with it.

Question: Does it help a Neptune person to meditate?
Yes. People with strong Neptune can use meditation to further expand and promote the way Neptune is intended to work best.

Question: I have a Pisces Moon and Neptune opposing it. I assume that the Neptune effect is a lifelong process?
Yes. However, there is an additional factor to consider when it is associated with the Moon. It is possible to do a whole class on how the outer planet strategy affects the Moon, but remember, if Neptune aspects the Moon it is with reference to the lineage. While Saturn and Pluto effects on the lineage (Moon) are drastic in their severity, because they disallow the talents and abilities of the Moon through violation or invalidation, Neptune's effect on the Moon is more amorphous. This is especially true if the person has a Moon position that is not validated by the current culture. Neptune

aspecting the Moon does not invalidate or violate the Moon; it obscures it. This is probably the only example where a person's personality traits are not necessarily like the Moon. It seems to work through a diffusion process, so a person might not know until they are thirty, or forty, or more, what the reality of their lineage is. I have seen this happen quite often with women who have fire Moons (Sag, Aries or Leo), and Neptune is aspecting it. These are cases where the qualities of the Moon rarely show up until later in life when an outer planet transit acts as a catalyst to trigger the reclamation process.

Now, back to the Pisces Moon aspected by Neptune. This case represents a sub-theme, or a behind-the-scenes base tone on who you are. It might be an extremely refined empathic quality, or dreaminess of some kind, but to what extent you own the Pisces Moon is another feature of the analysis. It depends upon whether the Pisces Moon is something you are addicted to and holding onto, or whether it is an area where you need to reclaim your power with reference to the current life intent.

Question: The transiting Uranus/Neptune conjunction happening now (in 1993) is squaring my Neptune opposition. Does that mean everything is breaking apart and I can't even see what is going on clearly, besides?
Yes. A portion of the population born between 1950 and 1956 can have three of the mid-life crisis cycles occurring at the same time, and they have those cycles impacting on the degrees of when the Uranus/Neptune conjunction was exact. It is almost impossible to have this take place in any other generation. There is good news and bad news about this. The bad news is those people are being hit with several life-changing cycles all at once. The good news is they burn through all of the mid-life crisis cycles a lot faster.

Comment: Somehow that doesn't sound like good news to me.
Actually it is, because the experience of the Uranus, Neptune, and Pluto cycle in the space of a few years creates an initiate ready to contribute to the planet, based on their profound experiences with these cycles. Many other generations don't even complete these cycles until they reach their sixties and seventies. Some generations don't reach Pluto square Pluto until they are seventy or eighty years old.

Question: So it kind of kicks you upstairs?
Yes, in a way. What we might ask is if this is all really happening or is it inside the great pyramid? Due to the intensity of the cycles we can assume it is inside the great pyramid, because these are the most powerful set of transits a person will ever go through in their life. As far as Neptune is concerned the intent is unknowable; experiences are designed to empty the glass out so new intent, new direction, new vision fills the glass. The best way to participate with the Neptune cycle is to give yourself total permission to be precisely in the space you are in, including feeling confused and uncertain. This requires trust in the process and faith that it will all sort itself out later.

Question: *What was the conjunction you were referring to in your last example?*

I was referring to the Uranus/Neptune conjunction of 1993. Uranus has an orbit of about eighty-four years before it returns to its starting point. Usually around age thirty-eight or thirty-nine Uranus reaches the opposition point, or Uranus opposing Uranus. Neptune has an orbit of one hundred and sixty-four years. It reaches its one-fourth point, or square, around age forty or forty-one. Saturn has a twenty-nine to thirty year orbit, and reaches its opposition point, or Saturn opposing Saturn, around age forty-four. This sequence of generational cycles from age thirty-eight to age forty-four are called the mid-life crisis cycles. One generation out of eight or nine has the Pluto generational cycle within the framework of these other three cycles. Pluto has an orbit of two hundred and forty-eight years. It reaches its one-fourth point or square, one generation out of eight, as early as age thirty-five to age forty-four. That means we are the Pluto generation, and there is something special and significant about that.

People born between 1954 and 1973 are the ones who experience Pluto square Pluto around age thirty-five to thirty-seven, even before the Uranus opposition. The Uranus opposition is the cycle usually associated with the beginning of the mid-life crisis cycles. I was born in 1948, and I had the Pluto and Neptune generational cycles happening at the same time. Another large group of people have their generational Pluto and Uranus cycles happening together. There are a couple of years where it is possible for all three cycles to happen simultaneously. Those born in the early 1940's had Pluto square Pluto occurring at the same time as their Saturn opposition. Those born from mid 1946 to mid 1948 experienced the generational Saturn opposition with an opposing Saturn/Neptune conjunction. In 1947 Saturn and Pluto were conjunct. This symbolizes a group that has taken on more karma than just their personal karma, and 1992 was their front lines year. People who have come for readings born in those years have stories of the most extreme scenarios I have ever heard describing the mid-life crisis.

All the principles of the strategy (the outer planets and their aspects to the inner planets on the natal chart) are applicable to any outer planet transit in hard aspect to a person's inner natal planet, and to all of the mid-life crisis cycles. Depending on the sign and degree of the sign on the natal chart, an outer planet initiation cycle can occur at any time in a person's life. There are three different types of cycles that impact our lives. First, there are the personal cycles that occur when a transiting planet hits something on the natal chart, and that can happen at any age. Second, there are generational cycles that happen when a person reaches a certain age, such as Uranus opposing Uranus. Third, there are collective cycles that have to do with what is happening with the planets in the sky at any given time; for example, the Uranus/Neptune conjunction of 1993, or the Pluto square Saturn cycle happening the same year. The collective cycles have a symbolic meaning for the planet as a whole, and can be seen reflected in worldwide events such as the fall of the Berlin wall, or the breakup of the Soviet Union.

PLUTO

The intent of Pluto strategy is to have a person go through something they don't know is going to happen before it happens; it cannot be prepared for or avoided. Pluto represents the descent into the underworld, the confrontation with the shadow, facing the deepest fears, and going into the darkness. In this case, darkness doesn't mean bad or evil. It refers to what has been repressed or denied, and Pluto's job is to call up the experiences that get us to look at these issues.

There are different kinds of initiation cycles, but they all have as their intent to move us in the direction we originally intended to go. An Aquarius, Sagittarius, or Gemini initiation sets up circumstances that are designed to expand the context of our experiences. They may involve learning a meditation technique to become more detached, going into meta-enjoyment, sending out one's eagle, and so on. Scorpio or Pluto strategy takes us into the unknowable, into chaos. In Greek thought, there is a statement that says, "Out of chaos comes the world." Chaos is defined by Webster's as: "Any condition or place of total disorder or confusion, or the disordered state of unformed matter and infinite space, supposed by religious cosmological views to have existed prior to the ordered universe." When a person is exclusively in logos, in clarity and detachment, they have not yet been in chaos. They have never even been truly on Earth, or fully engaged in third dimensional reality! Pluto represents the underworld initiation. The end result of a Pluto cycle is empowerment, but the initial strategy operates through disempowerment, or *The Acute Perception Of What Is Missing!* As a rule, a person goes through an experience that calls out what is most important to them by creating the acute perception of its lack, or circumstances completely beyond their control.

Similar to a Saturn cycle, Pluto cycles are often experienced as unfair, but a Pluto cycle in structural form is completely different. Pluto is the law of life, the law of nature. Saturn, on the other hand, is about human law. Pluto is organic, a natural process like "mother-right". A mother animal, with her babies, who is under attack, attains super natural powers to protect her children. This phenomenon is a Pluto effect. Pluto is also impersonal; it doesn't care about personal feelings at all. If we apply Pluto to the collective process of the Earth, we see the Earth has her own rhythms and cycles. What happens when human beings are messing up the planet? Pluto is not concerned with the personal feelings of someone who might be killed, injured, or lose their home in flood or earthquake or some other dramatic event. Pluto is concerned with the empowerment of natural law. When the Earth is out of balance, Pluto's job is to restore the balance, regardless of how that affects any individuals in the process.

Comment: Like in the midwest where they are spraying all the chemicals in the farming areas and then the Earth comes along and floods that off, as if to say, "Get that off my back! The earth is trying to survive and she doesn't care if there are humans living there or not, she is going to survive.
Yes. That's true. One of my favorite Pluto stories happened to a friend of mine at Mount Shasta. My friend liked to go to Squaw Valley every summer for two or three months to

write and meditate. It is a beautiful valley, almost at timberline. Over the years he noticed more and more people were trashing the meadow, and he felt he had lost the tranquility that was there. This feeling expanded into a concern about what was happening to the Earth. He decided to use prayers and meditation to ask the mountain what was happening. The vision that came to him from the mountain surprised him. The communication he received from the mountain was, "Don't worry, I have seen this happen before. Humans will come and go, and I go on and on. Don't worry about me, worry about yourselves."

Of all the mythical writings dealing with Pluto initiations I have come across, my favorite is Inanna and Ereshkigal. This is a Sumerian myth about Inanna, the queen of heaven, and Ereshkigal, the ruler of the underworld. Inanna is the most honored, most powerful, most loved of all women. When Ereshkigal husband dies, Inanna is obligated to pay her respects to her sister in the underworld. Inanna is forced to go through seven horrible destructurings during her descent into Erishikegal's domain. Everything is taken away from her, including all of her clothes and jewels. When she reaches the depths of the underworld Ereshkigal kills her and has her skewered on a spit. Inanna is eventually rescued and brought back to life, but there is no apparent logic as to why this happens to her, except that it is an initiation. As patriarchy took over, this story became the story of Pluto and Persephone, although the message is still ultimately about the cycle of death, rebirth, and transformation.

If you meet a person who is in a Pluto cycle, you will know they have just gone through, or are about to go through, something totally beyond their control, something that will challenge the deepest core of their being, in the area of life where their most important issues are. Most people need help understanding the process they are in. For example, one of the features of a Pluto initiation is the experience of deep loss ranging from physical losses to loss of beliefs and ideals. It is important to know how to grieve these losses. Women, at least, have a whole body of literature out there on how to deal with this, and are usually better able to deal with this grief than men are. When I have spoken to men's groups, I have found a lot of men are going through this now, and they are often surprised to discover other men are going through the same thing. In my talks I describe the experiences I have found to be the most common among men. For example, a man's experience might manifest as a situation where they love someone totally with all their heart, and it doesn't work out. This experience triggers their descent into the lower world. If men don't have the support system or the mythical substructure for how to understand this phenomenon, what do they do? If they attempt to deal with the situation without feeling it, they risk developing cancer, or serious heart problems, such as a coronary. The nature of a Pluto cycle requires a person to feel whatever their feelings are by producing melodramatic events beyond their control, so they have something to feel. That's why Pluto is a cycle that cannot be glamorized.

So far in all the readings I have done where I have explained the Pluto material, only once has someone expressed some sense of joy with it. This was a guy who had five or six planets in Scorpio. When I was telling him all the stories about death and rebirth and regeneration and shamanism, his eyes started to twinkle and he said, "Oh yes, that must be why my motto is, 'Today is a good day to die!'" If a person has Pluto conjunct the Sun, or Pluto square the Sun on their natal chart, it means they have made an agreement with the universe to have a regular pattern in their life of having the rug pulled out from under them, or just when they think everything is secure and together, they lose it all. Upon hearing this most people say, "Yes, Yes, that's my story, damn it, when is it going to end?" I have to say to them that it will never end until they *get* that this is the medicine they carry. This is not an aberration, it is not something a person guts their way through, hoping someday it will go away, but there does come a point, if a person incorporates these teachings within themselves, when they are no longer at the effect of any more melodramatic experiences designed to get their attention.

Question: *I think I was in a Pluto cycle when my mother died, but I have two brothers and three sisters, who weren't all necessarily in a Pluto transit at that time. Yet, I am sure they felt it was an overwhelming, uncontrollable situation.*
In my Pluto square Pluto cycle nothing happened to my parents, so there is not a direct one-to-one thing there. If we looked at all their horoscopes there may have been some other event in their charts corresponding to what they went through, however, since it happened to you in your Pluto cycle, then that creates the context for your reaction to the event. The events that occur in Pluto square Pluto are specifically formulated to get your attention. What happens is whatever it takes to wrest control away from your security system, and to get you to totally feel your feelings. Ultimately Pluto is a shamanic aspect. The definition of shamanism is death by intent, and a Pluto cycle is intended to be a cycle of death and rebirth.

Question: *Why have you said people should make a list of the worst that can happen for their Pluto cycle?*
In an effort to help people prepare for their Pluto cycle I tell them to make a list, whether it is in meditation, or prayer, or an actual written list, of what they feel is the worst that could happen to them. This flies in the face of a lot of the New Age strategy that says a person should always think positive thoughts. For those individuals in a Pluto cycle, or for those who are preparing for a Pluto cycle, making a list of the worst that can happen calls out the deepest fears, addresses them, and deals with them on their own level. What's wild about doing this process is that the thing that usually happens is something that didn't make the list! That's why Pluto transits are a curious paradox, because you can't really prepare for it. However, I still think it's useful to make that list.

The dominant feeling in the first phase of a Pluto cycle is powerlessness. Powerlessness frequently causes people to feel depressed. Similar to the depressed feeling found in a Saturn cycle. If a person has a Saturn and a Pluto cycle happening at the same time, it sets the stage for one of the most devastatingly difficult initiations imaginable. A Pluto cycle forces a person to deal with the shadow. For example, artists in a Pluto cycle often find themselves doing something similar to vast Heironymous Bosch canvases of entrails and demons of the lower world. A musician in a Pluto cycle may begin to do blues dirges. I know two New Age musicians in Hawaii who did the sweet Aquarian songs of love and light and inspiration, but when a Pluto cycle hit them, for the duration of the cycle they were unable to do their usual songs. Often these types of musicians are so attached to the sweet songs they completely stop performing during that time. The point of Pluto is to engage the dark force, the demons, and the deepest fears. Call them out. Jacob wrestling with the Angel is a biblical story that deals with this issue. The important thing is to concretize whatever the dark force is. Ask it, "What do you want of me?" Objectify it in some way, dialogue with it, but do not try to get out of it. This means Pluto and Saturn cycles share another similar feature that requires engaging them on their own level.

A curious thing happens at the end of a Pluto initiation. It's as if the changes begin at the cellular level. What was initially experienced as powerlessness shifts into a whole new kind of strength and power. It's as if the energy is coming up from the center of the Earth, energizing and strengthening the entire being. However, this only happens if the person has engaged the shadow on its own level and truly dealt with it. In Jungian psychology this is referred to as "the incorporation of the shadow material." The shadow side of our being is whatever has been disowned in the underworld, or subconscious. It is the repressed and denied areas of our awareness. Good or bad judgments are not useful when dealing with the shadow; rather the idea is to acknowledge what our own repressed energy is and then release it. People who have horoscopes that are mainly fire and air, with a detached kind of objective trip going, don't have any tools to deal with a Pluto transit. That's why we need Pluto support groups, too. I am even more serious about this one, because we now have a whole generation of people going through their Pluto cycle together. Wouldn't it be great if we were able to receive support and validation for our experiences from others going through the same thing? In addition, it might help to give us better clues on how to best participate with the Pluto journey.

Question: *Yes, but isn't it true that during a Pluto cycle all your friends think you are a jerk and don't even want to be around you?*
Not necessarily. For those with Libra Rising where their greatest issue is being liked by other people that might be true. What occurs in a Pluto cycle depends on what a person's most important issues are. Two things happened to me in my Pluto cycle. First, I thought the relationship I had been waiting for my whole life had finally arrived, and it turned out to be a hoax. The second thing was also in relationship to my Libra Sun and Libra Rising. Over the most intense six-month period of the cycle, literally everyone in my life that I cared about told me what a jerk I was. There was nothing I could do about it. When I tried to explain it was a misunderstanding, no one would listen. I experienced it as an airtight setup and I was forced to handle it. Six to nine months later when the cycle was over, my true friends apologized saying, "Daniel I don't know what I was going through there, but you will forgive me, won't you?"

People with Pluto strategy on their original horoscope, such as Pluto in square, opposition or conjunction with the Sun, Moon, Mercury, Venus, or Mars, are making an agreement with the universe to carry that medicine. It doesn't mean their life is constantly in the underworld, what it means is they are the ones who get to assist others with the knowledge of how to participate with the initiation. Therefore, those who carry strong Pluto are in a position to make the greatest contribution to those who, because of a Pluto transit or complex, are in the underworld and haven't gotten a handle on it yet. This is because the person with strong Pluto really understands the journey through the underworld.

The outer planets (Saturn, Uranus, Neptune and Pluto) by natal aspect or transit are the best indicators for knowing what a person is going through. The most important thing to remember is to give ourselves, and those around us, permission to be as we really are. We all created this multifaceted dance and the worst thing we can do is be in denial or judgment against ourselves, or others, for how we really feel or for how we really are. This principle is especially true when we are in initiation cycles. If Neptune operates through confusion so the new visions can come through, and Uranus pushes us to let go of outmoded habits so we can grow and change, and Pluto overwhelms us into transformation, we can cooperate with the intent by giving ourselves permission to be conscious of the process.

Comment: Someone told me you can't take back your power until you have really felt all the rage you have ever felt against everybody in your life in every situation. At that point you have some fuel going and you can really start using it to create what you want instead of being frustrated that you didn't create what you wanted, or feeling frustrated because you let others talk you out of creating what you wanted.
I agree with that. People are often afraid that if they take their power back they will become a monster, but the truth is they become complete. The bottom line is there can be no judgments good or bad about any archetype or strategy. There are thousands of astrology books that seem to be fond of making dualistic judgments. Even if they don't say a position is good or bad, it is written in such a way to make a person feel that some positions are flawed, or not healthy, or not strong. I think that is a dangerous and damaging approach. All astrological positions are equally valid. Yes, each archetype has its downside, or shadow side, when it's not given a healthy opportunity to fully express itself, but when each archetype has a healthy means of expression; they are all valid and important. We can't be truly free unless we know all the possibilities, and understand the full spectrum in a nonjudgmental approach. I am only judgmental against those who don't agree with that statement! (Not really--that's a little humor there.) The first principle of the new astrology, and all of life for that matter, is we must be tolerant of all the approaches to life that have heart and integrity.

Comment: So the initiation cycles are leading you to your true heart's desire and putting you right in touch with that.
Yes, all scripts are intended to work. No script is above and beyond the call of duty.

Question: *No matter how many quincunxes you have?*
There are many different strategies and some of us have more melodramatic ones than others. Some of us have set up more provocative challenges, but they are still intended to lead a person to the new territory.

There are millions of possibilities. For example, using the astrological model of twelve archetypes, then multiplying that times twelve tribes (Moon) and twelve mystery schools (Rising sign) gives us 144 possible paths for being human. Then we must multiply the 144 paths times the twelve masculine and feminine archetypes (of the Mars and the Venus). When we multiply 144 by 24 that gives us 3,456 possibilities. When you include the outer planet strategy along with the Sun, Jupiter, Mercury, and the Nodes of the Moon there are even more possibilities too numerous to count.

Question: *So if we look at the Rising sign as the destination point, then is it on you to make all your planets happy by making sure they are all serving the Rising sign, because if they are serving the Moon it is just an old record and there is no magic?*
Yes, there is the regressive approach and the progressive approach. All the planets need to be fed. Imagine we are giving a great banquet and there are places set at the table for all the Gods and Goddesses. Mars shows up. Mercury shows up. They all show up and there is a place set for all them. For a demonstration about how the drama might play out let's say Saturn is conjunct Mars. So, Mars is showing up in rags frustrated and angry. If anything is directed at the Mars energy that is seemingly judgmental, Mars will want to overturn the table, and scream, "Damn you, I no longer want to do what you are telling me to do!"

Comment: *That's why it is important to check in with all of your planets and notice what their needs are.*
Yes, that goes back to what we discussed about the internal dialogue between the Moon (the old Goddess) and Venus (the new Goddess) or the Moon (the old God) and Mars (the new God). The imagery here is of your central self inviting all of its component parts to the banquet, and your job is to see to it that each part is properly fed.

Comment: *And our new project is the Rising sign, so the challenge is to figure out how all the planets (or parts) work to fulfill the intent of that mystery school.*
That's right, along with the other angles of the chart.

A SHAMANIC LOOK AT RELOCATION CHARTS

Question: *Could you explain how relocation charts work?*

I agree that bringing relocation astrology into common understanding and usage today is one of the major breakthroughs happening in astrology. Jim Lewis with his Astrocartography and other astrologers working with relocation astrology, have come up with something quite remarkable that has made a major contribution. However, I have personally felt dissatisfied with some of the interpretations that are rendered by those officially associated with Astrocartography. To me, the approach is too traditional, and does not speak to the evolutionary model of astrology that I am sharing with you. Certainly there is value in looking at relocation charts and using them to a person's benefit, but I am finding other principles are emerging on how to use relocation astrology that are worth looking into.

The simplest way to create a relocation chart is to use the date, time and time zone of the natal chart, and simply plug in the new coordinates (latitude and longitude) of the new location. If you are using a computer atlas, you will need to remember to readjust the time zone to the natal time zone, if it changes. For example, if the person's natal chart is MST (Mountain Standard Time) and they are relocating to the east coast and the time zone is EST (Eastern Standard Time) be sure to keep the time zone at MST, but use the new coordinates. Some chart programs like Solar Fire will automatically compute the adjusted time zone for you. This gives you a chart with new angles, but all the planets stay at the same degrees, and that is how you know it is the right relocation chart.

For example, I was born at 7:07 AM Atlanta, Georgia. If I want to relocate to Los Angeles (three time zones away), I put in my birthdate, October 10, 1948, the coordinates for Los Angeles, and use 7:07 AM Eastern Standard Time. This generates a horoscope with the planets having precisely the same signs and degrees as the planets on my natal chart. For example, my natal Sun is 17Libra05 (17 degrees and 05 minutes of Libra or ☉ 17♎05) on my Atlanta natal chart. Every relocation chart for me all over the planet has my Sun at 17Libra05 (☉17♎05). The angles are what changes on the relocation chart. How far a person moves away from their original birthplace determines how much of a shift occurs with the angles. My Los Angeles relocation chart changes the Rising Sign, and the Midheaven, and all the intermediate house cusps, depending on which house system is used. Shamanic Astrology places great importance on the angles of the chart, especially the Rising sign and the Midheaven. That's why when I look at a relocation chart for someone the first thing I look at is the Rising Sign and the Midheaven. This tells me if there has been a shift in emphasis on the fundamental mystery school of that person's life.

It is important to remember the natal chart takes precedence over the relocation chart. If a person has Libra Rising on their natal chart they will be Libra Rising for their whole life, no matter where they are. However, different locations can emphasize different areas of the natal chart, and there might be times in a person's life when they would benefit from a location that stimulates or activates a specific area of their natal chart.

I found this was true for me when I moved to Hawaii. I have Libra Rising from the east coast all the way to the Arizona/New Mexico border. In Tucson I have twenty-nine degrees Virgo Rising, and I am Virgo Rising all the way to the west coast. The only place in America I have Scorpio Rising is in northern Maine. In Hawaii I have Leo Rising. Around age thirty-seven, during Saturn square Saturn, I was facing a major crisis. I had been laid off from my systems analyst computer programming job, and I had no idea what to do next in my life. I no longer cared about the work I had been doing, but I hadn't yet established my astrology career, either. I didn't know if I could make a living just doing astrology. During this time I moved to Hawaii (there I have Leo Rising) where all the doors opened for me and I came into my power as an astrologer. Everywhere I went I was running into people who knew me. In Hawaii I became a well-known astrologer and had a taste of celebrity status. I felt like I was always on stage and could never rest or relax, due in part to Pluto conjunct on my relocated Leo Ascendant. This relocation is a classic example of good news and bad news. The good news was that I came into my power as an astrologer, so it was a useful and needed experience. The bad news was that over time I discovered I didn't enjoy my celebrity status much at all. This was partly due to the experience of the elimination of my personal life, so my Libra Rising wasn't getting fulfilled there. After seven years of living in Hawaii, I finally realized I had to move.

In Tucson I have twenty-nine degrees Virgo Rising, which is the most comprehensive development of Virgo. Virgo Rising indicates a place where the sacred work is magnificent and wonderful, and that has truly been my experience. Tucson has been a marvelous place for my work. Just the right number of people came through for personal sessions, and I had more phone readings than I could possibly handle. Also, with the help of Carolyn, the book I wanted to write for several years got written. However, my natal Libra Rising was not fully activated in this area, either.

Debby, my wife, has Cancer Rising on her original chart. We are both from the East Coast. Debby's natal chart has no water on it except for Cancer Rising, but in the west she is Gemini Rising or all fire and air, so she feels dried out. There is no earth or water ground for her here.

These examples help to show how a person is affected by relocating when a different Rising sign or a different Midheaven is in place. Another example is Carolyn's husband, Jeff. He has an interesting relocation story. He was born in Germany with Scorpio Rising. In Tucson, Jeff has twenty-nine degrees Cancer Rising, which is the most comprehensively well-developed mystery school point for family and stability on the home and roots path. It is only in the Southwest all the way to the West Coast that he has Cancer Rising. He lived most of his young adult life in Colorado where he has Leo Rising. In Colorado he developed an identity that corresponded to Leo Rising. He was popular, well liked and known for being a lady's man. None of his friends or any of the other people who knew him there would have predicted that Jeff would choose the path of being a family man, raising four children, happily married, and enjoying his role as a husband and father. That just didn't fit the image they had of Jeff.

When looking at the relocation chart I look at both the Midheaven and the Rising sign to check out what mysteries are being emphasized. For example, in Asheville, North Carolina area, I have Libra Rising but my Midheaven is in the last degree of Cancer, and if I go slightly further east to Charlottesville, Virginia or on toward the coast, I have Leo on the Midheaven, even though my rising sign is still Libra. Leo on the Midheaven suggests a more dynamic powerful impact in my career. Cancer on the Midheaven suggests a close-knit group of family-type people around me, without the celebrity influence suggested by Leo on the Midheaven. This is another example of how to use the relocation information when choosing a place to live.

Question: *I had an Astrocartography chart done and it seemed to follow some sort of lay lines. Coming through Tucson was a Saturn line, and in the Oregon area I had a Pluto line.*

What they are charting is the angularity of the planets or whether they are close to the Midheaven or the Ascendant, and that is definitely on the right track as far as what a person looks for in doing a relocation chart. Shamanic Astrology is archetype-driven and based on the angles of the chart. Astrocartography is based on the angularity and is useful, but it doesn't take into account the actual sign energy of the angles. The Astrocartography chart does show where the sign for the angle changes from one to the next. It is only saying whether a planet is angular, without reference to what sign the Midheaven and Ascendant is in.

The principle of how Astrocartography works could be likened to taking everybody's birthdate in America and putting it into a massive computer. Then you could dial up exactly what kind of person you want. Chances are you could choose any city in the United States and find a person who has the greatest possible connections to your chart, such as karmic links, chemistry, or any number of different things. Then you find out who this person is and meet them only to discover there is no real mutual attraction, or you really don't get along with that person. This is similar to what one is doing when they get a world relocation map. A person might want to maximize personal relationship at this time in their life and the Astrocartography map indicates that Mexico City, or Upper Mongolia is the best place to have this occur. These places are not necessarily desirable or even practical for relocating. This broad-based approach to these issues is, in my view, backwards. The issue of finding the right person to be with, or the right place to live, is part of the *Great Mystery* and it functions best on a level of spiritual intuition. That's why I recommend that people allow themselves to participate intuitively with the Great Mystery. Then they can use tools like astrology to fine-tune their intuition, but not the other way around. Now there are some people who's astrological mystery school (such as Sag Rising) indicates a strong element of pure exploration on their horoscope, so going to upper Mongolia might be viewed as a feature of their mystery school. However, to get an Astrocartography chart to determine where in the world a person will meet the perfect partner is not always practical.

Another important feature to doing relocation work is not only knowing the life purpose issues, but also knowing the timings or initiation cycles of the individual. There may be times when a person feels strongly they must move, because life is not working for them where they are, but in reality what is happening is a feature of the cycle they are experiencing. That means no matter where they are living, they will still be going through the initiation. It is does them no good to leave, because they are taking who they are and the cycle they are in with them, and they can't escape the initiation cycle. Yet, there are timings when it is extremely healthy to try on a new identity. There are times when it is useful to get away from the parents, the family members, the friends, the rut. There are times when a person has completed a cycle and it is time to shift somewhere else. That's why it is important to know the timings when considering a move.

If a person is in a Neptune cycle (like Neptune square Neptune, or transiting the bottom of their chart, or transiting their Moon) and feeling confused and dissatisfied about where they are living it is not the time to be figuring out the ideal place to live. They might even have a vision or insight that they feel absolutely sure is their divinely appointed living place, but in a Neptune cycle they better not take that insight seriously, because it may change the following week. On the other hand, if a person is in a Saturn cycle and they have been living in the same place seven, fourteen, or more years and it feels like they have accomplished all they are going to accomplish there, or nothing has ever worked for them in that location and there is no reason to believe anything is going to change, then it might be precisely the window where a person benefits from moving to a different place. If their intuition says move to Colorado Springs, the best way to approach the matter is to pick three or four different places (including Colorado Springs) that interest them and run a relocation chart for each of those places. Then look at all four places relative to the timing or cycle they are in, and their current life mystery school. This process helps to fine-tune the person's intuition by looking at what is happening in those locations. Some places may be quickly eliminated due to outer planets conjunct the angles, and other places may totally resonate with what the person wants to accomplish. Sometimes the location is not so clearly resonating, but it doesn't hinder what a person wants to do, either.

I did a reading once for a woman living in Los Angeles, who was born in Bucharest, Romania. She was an attractive, successful international banker. She was wondering why she hadn't had any luck in relationships over the past ten years. There was no logical reason for her lack of relationship. My intuition told me the problem had to do with where she was living, since nothing on her natal chart indicated this type of trouble with relationships. From what she told me she wasn't personally doing anything wrong, and her sense of her self was accurate. As a successful, talented, and self-sufficient woman she felt she was capable of deep intimacy, but what was happening to her over and over was that within a week or two of meeting someone, the potential relationship fizzled. She found the men turned out to be superficial and uninteresting. When we did her relocation chart, we discovered that, precisely to the minute, Saturn was sitting on her seventh house point. Not only that, her natal ascendant is Leo Rising, but in Los

Angeles she is Pisces Rising. Los Angeles was a place for her that diminished her personal magnetism, as well as keeping her in limitation and bondage regarding partnership. My advice to her was to move, if she really wanted to have an intimate relationship.

Before going to press with this book in 1995, I learned that the above mentioned woman did move to Hawaii and almost immediately met a wonderful man!

Question: *Does this hold true if Saturn is in the seventh house, or does it have to be on the angle?*
The closer to the angle the more powerful the Saturn (or planetary) effect is. The further away from the angle the less extreme the planetary affect is.

It is important to remember that relocation charts are *not* the most important factor. Always start with what a person's lineage is, what the angles of their natal chart are, what archetypes they are working with in the masculine and feminine, and what the major strategy is they have going on in their life. Do they have a major Saturn or Pluto complex? Then look to see what cycles they are in. Always start with those ingredients. Relocation charts can then be added as an embellishment to the natal chart. I began doing relocation work as a way to complement and add to what I was already doing with the natal chart. All too often I see people doing relocation astrology and that is their main thing. They don't pay much attention to the things that I feel have a much higher priority.

Question: *You are saying, know the script, know the cycles, and then look at what places you would like to live?*
Yes. However, first and foremost tune into your own intuition for the places you would like to live. I get the person to tell me the places they feel drawn to or think they would like to live. They usually come up with three or four places they had in mind. Then it is easy to make adjustments by suggesting other similar types of places.

Comment: *If a person decides to go to a certain area because they think they might meet the ideal mate, they might be disappointed. However, if they went to that area with a partner they might have a good experience with their relationship.*
Great point! But if they went there during the wrong cycle it might not turn out to be what they anticipated. Say, if they got a world map and decided to go to a place where they had Venus on their seventh house point, or where their Saturn/Jupiter conjunction is right on the Midheaven, but they go in the midst of a Pluto square Pluto cycle, or a strong Neptune cycle, the initiation cycle takes precedence. It doesn't matter where a person is in one of these cycles, they will be going through the initiation associated with that cycle. During other timings, such as a cycle that has to do with bonding and relationship, it is beneficial to do a vision quest, or some other process to open the awareness, that helps a person know what places are best for them to live. Then the relocation chart helps to confirm what realities are associated with that living place.

Please remember, relocation charts are a tool to help us understand the effect the place we are living in is having on us, and to help us choose places to live. This is not an exact science, but rather an art, as is the whole approach to Shamanic Astrology. The best technique is to allow your own intuition to lead you, and then use Shamanic Astrology, along with relocation charts, to confirm or further guide your intuition. Remember, we are in the process of the Turning Of The Ages and the old law, the old operating manual, is being rewritten, and the new operating manual is not yet in place. We are now in the process of dreaming up the next 26,000 year cycle, so now more than ever we must tune into our inner wisdom, or intuition, and let it guide us into the next cycle. Shamanic Astrology provides a framework that gives us a vision of all the possibilities, and helps to guide us on our journey. The framework or artistic medium is there, it is up to us to create the final masterpiece!

RECOMMENDED READING LIST

ASTROLOGY BOOKS

Liz Greene *Any of her books. **Relating** is a good one to start with.*
Dane Rudhyar *Gives a great philosophical foundation for astrology. All are excellent!*
Stephen Forrest *Great 1990's textbooks of traditional astrology, clear, concise, practical*
Demetra George *Any of her books. Great mythological, matriarchal oriented works.*
American Ephemeris for the 20th Century 1900-2000 At Midnight Revised 5th Edition
American Ephemeris for the 21st Century 2001-2050 At Midnight Revised 2nd Edition
by Neil F. Michelsen
THE ASTRONOMICAL COMPANION and **THE ASTRONOMICAL CALENDAR**
> by Guy OHewell
> Phone 864-294-2208 Fax 864-294-3523 e-mail: guyvernon@furman.edu
> Astronomical Workshop
> Furman University
> Greenville, S.C. 29613

The Gods Of Change by Howard Sasportass
Myths of the Zodiac by Kathleen Burt

ARCHETYPAL AND JUNGIAN PSYCHOLOGY BOOKS

While not ostensibly about astrology these authors and their books have provided me with more useful and provocative material than the majority of astrological works.
Charles Ponce` **Alchemy, Papers Toward A Radical Metaphysics** and **The Game Of Wizards**
Jean Bolen **Goddesses In Every Woman** and **Gods In Every Man**
Sylvia Perera **Descent To The Goddess: A Way Of Initiation For Women** (An excellent understanding of Pluto & Scorpio from the archetypal perspective) and **The Scapegoat Complex; Shadow And Guilt** (Understanding Saturn and Capricorn Moon from an archetypal perspective)
James Hillman *All of his books stimulate the reader in the same realms as Shamanic Astrology*

NOVELS

Marion Zimmer Bradley **The Mists Of Avalon** And Most Of The Latter **Darkover** Series Beautifully Elucidate The Complexities Of Archetypal Virgo And Other Feminine Archetypes Damaged, Or Not Understood, By Patriarchy.

JOURNALS

Archaeoastronomy, The Journal Of The Center For Archaeoastronomy
Astronomy
Sky And Telescope
The Mountain Astrologer
Planet Earth

ASTRONOMY AND ARCHAEOASTRONOMY BOOKS

Echoes Of The Ancient Skies and **Beyond The Blue Horizon** by Ed Krupp
Living The Sky by Ray Williamson
Empires Of Time and **Conversations With the Planets** by Tony Aveni
Astronomy And The Imagination and **Sky Phenomena** by Norman Davidson
Movement And Rhythms Of The Stars by Joachim Schultz
Hamlet's Mill by Giorgio de Santillana and Hertha Von Dechend
Myth Of Replacement by Thomas Worthen
Star Names, Their Lore and Meaning by Richard Allen
Star Trek to Hawa-ii by Clyde Hostetter

Daniel Giamario

Daniel Giamario, creator of the Astrological Vision Quest(sm) and founder of the Harbingers of the Turning of the Ages, has been a professional astrologer for over 32 years. Since 1982, Daniel's specialty has been connecting astrology to the night sky at sacred sites, by taking groups to secluded wilderness locations including numerous tours to the stone circles of Scotland creating opportunities for the participants to experience their interrelatedness to the earth and sky. Since 1994 Daniel has personally been working extensively with two sites in Southern New Mexico and the Nevada Desert (near the White Mountains) and these sites are now recognized as complete astrological mysteries schools and are important experiential components of the Shamanic Astrology apprenticeship program.

The Shamanic Astrology Apprenticeship program is designed to qualify students as Shamanic Astrologers and for training counseling and therapeutic professionals in the use of the most important astrological tools. Ongoing research, personal consultations and workshops all contribute to the continued expansion of these mysteries, including a deepening understanding of the importance of the cycles of Venus, Mars and Mercury.

Daniel is available for personal and phone consultations, relationship counseling, lectures, and workshops. He can be reached through his California Voice Mail: 310-281-7651, email: daniel@ShamanicAstrology.com and website: www.ShamanicAstrology.com

Carolyn Brent

Carolyn Brent lives in Tucson, Arizona with her husband Jeff and their four children. In 1993 Carolyn began transcribing tapes of talks and workshops given by Daniel. This led to the collaboration and creation of *The Shamanic Astrology Handbook*. Additionally, Daniel and Carolyn have worked together on articles for the Mountain Astrologer, Ascendant Magazine, Four Corners Magazine and The Awareness Journal. Carolyn also writes a monthly Celestial Timings article for the Shamanic Astrology website, Savesite Internet Portal and free email subscription list. Carolyn is available for personal and phone consultations, classes and talks. Contact information
phone: 520-744-0506
email: carolyn@ShamanicAstrololgy.com
website: www.ShamanicAstrology.com

SHAMANIC ASTROLOGY CHARTS

These are high quality charts designed for those who know how to read a chart or for those who are learning how to read a chart. These charts do not come with interpretations but they do come with instructions on their purpose including hints on interpretation and how to read them. Consultations on the meaning of the charts are available. See contact info below. Prices are subject to change without notice.

NATAL CHART (With Aspect Grid, Chiron, Vesta, Juno, Pallas, Ceres are included	5.00
TRANSIT CHART-ONE YEAR (Outer Planets Only, Specify Time & Place Bi-wheel included)	10.00
TRANSIT CHART-ONE YEAR (Nine Planets-No Moon Specify Time & Place Bi-wheel included)	18.00
SUN/MOON ANGLE A.K.A. FERTILITY CHART-ONE YEAR (12 months)	8.00
NATAL/PROGRESSED BI-WHEEL CHART (plus 1 yr of aspects, Specify Date and Location)	8.00
RELOCATION CHART (One Location Only, Specify Location)	6.00
SPECIAL OFFER on Four Relocation Charts for four different locations (save $10)	14.00
SOLAR RETURN CHART (Specify year & location)	6.00
PLANETARY RETURNS (Specify planet i.e. Mars, Venus etc., year and location)	6.00
ASTEROID RETURNS (Pallas, Ceres, Vesta, and Juno generates closest current return)	10.00
LUNAR RETURN CHARTS (6 months, specify months, year & location)	8.00
YEARLY NEW AND FULL MOON CHARTS (12 New Moon and 12 Full Moon charts, 24 total)	12.00
SPECIAL OFFER #1 1 yr Progressed, 1 yr Outer Planet Transit, 1 yr Sun/Moon Angle (Save $10)	16.00
SPECIAL OFFER #2 Includes same charts in offer #1 plus a Solar Return chart (Save $12)	20.00
<u>**THE SHAMANIC ASTROLOGY HANDBOOK**</u> (INCLUDES $6.00 priority mail Shipping)	28.00

TRANSIT CHARTS indicate the current initiation cycles. They track the relationship of the planets in the sky to the planets on your natal birth chart. Many people confuse the Transit chart with Progressions.

SUN/MOON ANGLE CHARTS (a.k.a. Fertility Chart) Once each month both men and women experience a power point for conceiving ideas, inspiration, projects, etc. based on their Sun/Moon angle at birth. These charts also provide women with additional information about their fertility cycles. Women desiring to avoid pregnancy, or women desiring to plan a pregnancy can benefit from these charts.

SOLAR, LUNAR AND PLANETARY RETURN CHARTS provide additional information based on the annual return of the Sun, the monthly return of the Moon and the return of the other planets.

PROGRESSED CHARTS are based on progressing the planets one day for each year of life. This gives a subtler level of understanding about your personal timing, but does not reflect where the planets are now.

RELOCATION CHARTS aid a person in understanding the influences of locations other than their place of birth, especially supportive when considering a move.

THE NATAL CHART IS ONLY $3.00 WHEN ORDERING ANY OTHER CHARTS WITH IT

These charts are calculated to the specific parameters (orbs) of *Shamanic Astrology* and include *calculations for Geocentric, Tropical Zodiac, and Whole Houses* unless otherwise requested. We can do special requests. So, if you don't see the chart you want listed here, just ask. Faxed charts have an additional charge of *$1.00 for the first page and 50 cents for additional pages.* ARIZONA RESIDENTS ADD 5.6% TO TOTAL FOR STATE SALES TAX. Additional Chart Specials and charts are listed on the Shamanic Astrology Web Site with a quick order form and PayPal option for faster service. Allow two to four weeks for delivery once payment is received. *Send birth information:* DATE, TIME, AND PLACE, and any other required information, along with check or money order to: *JCA UNLIMITED, L.L.C., P.O. BOX 91498, TUCSON, AZ 85752-1498, (520) 744-0506 FAX (520) 744-6923, e-mail: carolyn@ShamanicAstrology.com,*

Please visit our web site for more information at www.ShamanicAstrology.com

SHAMANIC ASTROLOGY TAPES
By Daniel Giamario

Introduction to Shamanic Astrology
A 90 minute Tucson Talk
1 Tape Set is $8.00

NEW!!! The Venus/Mars Saga
Plus The Shadow Material
A recent advanced workshop on the newest Shamanic Astrology material expanding the reality of "As Above So Below" to a new level, through understanding the synodic cycles of Venus, Mars and Mercury. This is Daniel's latest research not found anywhere else.
A 4 1/2 hour Tucson Workshop
3 Tape Set is $22.00

PLUS! The Advanced Venus/Mars Saga
The Synodic Cycles of Venus and Mars
and Their Applications
This is a companion to the Feb 97 mountain astrologer article
A 4 1/2 hour Portland workshop, sep 96
3 Tape Set is $22.00

New!!! The Synodic Cycles Of Mercury From a Mytho-Shamanistic Perspective
A two tape set is $15.00

Relationship At The Turning Of The Ages
A 4 1/2 hour Tucson Talk
4 Tape Set is $22.00

The Goddesses In The Horoscope,
The Full Spectrum of Femininity
A 1 3/4 hour Tucson Talk
2 Tape Set is $15.00

The Spectrum Of Masculinity And
The Emerging Male Mysteries (Everything
Women Need To Know About Men)
An 80 minute Kansas City Talk
1 Tape is $8.00

Everything You Wanted To Know
About Scorpio
A Big Island Of Hawaii 2 hour Talk
2 Tape Set is $15.00

New!!! Right Livelihood at the Turning of The Ages. An exploration of the nature of sacred work
3 Tape set $22.00

The Twelve Paths Of Enlightenment
The Astrological Mystery Schools
(The Rising Sign Material)
A 6 1/2 hour Maui Workshop
4 Tape Set is $28.00

The Lineage Of The Soul
(The Moon Material)
A 3 hour Oregon Workshop
2 Tape Set is $15.00

The Initiation Cycles Of Saturn, Pluto,
Uranus, And Neptune At The Turning
Of The Ages
A 3 1/2 hour Kansas City Workshop
3 Tape Set is $22.00

The Lunar Nodes
At The Turning Of The Ages
A 3 1/2 hour Tucson Talk
3 Tape Set is $22.00

The Remythologizing Of Astrology,
Shamanic Astrology's Interface With
Jungian Psychology
A 90 minute Tucson Talk
1 Tape Set is $8.00

Unedited Tapes of Previous Chart Anyalysis Intensives are available. Contact Daniel for details.

Website: www.ShamanicAstrology.com

Mail Orders Add $5.00 Shipping And Handling For The First Set Of Tapes. Add $1.00 for Each Additional Set Of Tapes Ordered. (i.e. for two sets of tapes add $6.00 S&H) Prices are subject to change without prior notice. Check out the website, email Daniel, daniel@ShamanicAstrology.com or call Daniel's voice mail 310-281-7651.

SHAMANIC ASTROLOGY CONSULTATIONS
EVENTS AND APPRENTICESHIP PROGRAM

CONSULTATIONS

Daniel Giamario and Carolyn Brent along with a growing number of trained Shamanic Astrologers are offering Shamanic Astrology consultations. Please visit the website and the Shamanic Astrologers page for all the details concerning the procedures for obtaining consultations. If you do not have Internet access you can reach Daniel through his voice mail at 310-281-7651 or Carolyn at 520-744-0506.

EVENTS

There are also a number of events offered each year for those who are studying Shamanic Astrology and for those who are interested in deepening their connection to the mysteries of Earth and Sky. Again, please visit the website Events page for the most current information or contact Daniel or Carolyn at above phone numbers.

SHAMANIC ASTROLOGY APPRENTICE PROGRAM

This Apprenticeship Program is for those individuals with a serious intent to deepen their knowledge of the mysteries and/or practice Shamanic Astrology as taught by Daniel Giamario. Certification in this practice is useful for the following purposes:

1) Full time or part time Shamanic Astrology Counseling. A background in traditional astrology may be helpful but is not necessary.
2) Integration of the most powerful and useful Shamanic Astrology techniques into an already established therapeutic practice, such as breathwork, psychology, psychiatry, personal coaching, facilitating rites of passage, bodywork, etc.
3) General interest to quicken and deepen ones personal path of self- development and awareness.

There is a growing number of certified Shamanic Astrologers that have now completed the training. The first two to complete this process were Carolyn Brent of Tucson, Arizona who has established a successful Shamanic Astrology practice and Anyaa McAndrew of Atlanta, Georgia who integrates Shamanic Astrology with her successful transpersonal psychology practice. There are several apprentices currently in training to receive their certification. Contact Daniel Giamario directly, if you have questions about the apprenticeship program or in-residence programs.

For further details about the requirements for Certification please Visit the Website Events Page for the most current information or contact Daniel's voice mail 310-281-7651 or email daniel@ShamanicAstrology.com.

www.ShamanicAstrology.com